Magic of

# Qabalah

*Visions of the Tree of Life*

## Bringing the Tree to Life

The Tree of Life stands in the center of a secret garden of Western spirituality. It is the heart and soul of the Qabalah; a blueprint of the cosmos; a living symbol of the forces that comprise all of creation.

However, the path to understanding this great fount of knowledge has usually been made difficult by the obscure and scholarly nature of most of what has been written about it. It is often treated as an abstract, unapproachable monument rather than the dynamic structure that it is.

*Magic of Qabalah* breaks through these barriers by making the Qabalah something to experience rather than to study. Sphere by Sphere and Path by Path, you will climb the branches and taste the fruit of the Tree of Life. Myths and symbols, energies and entities are revealed as living beings that form the body of the universe of which you are a part—and of which you can partake as you remake your world in the image of your will.

## About the Author

Kala Trobe (England) holds an Honors degree in English Literature. She has traveled extensively and visited many of the world's sacred sites. Her experience includes working as a professional Tarot reader, medium, and vocational healer.

## To Write to the Author

If you wish to contact the author or would like more information about this book, please write to the author in care of Llewellyn Worldwide and we will forward your request. Both the author and publisher appreciate hearing from you and learning of your enjoyment of this book and how it has helped you. Llewellyn Worldwide cannot guarantee that every letter written to the author can be answered, but all will be forwarded. Please write to:

Kala Trobe
℅ Llewellyn Worldwide
P.O. Box 64383, Dept. 0-7387-0002-9
St. Paul, MN 55164-0383, U.S.A.

Please enclose a self-addressed stamped envelope for reply,
or $1.00 to cover costs. If outside U.S.A., enclose
international postal reply coupon.

Many of Llewellyn's authors have websites with additional
information and resources. For more information, please visit
our website at http://www.llewellyn.com

# Magic of Qabalah

### Visions of the Tree of Life

*Kala Trobe*

2001
Llewellyn Publications
St. Paul, Minnesota 55164-0383, U.S.A.

First Edition
First Printing, 2001

Book production by Peregrine Graphics Services
Cover photo © Digital Vision and © Digital Stock
Cover design by Gavin Dayton Duffy
Edited by Tom Lewis

Library of Congress Cataloging-in-Publication Data

Trobe, Kala, 1969–
  Magic of Qabalah : visions of the tree of life / Kala Trobe.— 1st ed.
    p. cm.
  Includes bibliographical references and index.
  ISBN: 0-7387-0002-9
    1. Cabala  I. Title.

  BF1611. T76 2001
  135'.47—dc21                                         2001029775

Llewellyn Publications
A Division of Llewellyn Worldwide, Ltd.
P.O. Box 64383, Dept. 0-7387-0002-9
St. Paul, MN 55164-0383, U.S.A.
www.llewellyn.com

 Printed in the United States of America on recycled paper

**Other Books by Kala Trobe**
*Invoke the Goddess* (Llewellyn Publications, 2000)


**Forthcoming Books by Kala Trobe**
*Invoke the Gods*

This book is dedicated with love, to:
Syd Moore and Steph Roche, for bringing
perpetual magick into my life;

to Beau McKernan, King of Pesks,
whose help has been immeasurable;

to Liz and Paul Davenport,
for healing the past and making me say
"wow!" all the time;

to Gwalchmai,
five-pointed Netzachian star
of the Qabalistic Tale;

and to my father, Peter La Trobe-Bateman,
who helped me channel my dreams from
Yesod to Malkuth.

# Contents

INTRODUCTION TO CREATIVE QABALAH / 1

Malkuth / 31

Yesod / 55

Hod / 83

Netzach / 105

Tiphareth / 119

Geburah / 141

Chesed / 157

Binah / 173

Chokmah / 189

Kether / 205

Daath and the Abyss / 219

The Remaining Paths / 225

A Qabalistic Tale / 257

APPENDIX: 555—PLAYFUL CORRESPONDENCES
TO GET YOU IN THE MOOD / 281

Bibliography / 285

Index / 289

# Introduction to
# Magic of Qabalah

hat is the Qabalah? Originally a Judaic path of ascension, as symbolized by the image of the Tree of Life, the Qabalistic system has maintained its structure over the aeons. It has never ceased in offering the aspiring soul a chance to reach higher planes, but with time its modes of use have changed dramatically. Adopted by spiritual aspirants from all walks of life, from medieval alchemists to nineteenth-century magi, then popularized on a wider scale by the "outing" of many High Magick techniques in the twentieth century, one might suspect the Tree to have bent under the weight of so many eager neophytes.

However, the very eclecticism found in modern Qabalah is one of the strongest and most essential features of this system. Much of the atmosphere of Orthodox Judaism, its "parent tradition," has now been lost, or at least absorbed into a much wider-reaching field of spiritual practice. No longer the province of a single philosophy or religion, it has incorporated the signs and symbols of many others, making it a transdimensional reference library, the living 777, to take an expression from Aleister Crowley. Indeed, Crowley's work is arguably the fertilizer most responsible for the Tree's latter-day luster, though cross-pollination would surely have happened sooner or later with such rich ground as this. Today's Qabalah is as diverse and eclectic as our current age. We can thank the psychically avant-garde work of Crowley, along with that of

Eliphas Levi, Israel Regardie, MacGregor Mathers, and Dion Fortune, for stimulating the popular magickal imagination of the last century, bringing diverse paths together and changing the import of the Qabalah forever.

While the system of Qabalah will be charted in depth through the course of this book, a summary of the tradition's structure can be offered here. The Qabalah describes ten main states of being, the *Sephiroth* or "emanations," and twenty-two states of becoming, the Paths. A negative framework to the Sephiroth's positive exists in the form of the *Qlipoth* or "sparks," also known as "shards" or "peels." In conjunction with these negative realms, the Sephiroth determine the shape of the Tree of Life, which itself describes the whole of Creation, including what existed before Creation.

Each *Sephirah* (singular of Sephiroth) exists under the rule of a different aspect of the Mother-Father God; that is, it represents a particular aspect of the relation between the Creative Intelligence and the Created Universe. The descent of Spirit into Matter, the development of duality, and the gradual divorce from our spiritual origin are all demonstrated by the Sephiroth as we scale down the Tree of Life on which they sit. The Sephiroth also contain all relevant archetypes, from world folklore and mythology: for example, *Binah*, the Supernal Mother whose name means "Understanding," encompasses Nuit, Kali, and other Terrible Mothers (as the givers and breakers of Form), as well as Isis and Mary, mother of Christ. As the facet of Understanding spans a great many aspects of experience, it follows that Mary's piety and Kali's apparent wanton destruction can both be ascribed to Binah, particularly as both conform to the "Vision of Sorrow" which is this Sephirah's spiritual experience, and both involve the dissolution of established form and traumatic transition into a new mode of being. Likewise, all sacrificed gods can be ascribed to *Tiphareth*, the mystical and solar Sephirah. This follows for all the other Sephiroth along the paths of the Tree. The same symbols attributed to each Sephirah play a microcosmic role, summarizing every facet of individual existence. This philosophy may in turn be encapsulated in the adage "As Above, So Below."

Where did Qabalah come from? The word itself comes from Hebrew, meaning "that which is received." Tradition holds that the teachings were passed from master to student, in a chain going back to the Archangel Metatron, Angel of the Presence, who descended from the Crown of Creation (*Kether*) to Mount Sinai in order to deliver enlightenment to Moses, the spiritual ancestor of all Jewish rabbis. Most of this occult knowledge was later condensed into glyphs, the first symbols of *Ets Chayyim*, the Tree of Life. Conveyed by word of mouth from one generation of learned men to another, Qabalistic teachings were not written down until around 1000 C.E. Following the collection and publication of the first texts of the Qabalah in the European Middle Ages, the creed underwent a renaissance. Again, in the sixteenth century, the development of Qabalah experienced a second flowering. That said, Qabalistic learning has never been so much a part of the popular mainstream as it is today.

In this book, "Qabalah" will be spelled in this way to differentiate it from the traditional Jewish Kabbalah, its parent—or should I say, its host. Modern Qabalah is a cuckoo child, a former impostor in the nest of Judaism, now an independent fledgling. However, as the foregoing survey of its history reveals, Kabbalah/Qabalah has long been subject to diverse influences. Like any living religion, it receives many tributaries—but the river which carries us here is the magickal river, and we are dealing with correspondences alien to Judaism, though not to Kabbalah itself. As Z'ev Ben Shimon Halevi points out in *Kabbalah, The Divine Plan*, the Tarot system so often dismissed as irrelevant is actually based on information gleaned from the *Zohar*, one of the central texts in Kabbalah. According to Halevi's account, the Major Arcana represent the twenty-two letters of the Hebrew alphabet, the four suits symbolising the Four Worlds (to be discussed below), and is highly conducive to Qabalistic development. The use of Tarot cards as a symbolic system, and the ability to adapt and relate anything—but anything—to part of the Tree, may be slightly unorthodox, but it is no less valid (indeed, in my opinion, it is more valid for being at least partially subjective). Kabbalah/Qabalah itself represents a long tradition of thinking in an unconventional and inclusive manner.

The Jewish Mystery Tradition has much to offer in the way of meditation, psychotherapy, psychology, and insight into the ancient folklore that informs the system, but the Western Mystery Tradition (the focus of this book ) encompasses a great deal more. Much that did not belong on the Tree at first now does, owing to the input of all who meditate on or activate the various Sephiroth. Thus, though Crowley's particular attributions may have borne personal significance for him at the time, their application by others in meditation and magick has since made them "real." Basilisks may arise in the mind's eye when *Geburah* is considered, though they originally had no place on the Tree. Astral elephants really do parade about the planes of *Yesod*, thanks to the much-invoked Thelemic thought practice, at least when the Tree is approached in the spirit of the Western Magickal Tradition. Whether they are "visible" to Jewish Kabbalists is another matter. Martin Buber and Gershom Scholem, two of those most responsible for reviving the increasingly obfuscated Kabbalah within their own heritage, might well rebuke the interloper(s), though I hope to be corrected on this point.

The cuckoo child has built its own nest now, and its host parent is once again freed of its uninvited presence. In the new Tree described in these pages, an ever-changing network of consciousness has formed, like a telephone exchange in which conversations on particular topics can be tapped. Within this system, all that was invested in the original Judaic model remains, but the correspondences of all mythological and religious traditions are also found here, equal in relevance, along with various types of magickal working and thought processes useful to the spiritual pilgrim. So too with the input of its travellers, Jews and non-Jews alike: the Qabalah is the embodiment of this far-reaching—and indeed infinite—eclecticism.

The present age is one founded on shared information, the mixing of ancient currents both intellectual and spiritual. In the West, even gender roles are changing, our personalities and looks becoming more androgynous, with the essential spark of polar magnetism left intact. Science is being brought into conformity with Will, allowing a soul to sculpt its own body. It is becoming possible to experience life-paths vicariously through informed empathy that we never would have believed in before. Travel is contributing towards this lessening of insularity, allowing us to perceive first-hand the living modes of other human beings on the planet. Cultures are mixing, influencing one another and creating new music, style, vocabularies, and thought patterns. Computers have caused an explosion of creativity and initiated an "Info-fest." Everything is merging.

That the Qabalah and other magickal systems should become commonly accessible was inevitable. With millions looking for ascension, every channel must be opened; a fact of which the late great magicians who first brought it to our attention were well aware. However, I feel sure that Eliphas Levi, Israel Regardie, Dion Fortune, and other original exponents of the craft would be the first to blanch at some of the side effects. Those early masters' emphasis was on strict training and self-discipline, with comprehension their highest priority. Unfortunately the system seems so complex at first sight, and was often so abstrusely presented, that those eager to taste the fruits of the Tree tend to neglect the groundwork needed to make a successful climb. Not only this, but climbing by the uncertain light of gibbous understanding, they leave foot and claw marks on the ancient bark and sweaty finger-prints on its appendages.

The Tree itself, however, still stands with its crown in the *Ain Soph Aur*, the endless light, and beckons to those who desire to scale it. Since it is nearly impossible to broach magick in the Western hemisphere without a good working knowledge of the Qabalah, aspirants must approach the Tree at some point in their education. To Dion Fortune, Qabalah was "the Yoga of the West," better suited to our lives and bodies than the Eastern art and indispensable for attaining coherent magickal form. It provides a form of deep introspection and meditation; there is a path or Sephirah for every facet of the human psyche. It provides a means of accessing energies and even entities for magickal or practical use. The original Kabbalah laid emphasis on the day-to-day application of its practical wisdom, and on seeking out the divine spark in the apparently mundane. Of course, for observant Jews the significance and symbolism of Hebrew letters and names literally *is* the mainstream of daily life, but for many unversed in the language, comprehension of its surface and deeper meanings has been a struggle.

It need not be so difficult anymore. Most of the necessary experience can be attained through thought image and meditation, and this is the purpose for which the visualizations in this book have been formulated. They are intended to impart maximum information and benefit with minimal confusion. This, in turn, will spill into the practitioner's psyche, and its conscious application to self- and dream-analysis, for example, will bring it into the provinces of practical Qabalah. The inclusion of Tarot symbolism performs a similar role. However, for the sake of clarity, this book should be considered a primer, as opposed to an exhaustive treatment of the subject. I have avoided the esoteric sciences of *Gematria*, *Temura*, and *Notariqon*, which strive to attain meanings from the numerology and lettering of key words. No doubt these and other ramifications can be of great value to those already conversant in the key symbols and correspondences of the Sephiroth, but simplicity and easy access to the material was the central goal in the preparation of this book. For those who wish to continue into the more esoteric dimensions of Qabalistic lore, some of the more detailed tracts are mentioned in the Bibliography.

Nor are these excursions magickally dangerous. They will, however, open up gateways to a great flood of experience. That said, do not undertake them if you are quite content with the way things are, thank you very much. Working with the Qabalah is like handling a psychological growth hormone: it gets under your skin and enhances certain areas of the psyche (which areas are affected depends on the practitioner's state of being and active mental and emotional affiliations). The exercises are designed to stretch and flex the psychic muscles, to progress the soul in one's personal and cosmic context, and to familiarize the participant with the key traits of each of the ten Sephiroth, the "apples" on the Tree's branches.

Some ideas for psychic self-protection are given in the next section.

## Preliminaries to All Exercises

Before any occult dealings it is sensible to protect oneself, not because the procedure itself is perilous, but because there are some peculiar entities around, and magick makes you more sensitive to them. Just as one would not arrive in the jungle without having had the appropriate innoculatory jabs and being equipped with mosquito spray, a hat, food, and a knife, it is madness to travel to the Inner Planes without any protective devices. For instance, one of the systems relevant to *Malkuth* is the acquisition of magickal weapons, and such a process is given in the Malkuth visualization.

As well as taking on weapons, one can form a protective sheath that should prevent them having to be used in the first place. This also protects from the more insidious entities on the Inner (and Outer) Planes.

There are several ways of doing this. A traditional occult method is to enlist the protection of the four Guardian Angels: Raphael, Gabriel, Michael, and Uriel. Writer/occultists such as Gareth Knight can furnish the interested reader with traditional methods for this and many other operations. Alternately, you could envisage yourself surrounded by cosmic energies, as such:

First, face to the East.

Send a request to the Cosmic Intelligence that your application for protection be heeded. Do not continue until you truly feel that it will be so. (This served to prevent haphazard workings when one subconsciously knows that the time is not right.)

Now, envisage a pillar of radiant yellow light before you. Feel how it shields you from face-on attack.

Behind you, sense a powerful pillar of blue, protective light.

To your left, a vibrant pillar of red vigilance stands your guard.

To the right, a black pillar prevents negative forces from reaching you.

Starting with the yellow pillar, visualize a ring of blue flame reaching out and catching the red pillar. Let it spread to the blue and black and back to the red until you are completely surrounded by a circle of fire, keeping off the wild beasts of the cosmos and acting as a beacon to benevolent entities. Seal the tube with blue fire beneath the feet and above the head.

Another means of protection is courtesy of one's personal Guardian(s); definitely easiest if you already know who your Inner Guides are (for example, a bona fide guru—few and far between on this plane), or an enlightened being such as an avatar of Christ-consciousness, Buddha, a Krishna embodiment, or even "the Master Jesus," if you are so inclined. Here I am not describing the suburban myth of these godforms, but their true, vibrant selves, very unlike the mundane expression we have constructed for them. Only you can know whether or not you have the energy, purity, and visualizing ability to make a true, noncomplacent link with such Great Ones. A regular godform is less effective, as these are specific to particular parts of the Tree. Only those who can be felt to have attained the *Ain Soph Aur*—which for our purposes here can be said to be equivalent to Nirvana or some other ultimately transcendent state—are suitable consorts in every realm.

Never be afraid you are duping yourself, for when we create the appropriate channel, the gods come. As the magickal adage goes, "Fantasy is the ass that carries the Ark," and its asinine nature in no way detracts from the reality or potency of its load.

A less personal approach to self-protection involves bringing the protective energies of the nonspecific cosmic consciousness into service.

To do this, stand facing East, take four deep, slow breaths, puffing out strongly and simultaneously envisaging all the tension leaving your body in dark billows, while your lungs begin to glow golden from the inside. With each breath, the glow increases until, with the fourth exhalation, your body is glowing brilliantly.

Now, tense and flex every muscle in your body, feeling the golden light creeping into its every tissue and bone as you do so. Soon your cells are alive with this vibrant prana.

Above you, the ceiling has turned a brilliant yellow-white. A crackling electricity has infused the room. Visualize the light strongly, so that your inner eye is dazzled. Feel the presence of the Divine Dreamer, the fusing of your two consciousnesses. Feel the excitement of the vastness that is.

Imagine a door in the back of your head, in the lower region just above the neck.

Now, draw that energy down, and look through the door. Surround yourself with this energy. Affirm that it is solid and pure, and that any negativity directed at it will bounce straight back at the sender. Visualize a bolt of black bouncing off the surface of your body-sheath. Be sure to concentrate on front, right side, back, left side, underneath, and overhead in turn. Let there be no part unprotected. Let the golden light be ever renewable.

Now, unless you wish to be totally conspicuous on the Inner Planes, tone the color and brilliance down but maintain the resolution, leaving you armored in dull silver-gold, with a warm feeling within.

It is a matter of personal inclination which protective technique is preferred. Malkuth will help you develop further tools, though weapons as such are anathema to the type of process we will be undergoing. This journey is one of respectful, joyous exploration. Hopefully you will never require weaponry for more than their symbolic purpose, and at this stage you can rest assured that you won't.

## The Four Worlds

There are four "layers" in Qabalistic cosmology, each representing a different aspect of reality. All of the Sephiroth exist simultaneously within the fabric of these layers.

At present we find ourselves in the world of *Assiah*, the layer of physicality and action. Here, symbols are perceived in material form; the spiritual luminary Tiphareth, for example, appears here as the sun. The occult symbol of Assiah is the Bull and its Tarot suit is, of course, Pentacles—a link to the earthly value that coins and other "hard currency" represent. In the system I have used in this book, Assiah relates to the four Page cards found in the Tarot.

*Yetzirah*, the next step up, represents the formative stage in creation. Its Sephiroth are those forming the "inner body" of the Qabalah; Yesod, Hod, Netzach, Tiphareth, Geburah, and Chesed. The Orders of Angels, deities, and godforms belong to this level. Yetzirah's symbol is cerebral Man, and its Tarot suit the intellectual Swords. In the system I use, the four Knights belong here.

The creative, receptive level is known as *Briah*, and to it are ascribed the Archangels. The Sephiroth encompassed in this level are Binah and Chokmah. Its symbol is the Eagle and its Tarot suit Cups, and the four Queens correspond to this level.

Finally, the layer of *Atziluth* represents the highest conceivable proximity to God. As far as the Tree goes, it is composed of Kether (some ascribe both Kether and Chokmah to this level). Its attributes are the Archetypal world, or the world of Emanations, the Lion symbol, and the suit of Wands. The God-names manifest through this level, and I prefer to associate the four Kings of the Tarot with Atziluth.

These four worlds represent the "thought" of God coming into being, descending through the planes from the very refined and conceptual to the solid and physical. Of course it is in the world of Assiah, the plane of physical fact and action, that we abide, but the whole nature of Qabalah aspires upward, towards Kether in Atziluth, the ultimate godhead. A key point to this aspiration is that this supreme state of divinity may be found at the heart of the apparently mundane. Malkuth is not only as important as Kether, but it also reflects and contains it. Likewise are all other Sephiroth interlinked, composed to a greater or a lesser degree of one another.

Each Sephirah exists on all four of these levels—hence the four different colors, popularly referred to as "the flashing colors," ascribed to each.

## Visualizing the Qabalah as a Whole

Probably the easiest way to visualize the Tree as a whole is as ten symmetrically positioned, colored spheres, or Sephiroth, each glowing with its own particular properties. All of the Sephiroth exist on all of the four levels. They are arranged into three columns, the middle of which is the longest and lowest. The columns to the left and right each consist of three regularly placed spheres. As you approach each Sephirah in meditation, you will feel yourself being drawn into and assimilated by the position and color of that sphere, quickly leading you to its inner properties.

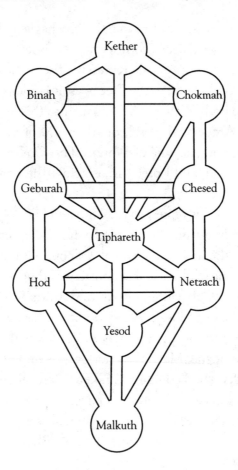

To visualize the Qabalah as a whole, and thus establish a "map" for your later meditations, first envisage yourself surrounded by a tentlike sphere of four colors, as if you were inside a giant juggling ball or beach ball, its segments yellow, green, dark red, and blue respectively.

You are standing at the center of this construction. Their colors unite at the top and bottom of the sphere, at the points above your head and beneath your feet.

Facing you is the yellow sector, representing air. To your right is the red of fire. Behind you is the cool blue of water. To your left, the verdure of green earth.

Make a concerted effort to invest your sphere with the Elements—be aware of the fresh, redolent earth; the sighing, lapping ocean; the crackling brilliance of fire; the relief and freedom of air.

With the wind comes the spirit world, whose denizens are all the beings who abide with us, yet are rarely perceived by us, nor us by them. Some of these are elementals, others restless spirits caught up in their personal woes, long obsolete in the worlds from which they came, but still fresh as yesterday's dreams. Still others are intelligent entities on missions between the planes. Some, of course, are good, some neutral, and others malign. Obviously, any occult work increases one's sensitivity to the astral/spirit realms, and psychic self-protection is a good "antispook" device. The Qlipoth abide in the Sephiroth as entities engendered by an imbalance in the spheres. Certain areas have become populated with Qlipoth, whose sustenance is this pernicious (because imbalanced) energy. These *prana*-draining mosquitoes of the spirit realms are troublesome, but can be kept at bay using the simple techniques described above.

Inside this tent of four colors exist all material things, and everything that you connect with your life as an individual personality, especially those aspects which are obvious to your waking mind. The tent, as you have no doubt gathered, is symbolic of the first station of the Qabalah, Malkuth, "the Kingdom."

## Drawing Your Map of the Tree

Now, to begin your mental map of the Tree, focus on the properties of the Earth Kingdom, of Malkuth:

- See your abode (you do not have to own it), your possessions, your work.

- Think of all the practical skills you possess, and those you would like to develop.

- Consider those companions with whom you have the most dynamic and enjoyable conversations.

- Feel your animal presence in this realm. The stamping of feet usually facilitates this.

- Prepare to explore, knowing that you are strong on this most fundamental of levels.

When these thoughts are established and you feel ready for anything, you are ready to progress—or regress—to Yesod.

This purple-silver orb hangs directly above you, like a strange moon whose tides you know on a semiconscious level, but whose laws elude you. It reminds you of half-remembered dreams which slip away under scrutiny; you know you will have to induce a semiconscious state to tune in to the reality of Yesod.

- Lie down flat on your back on your bed, arms to your sides, shut your eyes, and focus on the inside of the middle of your forehead, at the top of the bridge of the nose. Allow whatever thoughts and images you have to float through your mind and drift away.

- Now, think back through your life to those events and personalities that have affected you. Try to maintain objectivity while doing this; view these life memories as you might someone else's televised biography. Try to observe any patterns or astral networks you may perceive cropping up.

- See your soul in silver, ascending the line which connects Malkuth to Yesod. As you ascend feel the increased lightness of being—a shedding of burdens, a mental holiday. Here, all is less personal and more essential. It is by inner nature that all is defined on this plane.

The beautiful and the strange process before you on this level, and many seem familiar, like the forgotten paintings of childhood. Others give you the feeling of dreamy déjà vu: did you dream them only yesterday?

Don't fall asleep! There are further tasks to perform.

Now you must fly to the strong, orange sphere of Hod, which hangs above you to your left.

- Still lying on your back, concentrate on travelling up and to your left.

    Even on thinking this, the subtle forms of Yesod disperse and seem unreal again; in Hod you know there lies a defining strength that emphasizes rather than romanticizes the inner nature of things.

- Take time to perceive the qualities of Hod, a very different genre compared with those of Yesod.

    This is the realm of mental energy, the seat of empirical learning, patience, and effort. The geniuses and thaumaturgists of our realm are strongly affiliated with Hod.

- Note how, even on so brief a visit, you feel a similar respect to that which you might if, visiting the British Library, you suddenly discovered that all the Nobel Prize winners were gathered within. The atmosphere is distinctly intellectual, but do not be intimidated by your own shortcomings in that respect (or overly proud of your own achievements!). Any entity worth its protoplasm knows that intellect is a component often latent in the human condition, and that emotional intelligence is its equally worthy counterpart. Many to whom Hod is a natural abode have lessons to learn in the more emotional and often practical spheres.

    Here, ideas manifest in the abstract, and civilization progresses to the ticking of the mental clock.

- Feel yourself assimilating these qualities along with the deep burnt orange of their vibration.

As Charles Seymour says in his magical diaries, every day the Magician should ask him or herself: "Is my brow wet with mental sweat?" For it is the vice of the magician to spend time creating fancies rather than on progression, and when the temptation to stray from the path of mental evolution is particularly strong, defining Hod will help us turn our back on fanciful distractions.

After the effort you have exerted in the close atmosphere of Hod, you will be pleased to take a break in the verdant greenery of Netzach. There is a strong relationship between this sphere and our own Malkuth: it is faery country. Those who are attuned to nature will be very at home here, and the urban pagan will find a refuge cheaper and more accessible than a trip to the countryside.

- Reach Netzach by travelling right in a straight line, or, if you prefer, touch down on purple Yesod, slightly below and to the centre of your line, before ascending to brilliant green Netzach. You may undergo some discomfort, like the change in pressure when diving underwater, but do not be alarmed. Remember your strong protective armor.

- Relaxed, still supine and smiling slightly, explore the Sephirah.

  In the earthy, elevated natural world of ultragreen Netzach, refreshment pours forth from the ground and is innate in the vital elements celebrating themselves here. To a true Taurean this is home, with its ingredients both nurturing and natural, a place steady yet creative, rewarding considered participants in the dance of life.

- Consider the most sublime aspects of your love life, past, present, and future. Allow the ensuing feelings of pleasure to infiltrate your heart and soul.

  This beautiful faery-realm is the starting place of many a true romance; its qualities are rapturous, enchanting.

Opposite a sun of white-hot radiance, aureoled by rainbow hues, the violet moon of Yesod hangs in the sky. Energy is everywhere: you can feel the force of every object you encounter pushing out, externalizing.

Perspective here is not what we are accustomed to. Angels follow strange rules of elfin geometry and many objects seem out of kilter and likely to slip through dimensions at any moment. A large seven-pointed star hangs in the blue-purple sky, along with other celestial bodies of deep buttery yellow and startling silver. Here is the perfect place to recline beneath a tree, like Omar Khayyam, and write or dream about the lifting of veils, the dissolving of *Maya*, taking part in the emotional truths inherent to the religious urge itself.

- Abide here for as long as you feel inclined; there is plenty to explore and many paths of fancy to be skipped along. This trip to Netzach should leave you feeling sprightly and inspired.

Next stop, Tiphareth.

Remember the sun of Netzach? It hangs above you, to your right, and you are going to surf the cosmic ley lines that attach it to your present station.

- Imagine the line linking the green orb with the yellow; feel yourself positioned at its base, and then, by the power of your Will, feel yourself impelled along it, slanting upwards towards Tiphareth.

- You enter through the outer atmosphere and feel a change in your constitution as you do so. This is a mystical realm of elevated love, of soul mates and infinitesimal beauty. It smells of strange, heavy, entrancing perfume, one likely to make you lose your head at any moment. Remembering Malkuth, however, you resolve not to do so.

- This is the Leonine sphere and it emanates strength, solar power, and love. Healing is performed here and sent down through the planes. If you have any requests of this nature, now is the time to divulge them. There are many golden beings of light ready to receive every twitch given off by your thought processes. If you can focus your wishes and visualize the desired end, so much the better.

- Bask in the life-giving properties of Tiphareth, and feel the excitement they engender. This is also a good place to visit when faced with a difficult choice or decision, particularly between two possible paths. You may, if naturally psychic, find yourself involved in high-level communications of an emotional nature (as opposed to those more academic concepts of Hod) with a particular guardian. Try to maintain equilibrium during this procedure, and especially afterwards. Pride is one of the pitfalls of this level, and self-respecting humility a boon.

As you find yourself heading for the red sphere of Martian Geburah, you may feel arrogance rising in your blood, for you have seen and experienced much on this short preliminary journey. Do feel strong, but try not to approach Geburah in a bombastic manner, or you will have the stuffing knocked out of you. Geburah is, on a microcosmic level, the harsh part of ourselves necessary for self-protection. Here we can shed what has become obsolete in our lives, rid ourselves of unwanted influences, and fill ourselves with warrior strength.

- Travel up and to the left.
- Note that everything here is red; the tone is either positively sanguine or sacrificially bloody, depending on your personal state of being.

- The forceful atmosphere of Geburah is a philosophy in itself. Denoting war, it embodies possibly the oldest impulses of man: to protect and acquire.

Consider these properties and their ambivalence. Uplifting and courageous, the spirit of Geburah has frequently degenerated into wanton cruelty and destruction. Still, for those with a gentle nature, possibly self-sacrificing and too emotionally generous, Geburah provides a healthy antidote to self-dissipation.

Theoretically, Geburah is one of the seats of justice, especially when counterbalanced by Chesed, and it should be possible to have wrongs righted courtesy of this sphere, if the Powers deem that they are indeed wrongs. It is not a particularly pleasant stop, but its might is impressive. Walls, forts, and military constructs define it; stone, metal, and spilt blood are its main components. This is, of course, the sphere in which wars are fought and lost . . . or won.

Before it all gets too much, let us counterbalance the experience with a visit to the calm blue sphere of Chesed, also known as Gedulah.

- Travel up and to the right.

   This blue-violet sphere is also known as the Mercy Seat or the Temple of Love. It is the abode of gurus and masters, and the atmosphere is at once challenging and reverend. You may well hear an inner narrative while visiting Chesed; chances are, it will instruct you. As obedience is one of the virtues of this station, it is well to follow the dictate you feel is authentic.

- This is a place of dedication to a path or discipline, an astral hermitage. Here you may consider your life's greater purpose and the steps necessary to secure its coming to pass. This will involve effort, for the rewards of the gods are not easily earned. However, one's shortcomings should be given a sympathetic appraisal in Chesed.

- Meditate on the following theme.

  The nature of gurus is various, but it is fair to say that the number of true gurus incarnate in Malkuth today is minimal, while there are many false prophets and unsavory self-proclaimed spiritual leaders who are more likely to lead us into the Abyss than to the bright lights of Kether. It is foolish to trust such figures on the Outer Planes, but on the Inner Planes one's intuition may be employed. There is too much room for confusion on the material level, where countless forces prevent us from making accurate judgments, but with the help of one's guides in the sphere of Chesed, disinterested help may be sought. The guru devoid of personal motive is so rare, especially in the West, as to be unicorn-like in its elusiveness. Still, it is good to know that such beings exist, somewhere.

Chesed is quite a solemn place, with an atmosphere akin to a Court of Justice. It will be a relief, especially to feminine spirits, to prepare to ascend further still, this time into the bitter, receptive sea that is Binah, the most menstrual of female planets, at once pregnant, menopausal, and steeped in mystery.

Placed at the top of the left-side column, black Binah feels as if it might at any moment absorb all of the other Sephiroth into itself and fold creation up like Sylvia Plath reabsorbing her children in her poem "Ariel."

Indeed, one of the paths to Binah is "Plathological," borne of deep neurosis and masochistic pain. However, in a balanced state Binah is healthy understanding, compassion, the ability to empathize.

- Try to free your mind of analytical thoughts. Center on "blind" feeling.

- Allow thought-forms to rise in your mind as you intuitively explore this dark Sephirah.

    Binah has a very special relationship with female mysteries and Goddess-related issues, and emanates primal femininity in its most potent aspects. Binah flows with the tides, and women often access it through lunar Yesod, though this path is not commonly, or deliberately, used. There is a telling silence in the atmosphere of Binah, a tacit sense of knowing. Much is thought here in the caves of intuitive and atavistic wisdom, and little spoken.

    The light of Kether bathes the top of this sphere, which revolves and sends reflections scudding across its dark, miasmic surface. The heat of Geburah filters up from beneath, but there is no reflection of its brilliant red. This is absorbed into the dark seas of Binah's strange antimatter.

- Abide here for as long as you feel comfortable. Note your reactions: do you feel at home, claustrophobic, restricted? Do not interpret these reactions yet; simply feel them. You can write down your experiences and interpretations when you return.

Opposite this disturbing yet restful sphere—rather like a graveyard just prior to mass resurrection (Stanley Spencer's paintings, though bright, evoke this atmosphere admirably)—hangs the gray sphere of Chokmah.

- Journey straight across to your right.
- Meditate on the following.

    Chokmah is the top Sephirah in this vertical column, the so-called "Pillar of Mercy," and is solemn as a cathedral, while still joyous, for the goal of the ascent is imminent. The Creative Intelligence permeates this sphere

like hallucinogenic incense, and faith in oneself and the
benevolent nature of the sublime infiltrates the still soul.
The traditional imagery, as with all of the Tree, is deeply
biblical. Needless to say, the system is peopled with Rab-
binic men, bearded and with robes, for the imagery is
archetypal and born of thousands of years of Judaism.
However, the mind conversant in many cultures should
not find this an obstacle; alternately, it may translate to
your own inner tongue and imagery as quickly as a spiritual linguaphone. Take what comes to you; as time goes
on the impressions will change and deepen.

Remember that Chokmah is the place where one identifies
one's own Yahweh/Buddha/Vishnu/Isis, preparing for personal dissolution in its most positive form. Such tasks are not lightly under-
taken, and there is a nervy feeling in the air, for this is the vestry
that leads to the Temple of God. There is also a sense of great
accomplishment within this sphere.

The living light of Kether is growing ever more attractive to
you, the astral pilgrim. Standing in the gray stone vestry that is
Chokmah, you yearn toward the light that has informed you during
the entire journey.

Your mind flicks over the nine stages you have so far accom-
plished: the rise from earthly Malkuth to dreamy Yesod. The left
turn to determined, orange Hod and right turn to emerald Netzach,
the Ireland (or, mythologically, Tír Na-n'Óg) of the Tree. You recall
the solar resplendence and beauty of central Tiphareth, then the
left-hand turn to bellicose Geburah. Remember how pleasant it
was to zig from there to Chesed, the violet-blue home of guides and
gurus, then zag to dark Binah, place of female mysteries.

- Now, here you are, at the top of the right-hand pillar, so close to the light you could almost touch it. Feel yourself drawn upwards at the very thought of it, up into the impossibly resplendent Temple of Kether.

- White light engulfs you, pouring in through your now-permeable astral armor, dissolving it (though it will return when you descend), filling you with divine acknowl-edgement. Let this be two-way; draw yourself close to your God, however you imagine the Creative Source. Give, do not just take. Stay bathed in this refulgence for as long as you feel inclined, vaguely aware of the Veils of Negative Existence above you, those aspects of the creation for which our minds can only draw an analogy of concealment.

- When you are sated on Ketheric light, it is well to bring yourself back station by station, thus recomposing your nature and grounding any energies you may be bringing back with you.

- So, zigzag back through each of the radiant spheres. If you can do so without my prompting, all the better. To travel back by memory will help fix the positions and qualities in your mind. If this proves too difficult, then reread the process described prior to visiting Kether, going backward, starting with Chokmah and ending at Malkuth.

## Encountering the In-House Divinities

Before entering any Sephirah it is beneficial to apply for permis-sion from the powers ruling it. This is not strictly necessary, but it will help fix some of the traits of the Sephirah in your mind, and it is good form. You may wish to skip this preliminary overview until you have the areas firmly fixed in your mind; initially, there will be much to remember. However, if you are primarily visualizing as you read, or if you are ready to "go for it" on the Inner Planes (as opposed to just imagining your journey—you will soon learn the difference), then an introduction to the following would be wise.

The first trait is of course the expression of God in the Sephirah, known by a different name according to its aspect. The second is represented by the mighty Archangel who presides over the sphere and its qualities, while the third is the Order of Angels. In all cases these are very specific levels of energy "personified" in order to make them more easily accessed and identified. Giving anything a title and imaginative form helps to classify and thus clarify it.

Each section in this book includes details of the God aspect, Archangel, and Order of Angels to be found within each Sephirah. Many of the descriptions of the Angels will seem peculiar to the Western perception, accustomed as it is to images of tinselled humans descending from the heavens; or else of winged beings made of golden-white light.

Angelic images may be built up telesmatically, using the properties of the letters in the entity's name in the world to which they are ascribed, or they may be visualized in a simpler, more generalized way. The manner of building these images depends on which technique gives you, the practitioner, the biggest bolt of psychic lightning. The names of the energetic personalities are translated letter by letter, using a code of telesmatic attributions: first, the Yetziratic or celestio-physical details, such as whether or not the energy is mystically construed of as winged; then the color of the energy. We learn a great deal from the color details, such as affiliation to other Sephiroth, and elemental qualities (elemental, that is, in the highest sense: these properties are far removed from earth, air, fire, and water as we know them in Malkuth).

Each Sephirah exists on four major levels, as described at the beginning of the section on visualizing the Qabalah as a whole.

These reflect the impulse of creation from its archetypal expression in Atziluth, at which point it is very pure thought, through Briah, where the concept is created, into Yetzirah, where the concept grows and becomes evident, and finally through to Assiah, where it manifests in its fully tangible state. These stages are represented by a different color in each Sephirah.

Likewise is each deity force attributed to one of the four different "worlds" of the Tree. When translating the name-keys of these energies, this is taken into account. The letter *Aleph* (א) for example is the first in "Ashim," the choir of Angels in Malkuth, and the penultimate in "Raziel," the Archangelic force of Chokmah. Its general properties are the same in both cases, denoting a highly refined, airy form. However, in the former case it manifests predominantly as emerald, a color particular to Netzach, which denotes elemental properties relevant to Malkuth, while in the latter it is celestial sky-blue, relating to Chesed, the sphere of mercy.

Though many of the ingredients might be the same, I doubt that two telesmatic images ever agree on every point. Indeed, the task of describing the energies is a tall one, even with the prop of telesmatic codices. Imagination is the vivifying ingredient; without this the telesmatic images are a lifeless Frankenstein's monster with a bit pulled from here and a bit taken from there. And because imagination is deeply subjective, everyone's telesmatic vision will be a little (if not very) different.

Energies may be subjectively perceived through the filter of what is palatable to the onlooker, but it is closer to the celestial bone if they are visualized at least approximately as their name describes. Consequently readers may, for example, find themselves confronted by androgynous Angels of green, purple, and blue. These are certainly not angels as we popularly perceive them, but rather, concentrations of very specific types of divine intent. Essentially, they are security guards ensuring that the Tree remains in creative equilibrium: intelligent, independent entities, honed to particular functions.

The descriptions I have given are necessarily limited, intended to give the subconscious a few accurate clues rather than the consciousness a full, empirical description. The Qabalah itself does not operate on that level. As with all such exercises, it is for the participant to tap into the source.

# The Paths

Originally, I had intended to describe only the Sephiroth in *The Magic of Qabalah*, fixing the static conditions of each in the mind and allowing the individual to intuitively perceive the possible processes of arrival at that state. However, I have since decided that the signposts or symbols of the twenty-two paths between Sephiroth are too helpful to be overlooked in this book.

As a result of this I have included a short visualization or description in each chapter, in which one might encounter the major symbols between the Sephirah last described and the one about to be experienced. However, by zigzagging imaginatively up the Tree we only travel nine of the twenty-two routes. The remaining thirteen are described at the back of the book.

One point worth noting here is the feature of godforms upon the paths. This is a contentious point; Dion Fortune, with whom I find myself in agreement on practically every other point, confines the gods to the Sephiroth for the reason that the latter are objective, and thus the proper place for fixed manifestations. However, my own experience is that the gods are evident when one is travelling between spheres, and so I have adhered to the Crowley/Regardie system of attributing godforms to the Paths. Fortune is perfectly correct in that this is messier—and more confusing—and, though I wish it were not so, this is how I perceive it, and have thus recorded it as you will find it here. The different states bleed into one another and godforms seem to thrive off the crosscurrents. However, as the Paths are distinctly subjective, the reader will find him or herself drawing a personal conclusion on this point.

# The Veils of Negative Existence

There are three layers, or "veils" of the unmanifest lying just beyond Kether. *Ain*, meaning "nothing"; *Ain Soph*, "limitless nothing"; and that which lies closest to Kether, *Ain Soph Aur*, "boundless light emanating out of nothing." The last is the easiest to imagine, but all three are by their very nature incomprehensible. They symbolize the concept of pre-existence.

Regardie compares this concept to that of "the thrice-great Darkness of the Egyptian sacerdotal caste," which is worth mentioning if only because it is such a resonant allusion. It connects nicely with Nuit, whose boundless star-spangled body is another attribution of these strata of the infinite. However, both have human or semihuman referents, and thus do not properly echo the "nothingness" of the Three Veils. They are the space behind all perception and possible thought. They represent one of those metaphysical migraines children suffer when they first contemplate the sky at night. Where does it end? It must end somewhere: that's the rule!

Another correspondence is the Indian *Parabrahman*, "the causeless cause." It is the best we can do to note the comparisons, meditate on them a little perhaps, and then move on. They exist on the Tree to maintain a humbling perspective on man and his universe. Even in our most sublime moments we are unable to conceive of God's boundlessness.

# The Pillars

The Tree of Life is composed of three Pillars, on which the Sephiroth are placed. The right Pillar, comprising Binah, Geburah, and Hod, represents form, severity (because form is restrictive), and the *Ida* currents of Hinduism. It is construed of as feminine, though, as we shall see, it is in fact balanced equally between the genders.

The left Pillar, comprising Chokmah, Chesed, and Netzach, symbolizes force, mercy, and the *Pingala* currents of Hinduism. It is construed of as masculine.

The Middle Pillar is the Pillar of mildness, or equilibrium. Its four visible Sephiroth, Kether, Tiphareth, Yesod, and Malkuth, represent a balance between the polarities of female/male, form/force, severity/mercy.

There is another balancing act immediately evident in this arrangement. Rather than being entirely composed of feminine Sephiroth, for example, the Right Pillar is made up of Binah, which is feminine; Geburah, which is masculine; and Hod, which is hermaphroditic. Likewise the Left Pillar encompasses Chokmah, which is masculine; Chesed, exhibiting both male and female traits; and Netzach, the feminine sphere of Venus. Because all Sephiroth are emanations of the same Original Consciousness, they also "contain" one another, like interlocking bands of a mandala. However, the qualities exhibited at the "top" of the mandala so to speak—those most immediately in evidence as one studies the Sephirah—are their primary traits. Thus, looking at Binah, we may safely say that although the Sephirah is connected with many others (not least our own plane, Malkuth), its primary qualities are those of reception, form, and restriction, as represented by its planet, Saturn.

As power descends the Tree, it zigzags in a manner that takes into account an equal proportion of each polarity. This descent of consciousness is popularly known as the "Lightning Flash."

## Tarot Attributions

The Tarot and the Qabalah of the Western Mystery Tradition are so intimately linked that it is impossible to have a good working knowledge of the latter without an in-depth understanding of the seventy-eight Tarot cards and their meanings. A Tarot reading, conversely, may be performed without a working knowledge of the Qabalah, but it is greatly enriched by mental reference to this system. Besides, many packs have been designed with their Qabalistic correspondences in mind, and the pamphlets and books accompanying them describe the meanings of each card with reference to this esoteric system, even if this is not overtly stated in the text.

The interested reader is strongly advised to procure a pack of Tarot cards if (s)he does not already possess one. Apart from being an indispensable occult tool, it will help greatly with visualizations of the Sephiroth and the Paths between spheres. Meditation on the cards is an old and effective technique, opening astral doorways and familiarizing the participant with the various energies and their symbolism.

There are numerous Tarot packs available today, one for every mood of the month and still a few to spare. The occult's touchstone is without doubt the *Rider-Waite* deck—a classic, it is easy to learn, as each card is illustrated with an action-packed picture which a little imagination renders self-explanatory. This is the pack I always recommend to learners, and the main deck referred to in this book.

Several others deserve a mention, however, as each deck (including those too numerous to mention here) has its own particular strengths. *The Tarot of the Old Path* is a particular favorite, full of Wiccan, Netzachian energy as well as being an absolute delight to read. Many of the illustrations, such as the Karma, Temptation, and Strength cards (the former corresponding with the traditional Judgement and the Devil, respectively) are stunning in their innovative symbolic clarity. This pack is especially recommended for Pagans and neophyte Wiccans.

*The Witches Tarot* has the advantage of including in each illustration the edges of the Sephiroth closest to it, which makes it ideal for use when learning Qabalah. Ellen Cannon Reed, its co-designer and author of the accompanying book (*The Witches Tarot*,

Llewellyn 1997), has much of value to say on the subject of fundamental Qabalah.

The *Morgan-Greer* pack has all the advantages of the Waite deck, on which it is heavily based, but where Waite is grim, the *Morgan-Greer* is sassy. It is brighter and evokes less of the "maudlin Victorian drawing room" than its counterpart.

For lovers of Greek mythology, *The Mythic Tarot* is the obvious choice. Each card of the Major Arcana is related to a Greek god or goddess, and the Minor Arcana tell four stories relevant to their suit.

I will not overwhelm the reader by giving further examples, but suffice it to say that there is something for everyone, whether your inclination be Egyptian, feminist, Norse, Celtic, Qabalistic, Russian, or medieval. If you are not already well versed in Tarot, find a pack that suits you and break it in—this will aid you immensely in your quest to learn and experience the Qabalah.

# Malkuth

## "The Resplendent Intelligence"

### SEPHIRAH 10

*M*alkuth is the kingdom in which we operate when carnate, and includes all of our experiences of physicality. It is "the real world" in its most tangible, earthly form. Our experience is not merely mundane in Malkuth, but embraces the optimum achievements possible on the earth level. The actions and experiences here have a considerable impact on us, both intellectually and spiritually.

Mundanity is Maya, the delusion of individuality, the sense of divorce from the cosmic intelligence and the subsequent futility that continually tempts us to believe in it. Malkuth, protruding from the bottom of the Pillar of Equilibrium and "exiled" from the rest of the Tree, is deeply concerned with the issue of reclaiming oneness with the Divine. In Jewish lore, Malkuth represents the *Shekhinah* or female half of God, and, on an interpretative level, humanity itself striving towards reunion with God. It is a state of sorrow, but also of potential redemption. There is much to distract us from our quest to regain divine consciousness, such as the Maya just mentioned. Brute sensation is its brother, and if uninformed by the rest of the Sephiroth our experience of Malkuth would consist of nothing but sight, smell, touch, sound, and taste. We would have no reflective capacity, and our consciousness would resemble that of primeval man prior to his ruminations on the source of natural forces.

31

Malkuth is changing. Physically and sociologically we have evolved immensely over the centuries—particularly during the twentieth century—in which human consciousness has quantum-leaped. Society as a structure has made it possible for some people to cease the continual battle for survival, to look for God again (shamans, yogi(ni)s, nuns, and monks of course have been leading contemplative lives throughout history), and is involved in guarding against what is pernicious to its weaker community members. Society has brought us civic rights, education, protection from disorder; that is, shelter from the experience of Malkuth. However, it is a fact that spiritually speaking, the sophistication of man, far from indicating a step up the evolutionary ladder, has instead taken us one step away from our primary goal—that of return to the Cosmic Source.

Long ago the species was delivered into matter, into Malkuth, and gradually we assimilated it and made it work for us. Qabalistically this would take us back to Eden and the fall from grace. One interpretation of this ancient allegory is that the Fall represents the dawning of awareness of humanity's "difference" from God, the first seeds of duality in human consciousness. Suddenly Adam and Eve realized their vulnerability and fallibility in being separated from the Cosmic Source. This principle is represented by Malkuth and its many sensual cul-de-sacs of consciousness.

Currently, the ascetics among us believe we must conquer Malkuth by transcending the materialistic cravings it engenders, by quieting its noise in the minds that could be otherwise involved in celestial meditation. The hedonists disagree, seeking the Palace of Wisdom via the Road of Excess, seeking to experience the divine or the Kether in Malkuth. The former are working the Mystic Path, the Middle Way of Devotion. The latter are experiencing the Orphic Path in which music, dance, and revelry may lead to an expansion of consciousness. On the Tree of Life, this system belongs to the Right Hand Pillar. Then there is the approach of intellect, analysis, and conscious manipulation of matter in conformity with will; this constitutes the Hermetic Path which belongs to the Left Hand Pillar, that of severity. Most of us in the West follow a combination course: there is more than one way to crack the Malkuthic nut.

The cosmic doctrine is full of paradoxes—called euphemistically "variety"—and evidently it was designed thus. Some mystics describe God as a lonely individual dreaming us into consciousness; as Paramahansa Yogananda puts it, our lives are the "big movies" on the cinema screen of God's imagination. The fundamental point of Malkuth is to recall the truth that lies latent in all our soul memories: that we are not merely flesh, but immortal sparks of cosmic fire. Having truly perceived this, the natural impulse is to aspire to ascend. This ascent should, of course, end in the dissolving of the personality and subsequent re-assimilation into the mind of God—the *Samadhi* to which yogis of the East aspire, the ecstatic trance with no end.

However, here we are in *this* reality, with its bustling cynicism, its bills to pay, with harsh unreality pressing in on every side. Even when we dedicate ourselves to the spiritual path, the negative side of Malkuth, Maya has a way of stepping in and reasserting itself with a vengeance. Consider how many religious communities, occult fraternities, and churches exhibit pride, materialism, and low-level objectives concerning status, etc. Indeed, Maya redoubles its strength in situations in which it is threatened. One of the challenges of Malkuth is to rise above the vices and illusions with which we are plagued on this base level.

We can envisage Apollo shooting his arrows from Tiphareth down at Malkuth. Some of these are rays of illumination and healing that pierce the darkness of Malkuth. Some possess the illusion of either being positive or negative, having passed through Yesod, sphere of imagination. Others are pestilential, the result of duality, sent to cause madness and disease. We must decide which to receive and which to take shelter from.

Contrast can be beneficial to the imagination: the Sephirah immediately above Malkuth on the Tree, Yesod, offers thrills which appear exuberant compared with those of Malkuth (though against Tiphareth, Yesod's excitements pale in their own illusion). This leaves the spiritually inclined and the occultist with a double battle. First, against regular-strength Maya, we strive with the gravitational force continually reminding us that, though our astral bodies may fly, our physical ones cannot in an everyday context. Secondly, against the change of levels, which challenges what is commonly regarded as sanity. The magician and Qabalist work with many different types of consciousness, as represented by the different Sephiroth, and are capable of being "all things to all men," and are conversant with many different modes of consciousness and their denizens. What is perfectly natural on other planes is anathema to the mass consciousness of Malkuth, the physical—just as fish can breathe in water but will suffocate in the open air . . . except, that is, for a few flying fish who are fortunate enough to experience both worlds. The occultist too is able to exist in more than one set of circumstances. When journeying in Yesod, we follow the laws of the cosmic ocean; at home on Malkuth we have other currents with which to contend.

The question of sanity within the perceived "real world" is a trying one, and one which is unlikely to be resolved for as long as there is intelligent life on earth. It is our nature to have diverse opinions regarding nearly everything, and there will always be stick-in-the-muds who refuse to contemplate anything outside of their personally defined norm. This is a necessity within Malkuth. Of course, in other astral dimensions there are groups and societies with equally staunch rules, those bodies demanding that individuals define themselves, to keep their forms together. Likewise, if

every being on earth ceased to believe in gravity, and wholeheartedly believed they could levitate, we would find ourselves in a state
of uncontrolled chaos as untrained minds expressed their new-
found freedom. We need these ground rules, and it is quite natural
and healthy that the majority will reject unusual thought-forms,
even if the nonconformist individual must suffer occasionally for it.

Gullibility, of course, is the weapon of many a false guru, and
active discrimination is essential; but to limit one's credulity to
what is already accepted is to halt evolution in its tracks. For a
healthy life in Malkuth, one's imagination should be continually
stretched, one's discrimination perpetually exercised. This state of
being is an adventure, a physical analogue of inner reality. We
should be breaking new ground, developing from day to day, questioning ourselves and others, challenging complacency, because,
by the sheer fact that we are here in Malkuth, we know that we
have a long way to go. As William Blake puts it in his *Proverbs of
Hell*, "Everything Possible to be Believed is an Image of Truth."
Bearing in mind that divine energy from Kether reaches us via the
Sephirah Yesod, the sphere of dreams and imagination, this makes
even more sense. Importantly, we should check out the facts and
refer to our intuition before condemning or extolling a concept or
its exponent.

Look at the pioneers of science and spirituality, especially the
ridicule they were and subjected to by the dominant society. "The
world is round? Heresy! Burn him! How dare you escape from your
pigeonhole?"

I am not saying we should upend our lives in accordance with
every crackpot theory, but what a terrible waste when we laugh
cosmic truths to scorn! To quote Blake again, "What is now proved
was once only imagin'd."

Public scorn is the potential karma of the individual who presents new ideas to a necessarily defensive society. Like Prometheus
stealing fire from the heavens, those with strong convictions are

impelled to act, the evolution of the species being at stake. Nor is any seed of consciousness ever wasted—it either takes root in a living mind or returns to the Akashic Records, where all that has ever been thought, felt, or experienced is cataloged (one of the most useful tools for the occultist is knowing how to access this information—see Dion Fortune's *Secrets of Doctor Taverner* for examples)! Some of the wildest, most improbable theories have forged living links with a complex and powerful "other" consciousness. We need to be challenged at every juncture; it is from this friction that we learn and grow. The presentation of new concepts is a great work, but this does not protect the individual from being publicly condemned. Having received the seed-thoughts, we proceed to shoot the messenger (or elevate them to unrealistic guru-status). On the Malkuth plane we like nothing more than to make ourselves feel secure by ousting others, creating a pecking order of beauty, riches, prestige, and so-called sanity. What could be easier or safer than laughing at the new?

The banal can be potent when kept dammed up for a while, revealing just how strong it has become when it's given an excuse to pour forth. The sacred space is often desecrated by such tidal waves and the debris released by this flood of the trapped mundane. It will always be this way on this plane, where consensual opposition exists against ascension. With performed magick, however, the skeptical group-mind can have no effect except on one's perception of present reality. Unfortunately, in Malkuth it is this—the immediate and one-dimensional—to which we are primarily attuned.

As the magickal adage goes, "Malkuth is in Kether, and Kether is in Malkuth, though after another manner." In other words, there is a direct link between the immanent world of the flesh and the creative source. This is less obvious than it may sound, for the link is primarily a function of the mind and body *in conjunction with* the spirit. All are necessary, none is redundant. A balanced personality is as reliant on sweeping the floor as it is on a knowledge of metaphysics. The tale of Malkuth is the tale of the true Sorcerer's Apprentice, who is forced to complete numerous paltry tasks before reliable magic even comes into the equation. All of us are forced to do our time in the long slog of banality, but if we complete our tasks with competence and good cheer, our faith and effort will bring their own rewards.

Grounding on the physical plane is absolutely essential in magick: without being "earthed" it is impossible to maintain a strong mental image, for grounding is in some sense the key that unlocks the door into the beyond. It is not for nothing that witches of yore pissed into the cauldron and had their neophytes eat from the brew straight afterwards; for a neophyte with neither the humility to do so nor the ability to decently purge the cauldron of its immediate past was not worth the training. My own training involved endless chores, as I was utterly unversed in the fundaments of physical existence at the time. I learned to clean, cook, and concentrate *even on the undesirable* before I was allowed to be consciously active on the Inner Planes, despite having performed advanced rituals prior to this training. It was dull and frustrating, but it worked. The undisciplined forces of my own psyche—which had hitherto blown me about like a dry leaf on the wind—were brought under control, and the unwanted elements became grounded in physical experience. There is nothing to say that the street-sweeper and toilet attendant are not undergoing just such an apprenticeship on the cosmic level; in fact, there is every probability that they are.

Each incarnation is intended to bring us closer to our goal of return to the cosmic source by providing us with the opportunities to develop certain areas of our psycho-spiritual constitutions. Always bear in mind that the goal is not obliteration of the body, or of the psyche; rather, the aim of this practice is to achieve the enhancement of the essential spark to ecstatic proportions. This is the gift of Malkuth; the practical opportunity to improve ourselves on the most grounded of levels. It is a realm of tutelage, and capable of being either a prison or a Narnia, depending on how we are placed both physically and constitutionally.

Malkuth can be great fun, especially when negative experiences are viewed in terms of nullifying karma—one's own, that is. The attitude that other people may deserve their negative experiences is one of the most pernicious in existence, just as compassion is one of the greatest. With so many unseen forces at work, we are unable to accurately assess anything in this realm; we may react, we may protect ourselves and others, but judgment itself should be left to the Gods.

## Meditation on Malkuth

As the essence of Malkuth is the use of physical tools to attain assimilation and ascension, the meditation will mirror this. It is also worth considering the thought from *The Lost Book of Paradise*: "all is inside the Garden/now we have climbed outside/to find all things hidden/like the gods."

The process of Malkuth is one of assimilation of the lessons of Matter, and a reclamation of our original unity with the Father/Mother God. All that we require for ascent is available in this sphere, which contains doorways to all of the others. All that is above is represented here, particularly by Nature, the *forêts de symboles* referred to in Baudelaire's *Correspondances*.

One of the dual meanings of Malkuth concerns the balance between healthy awe (of Creation in its entirety) and perspective, so that one is neither swept away by spirituality nor overly cynical about it. Being grounded, but not too grounded, consciousness is a kite with its string held firmly in the hand of reason. The height gives perspective; the string provides a means of touching home base.

In Malkuth we have the choice of discrimination.

The names by which Malkuth is known are various, but several include an allusion to a gate. She is "the Gate of Death," "of Eden," "of Prayer." Thought-matter has descended from Kether (fallen from grace, or Eden) and become material, thus apparently finite. Death is the illusion we must bear from the standpoint of the final (but equally valid) Sephirah. Death is a gate into the Astral, just as birth is the gate into Malkuth; it is not difficult to see why this metaphor was chosen.

At the gate between Yesod and Malkuth, the first of the higher realms, we pray for redemption; that is, for "re-ascension." Malkuth is also called the Virgin, which, coupled with the idea of intercession, is highly reminiscent of Mary, Mother of Christ. This relates, via Isis, to Binah, one of whose titles is *Ama*, the Superior Mother. As another of Malkuth's appellations is "the Inferior Mother," we can recognize a strong relationship between Binah, representing the idea of form, and Malkuth, which is form's ultimate expression. Thus she is also "Daughter of the Mighty Ones," the "youngest" Sephirah, the final deliberate expression of Godhead. As the Bride she is also God's female side, the exiled Shekhinah mentioned before, she who is invoked by Jews every Friday night, as dusk falls and Sabbath begins. More detail about this essential facet of Deity may be found in the section on Binah.

Yet another title for Malkuth is "the Gate of Justice." We play out a great deal of our karma on Malkuth, and the name befits this role. That it is also the Gate of Tears goes without saying. Here, we suffer to learn.

The particular spiritual purpose of the sphere is the Vision of the Holy Guardian Angel, meaning the belief and understanding that there is more to life than working, eating, sleeping and partying, or suffering. As well as giving insight, the Angel imparts a feeling of protection that predicts the gift of the next sphere, in which a sense of cosmic rightness is established. There is more to it all than Malkuth, of course, but Malkuth is as valid as the rest. This earthing element can be of particular help to the neophyte, preventing the glamouring influences of Yesod from taking full sway.

The Tarot cards attributed to Malkuth are the Ten of Pentacles, Ten of Wands, Ten of Swords, and Ten of Cups. Of these, two are good and two not so, reflecting the general state of ambivalence on the earth plane.

The Ten of Pentacles represents progeny, the fruits of the earth, the establishment and continuation of family tradition, the zenith of a lifetime's work in Malkuth. The card, as depicted in the *Rider-Waite* pack, shows a gray-haired, bearded patriarch surrounded by coats of arms, fruitful vines, his hunting dogs, and his youthful family. One feels he is halfway through a well-deserved, affluent retirement: this man has worked hard, and succeeded in his endeavors. Prosperity, love, and progeny are his and, indeed, are to be inherited by his family. All that is good in Malkuth has been harvested by this man.

The Ten of Wands is also a card of success, but here the querent faces up to the problems of overachievement. The figure in the card is struggling with his load of ten wands, back bent, unable to put them down just yet. He has taken on more than he can handle, has too many projects, interests, and ambitions on the go; he needs to shed a few of them in order to gain a little time for himself. The lesson here is obvious: we need to participate fully in Malkuth without getting bogged down by its numerous activities and neglecting the inner life, our passport out of here.

The Ten of Swords is never a cheery addition to a reading, depicting a man cast down with ten swords sticking out of his back. Still, it is an image most of us can relate to in one way or another: the feeling of being at an all-time low, desolate, utterly wretched. Nobody escapes this unpleasant state of being at the bottom of the Wheel of Fortune; it is a function of cyclic Malkuth. At first, looking at the card, it seems as if the figures life-blood is draining away; but, on closer inspection, it becomes evident that the red "fluid" is in fact a red blanket or cloak. Likewise, though the image seems dark, dawn is breaking on the horizon. That old cliché springs to mind, "It is always darkest before the dawn," and is perfectly applicable to this card.

In Malkuth, of course, it is often difficult to have faith in this oncoming dawn: our self-pitying thoughts and negative actions pierce us like swords. In a way, our intellectual capacity, represented by the Air element and its sword symbolism, has thwarted us, causing us to believe ourselves independent of any cosmic creative intelligence. This also abnegates the possibility of redemption and, indeed, causes one to conclude that there is no purpose to this complex life of ours. Certainly a depressing state of affairs.

In the Ten of Cups, on the other hand, a man and woman stand with their arms uplifted to the heavens, where a rainbow spans the sky. Two infants dance nearby. In the background the red roof of a house can be seen, probably their homestead, as well as a river and trees. Generally, the card reveals a fertile environment. Peaceful exuberance characterizes the image. These are people who have mastered the material side of Malkuth, getting just enough of it to make them happy; they are predominantly concerned with their emotional lives, represented by their children and the way the man's arm spans the woman's waist, and the spiritual, represented by the rainbow. The colorful archway also indicates the proximity of the dream-sphere, Yesod.

These four cards illustrate some of the major components and challenges of Malkuth.

The goddesses allocated to this Sephirah are Persephone, Demeter, and Laksmi, among others. The first represents seasonal changes—the myth of Persephone's abduction to the Underworld is one of the cornerstone myths of this sphere. Spring and summer become autumn and winter. The goddess was here, now she is underground— when will she return? It is not difficult to understand the significance of seasonal myths in the light of Malkuth and its levels of operation, in which the present moment always seems the most real, and all seems finite.

Demeter, as well as being active in the Persephone-Hades myth, is relevant in her role as Empress, fertile corn goddess, bringer of plenty. Likewise is Laksmi relevant, representing wealth and fortune, sustenance, and physical fertility. These are the things most popularly craved in Malkuth.

One of the creatures ascribed to Malkuth is the sphinx. Echoing the entrance to the Egyptian Mystery Temple, this attribution encapsulates the fundamental riddle of our presence here. Even enlightened beings wonder that we exist, and are exiled; the whole thing seems so ridiculous. We live, we suffer (we laugh, too, if we are lucky), we die—to be born again, no doubt, but why, O *why*? The smug sphinx looks as if she might know but, typically, her defining trait, apart from her human head and lion's body, is her silence. Silence, the same characteristic that typifies Binah.

Of course, rather than answer a riddle, the sphinx is more likely to set us one. Her very name means "one who binds fast": we are held captive by our inability to crack the code of life. Malkuth itself is similarly full of questions and not answers, for we cannot really begin to be answered until we reach Yesod, and rise. The question asked of Oedipus by the sphinx—which is the animal that has four feet in the morning, two at midday, and three in the evening?—was of course a reference to the progression of man from infancy to old age. Had Oedipus failed to recognize the fact, he would have been instantly consumed, just as we are consumed by time if we fail to take stock of it. It is easy to go through life oblivious, but a lack of consciousness will lead to our being eaten by the enigma itself. Matter will be consumed by matter, but spirit will rise.

Just as the sphinx is a composite, a hybrid of lion and human, so too do we aim to combine our animal nature and qualities with a higher understanding that (hopefully) typifies our ascent to the

MALKUTH 43

top of the evolutionary ladder. In its animal torso we glimpse our own atavistic past. Likewise, as the sphinx is usually depicted as *couchant*, so too is our potential lying in wait, barely exercised yet.

Finally, the sphinx, frequently depicted on tombs and in Egyptian papyri relating to the Underworld, was the guardian at the Gate of Death. What could be more appropriate to Malkuth than this tacit, placid, yet potentially lethal totem?

Assumption of godforms in ritual situations is the method of ascent natural to Malkuth. This means adopting the qualities and perspective of deities and astral archetypes. However, a gentler form of working is possible through the elemental energies, namely Earth, Air, Fire, and Water, and acquaintance with the elemental beings inherent in these. This provides a natural bridge to Netzach, home of the elementals and other entities whose evolution runs parallel to ours.

Spiritualist work and high-level mediumship provide a link with astral Yesod, as do the healing arts and work with the dying and bereaved. It is common in these situations to experience a sensation of detachment from the physical body and from the world at large. Dream work also leads to the subtler lunar sphere of Yesod.

In its relation to the other Sephiroth, Malkuth might be described as a basket hanging beneath the balloon that is the astral sphere of Yesod. The comparison is apt, as we can gain a great deal of insight from the lofty vantage point proffered by Yesod, but occasionally we need to touch down, gather supplies, and reacquaint ourselves with a more naturally human lifestyle lest we become airsick and/or starve. Leaving Malkuth altogether, we "die," or cease to be physically evident. Yesod is a "'basket" as well, hanging between two balloons, those of Hod and Netzach. The ascent is infinite, but a grounding in Malkuth is vital. Why would we be here, if we did not require it?

Let your senses be drawn by the positive components of Malkuth.

The tricksters of this realm, the stomping ground of Maya, include entertainment-addiction and arrogance. The latter is caused by the half-baked intellect so common in our species; the sense of "knowing it all." It is also facilitated by the idea that we are perfectly all right as we are, and need not bother to strive. This, of course, is a species of indolence.

The vices of the tenth Sephirah have a tendency to end nihilistically, as all blunt the finer senses and are prohibitive to astral manifestation. Following the first glowing signs, which only become visible with some effort, will lead us out of the comfy confines of Hotel Malkuth. This is not to say that nonspiritual activity is wrong, or a waste of time—personally, I am partial to a glass of wine and a soap opera some nights—indeed, pleasure aside, such periods of "tuning out" can be extremely useful for grounding. (As Dion Fortune's *The Sea Priestess* is well aware, alcohol may be used to finely tune a mood, even for ritual purposes; and no true Wiccan or occultist fails to appreciate the symbolism of red wine.) It is simply a fact that, under certain circumstances (such as continual, exclusive usage), these sense-stimuli also act as barriers to subtle perceptions. How many of us drink, watch TV, busy ourselves with the trivial, in order to forget? These activities blot out thought and time. Dismissiveness, concentration on "the inevitable facts of life" to the exclusion of what is challenging in life—whether it be sociological, spiritual, or intellectual—does the same.

In comparison, we have the unsullied perceptions received during deep meditation, or following a good night's sleep, or when walking in sunlight down a street or by a body of water: those moments of lucidity when life feels great and everything fits, even the apparently irrelevant. These are the routes out of Malkuth. I will not describe them further at this point. We must stay "grounded" for the time being, and further meditation on higher experience will cause us to ascend prematurely into Yesod.

To be, and to will to fulfill one's optimum potential: these are the groundworks of ascension from Malkuth.

# Encountering the In-House Divinities

The God-name at Malkuth is *Adonai ha-Aretz,* "Lord of Earth."

Its Archangel is Sandalphon, who rules over the atomic structure of all the forms on Earth. He is also regent of all the countries of earth and their group souls, these being at varying stages of development. He works in conjunction with Uriel, the Angel usually invoked in relation to the element of Earth. Uriel is responsible for the vaster structure and development of the planet itself, independent of its present inhabitants. The Ice Age, for example, would have been ordained by Uriel, as well as the eruption of volcanoes, tidal waves, and other natural phenomena which come under his jurisdiction.

Uriel therefore controls the elements themselves, while Sandalphon rules over the evolution of all species and the paths of all atoms through matter (after all, each atom may be undergoing its own evolution). We are comprised of matter that has always been here; we did not "create" it. It is quite mind-boggling to consider where our own body's atoms may have been before. Each of our physical structures was produced by our mother in the womb, true, but she got the energy to duplicate the cells from her own cells and from the food she ate, the water she drank, and the air she breathed. Everything she assimilated became a part of our original makeup. In turn, the substances she took in had their origin elsewhere. Vegetables grew in the soil and took in the blueprint of whatever elements were in the earth at that time, from the minerals of other vegetation, long transformed from plant to compost, to the DNA of whatever persons or animals may have died around there, millennia before. In a worst-case scenario, the vegetables were sprayed with chemicals that also infiltrated her bloodstream. All of this went into the "manufacture" of your body.

The evolution of the atom is no simple matter, particularly when we consider the belief that we were put here to conquer dense matter. This does not mean treating all but the spiritual with disrespect; rather, we are encouraged to avoid the pitfalls of materialism. There is also the belief that matter may be redeemed and sanctified by being incorporated into the body of an initiate, thus "enlightening" the atoms. One who thinks in this way would believe a skin cell on an initiates arm to be of greater value than the cell on a cabbage leaf, which of course it would be, to him or her. However, Sandalphon might argue that every single atom is essential, and that the loss of one might cause unimaginable disruption to the cosmos. Likewise, the ultimate Deity might feel that no soul on earth, however wretched and downcast, was of less value than another, however spiritually adept that soul might be. Indeed, isn't there supposed to be more rejoicing in Heaven at the return of one "lost sheep" than at the continued faithfulness of an established flock member? We always want what it is more difficult to have, it would seem, even on High.

Under Sandalphon's watchful eye are the angelic *Ashim*, also known as the Souls of Fire, or the Perfect Men. This fire relates to the aforementioned consciousness of atoms, the spark of consciousness, of intelligent potential, which often appear as a flame on certain levels. William G. Gray attributes the "cherubs" or *Kerubim* to Malkuth, since they represent the four elements, a correspondence obvious to the earth Sephirah. Likewise, the Souls of Fire are appropriate to Yesod, the Sephirah that rests between lives and the plans for reincarnation. It is easy to visualize these angelic flames guiding us during such an interim stage, and also to imagine the souls of the discarnate as flames, or sparks of life consciousness. The choice, as with much in this hypereclectic era, is purely subjective.

## Entering the Sephirah

If you are not already familiar with the Magician card of the Tarot, look it up prior to beginning this visualization. This will help establish the relevant scenario in your mind.

Traditionally, this card has related to the twelfth path, connecting Binah to Kether. As Binah is the Sephirah of understanding on an intrinsic level—and the next stop from Malkuth is Yesod, where understanding begins (one learns of life as a metaphor, past incarnations, etc., on approaching Yesod)—the shared symbolism is appropriate. Here, however, we are learning to be the Magician on a practical level. The card takes on symbolism of greater spiritual energies higher up on the Tree.

## The Temple of Malkuth

The Temple of Malkuth appears to me as a functional black-and-white tiled chamber with columns, made of cool, smooth marble. The tiles are regularly placed, yet there is something infinitely fascinating about their pattern. The vibrant black and white tiles seem to speak volumes.

The Temple is quite plain except for vases of luminescent peacock-feathers, symbolic of the senses and earthly vices. When the Temple is first entered, the eyes of the feathers seem to follow you like those of a lusty satyr. However, these are facets that have been gathered up and controlled; their function could even be described as decorative. You realize their presence to be an analogy for sense-slavery, and that, as you have entered the elevated worlds of the Qabalah, your sense perceptions have become servile, while you hold mastery over them. The pervasive atmosphere of holy calm soothes your troubled nerves.

In the middle of the chamber is a white marble bath, or lave, full of lustrous salt water. It is effective to have a salty bath on this plane while visualizing yourself in the elevated Malkuthic version.

Hold the terrestrial salt high towards the East and ask for it to be blessed with formidable cleansing properties, so that any factors hindering your search for the Divine, both within and without, might be neutralized by it. As you sprinkle the sanctified salt into the clear bath water, see the whole bath glowing white. As you step in, be aware of the tiled black-and-white floor, the attentive vases of peacock feathers, the fact that the very moment your foot hits the aura of the water your leg becomes first radiant, then brilliant white. Submerge your entire body bit by bit (it is better to give your head a quick dip, but if this is not possible, flicking water at it will do, so long as you strongly visualize it causing your head to irradiate brilliance), and watch as flakes of unclean matter dissolve from your body, bringing a feeling of relief and spiritual freedom. As you do this, the peacock feathers also dissolve, first turning white, then dissipating. Tiny swarms of light hang in their place, a vision of atomic purity. They cluster together and form a single candleless flame, then another . . . and before you know it, you are surrounded by these slender, graceful souls of fire. Their radiance is different from that of the bath—the luminous salt water made you feel clean, but these luminaries seem to tell you that all experience is good, there is no right and wrong, no clean and unclean. All that you are exists for a reason, is sanctified.

You step out of the bath in your body of light, full of hope.

First, let's come to grips with the body. After all, this is the most fundamental gift of Malkuth, and without it we would not be able to visit this plane in so definite a manner.

The body proffers many of the tools required in Malkuth: limbs to perform practical tasks; the faculty of speech and thus communication; the mind and all its wonders; the opportunity to consolidate affection by, for example, holding hands.

Activities such as massage and reflexology are very good for getting us in touch with the positive aspects of Malkuth, as is partying with good friends, walking in the park, having fun . . . *but remembering that there is a Beyond*. This is not a maudlin realization. Rather, such a deep understanding provides perspective from which the pleasures of life can be redoubled.

One of the best ways of assimilating Malkuth is to do what you love most of all. Music is a great uplifter (and confuser) on the plane of Malkuth, and listening to favorites can on occasion carry us direct to higher spheres. Food is another excellent manifestation for Malkuthic purposes, being the source of both pleasure and nutrients for the human body; eating is by its very nature a grounding action. Appreciating every mouthful, its source (the earth, not the supermarket!) and its transformation into body-energy, is a good place to start.

Stand facing East at the center of your most comfortable room, raise your arms so that your body forms a Y, then plant your feet directly beneath your shoulders.

Feel the power of your physical presence and your control over the machine that is your body. Resolve to control the expression and flow of every aspect of yourself: physiological, neurological, spiritual. Of course, this is a very tall order, but every achievement begins with the impulse of will.

Your body and mind, as well as those material attainments you have gathered during your present incarnation, will provide your tools on this level. But bear in mind that you intend to journey to other spheres. Therefore you require tools and weapons that are not of this earthly realm.

Maintaining the posture of conducting cosmic energies, feel these energies spilling into your receptive hands, arms, and cranium, until your body is aglow with potent creative light.

Now you are going to apply this energy to the elemental forces of Malkuth in order to craft yourself a Class-A set of astro-spiritual tools and weapons.

Visualize yourself at the center of the yellow, dark red, green, and blue tent-sphere (see Malkuth section of the Introduction) as a magician preparing his or her tools—as seen in the Tarot card image. In Malkuth you are playing the part of the Hermetic Mage, using physical laws and properties in conjunction with directed Will. Spiritual qualities, though of paramount importance, are latent on this level, while those elements which are active are denser and more coherent and tangible, related as they are to the deliberate discipline of human personality forces.

You, the Magician, stand at the center of this circular, circus-like canopy, dressed dramatically in a robe of red velvet, beneath which a simple white tunic of cool, clean cotton covers your torso. You enjoy both the simplicity of the tunic and the thespian quali-ties of the blood-red cloak, hence your choice of garments.

Beneath your bare feet you feel the power of the earth. A slight breeze ruffles your hair and ripples through the trees that flank you. Birdsong drifts from their abundant canopies, and the smell of recently cut grass delights your nostrils. This is your circle of con-tainment and concentration, now a sphere. The atmosphere is fresh, as after a downpour.

Before you is a table of stone, and on it the implements of your craft: a pentacle, a sword, a chalice, and a wand. They are fine specimens, each item seeming to perfectly represent the archetype of its kind. However, there is something in their composition that lacks luster. You pick the implements up, one by one. They have weight all right, and form, and a degree of color—but they require that subtle quality which will make them fit for magickal use.

Pick up the pentacle and consider its properties.

The disc is thick and sturdy. If you drop it, it will dent the ground rather than itself. It is probably worth a lot, considering that it was forged from such good metal.

You admire the craftsmanship that has gone into carving the five-pointed star with its encompassing circle onto the surface; this object has been concentrated over, and is the fruit of honest toil. You recall the adage, "The Gods give their rewards only to those who sweat for them." This reminds you that there is work to be done.

Still holding the pentacle in your mind's eye, you imagine your-self standing at its center, your head at the uppermost point, a position representing the faculty of thought. Your arms are out-stretched to the points representing Air and Fire, your feet are planted on those below, of Earth and Water.

You know that the tools on the table before you are dedicated each to a particular element—the pentacle to Earth, the sword to Air, the wand to Fire, and the chalice to Water. The vivifying element you need is that of Akasha, the fifth element of spirit-thought, and this you must direct through your individual Will. You, the Magician, must make of your body a channel for cosmic forces, and learn to capture and control them, like electricity.

Holding two conjoined fingers of your right hand skyward as a living wand, the imaginary pentacle clasped in your left hand, begin to direct cosmic energy down into the pentacle until it glows with golden light. When you are satisfied with its energy level, you must then consecrate it to Earth.

As you think this, green and brown intertwining vines seem to leap from the ground at your feet and bind themselves about and through the glowing pentacle. Steady currents of Earth energy, full of vitality yet slow and deliberate, pulsate into the tool, now glowing green and brown in conjunction with your thoughts.

Say out loud: "Astral Pentacle, I consecrate thee to the Powers of Earth. You will be available to me when I require grounding, or when the element of Earth is necessary to me. So mote it Be."

Pleased with your work, you place the firmly established magickal pentacle back on the stone altar (for the table has become an altar now, bearing witness to such rituals), and raise the chalice. You briefly admire your own reflection in its surface. It makes you want to daydream, this object: it is the cup of the Muse, from which a Nereid might drink.

You look at the pentacle and find yourself refocusing on the practical. The chalice is enchanting but, again, it requires that certain subtle fire you have successfully invested in the pentacle. As you think it, a tendril of ocean mist seems to stroke your face, a taste of sea salt tingles on your tongue. As yellow light floods into it and jiggles its particles around, the chalice, uplifted, vibrates in your fingers. Yet it still feels solid, in an elegant and distinctly feminine manner.

The powers of Water rise in the room; you begin to feel fanciful, rather more emotional than you might like—you remind yourself that it is in order to develop your tools that you are engaged in this process, but the water nymphs filling the room seem to gurgle with laughter at the thought. They shimmer naturally around your upheld chalice and you take the opportunity to consecrate it to the element of Water, saying:

"Astral Chalice, I consecrate thee to the Powers of Water. You will be available to me to contain and enhance the female and emotional force, and when the element of water is necessary to me. So mote it Be."

Replacing the chalice on the altar, your eyes fall on the sharp, cold sword by its side. A pang of neurosis assails your system. Are you merely deluded, misguided, mad even? Surely your intellect should be informing your actions, rather than mere intuition?

Lifting the weapon aloft you wish vehemently that you could slice through the bullshit and cut straight to the heart of the matter.

Anger infiltrates your blood and your jaw clenches with determination. You will succeed in your endeavors, on every plane. You make a conscious vow to use your mental powers and discrimination to redouble the resolve of your quest. And woe betide any that stand in your way!

As you think this, the sword begins to vibrate with red cosmic energies, so strongly that it seems to threaten to snap the tensed weapon in two. Realizing that force must be regulated if it is not to implode, you quieten your thoughts, through an effort of will, to "what is necessary" rather than "what is indulgent." The sword glows golden now, as your other tools did. Eddies of air caress its surface; the sylphs cannot be cut by it, for it is of their own substance; they can *become* it and *endow* it, however. Indeed, they seem intent on the latter, and even as you glance upon their slender forms you witness the elementals of air blessing your sword of their own volition. In conjunction with this natural cue you say:

"Astral Sword, I consecrate thee to the powers of Air. You will be available to me when I require an intellectual boost or strength of Will, or when the element of Air is necessary to me. So mote it Be."

You replace the astral sword on the altar, resolving to use its blade, not to do harm, but to cut away the obsolete or to protect.

Rather self-satisfied, you take a small step back and smooth the folds of your velveteen cloak down your thighs. Your eyes rest on the final sacred item—the Magician's most essential tool. It is the conducting-stick or wand, the symbol of directed force and controlled creativity. Even glancing at it brings ideas teeming into your mind.

You raise the wand aloft, and as you do it seems to sprout and a blossom of potential burgeons from its wood. A delightful fragrance assails your senses; you think of how much you love this realm with its natural beauty and bountiful verdure, of the myriad species it nurtures, creatures whose evolution runs parallel to our own. This is true, cosmic magick—the creation of intelligent matter out of a vortex of antimatter. The fire of vitality that separates the empty corpse from the living entity—the subtle fire of Being—this is what your astral wand can channel.

Excited by this thought, you perceive tiny tongues of flame leaping from the center of your forehead and entering the tip of the wand. Salamanders, the sprites of Fire, flicker and fly about the upheld branch, giving it the curious appearance of a flaming torch unburning at the center, investing the branch with their elemental vitality.

You experience the boltlike sensation of energy levels changing as the wand upgrades itself to the same astral status as your other tools. As it does, you say:

"Astral Wand, I consecrate thee to the powers of Fire. You will be available to me for inspiration, and when my soul lacks luster may it be refreshed by you. When the element of Fire is necessary to me, be thou at my disposal. So mote it Be."

Your four consecrated tools now sit glowing on the altar, each divested of a slightly different wavelength, so that they all seem a little out of kilter and shimmer in subtly different ways.

You, the Mage, have worked hard, and you are pleased with the results of your efforts. All that remains is to consecrate yourself as the Akashic force, thus completing the pentacle.

To do so, imagine a stream of brilliant light entering the top of your head, and say:

"Here I stand in Malkuth, aspiring to the Ain Soph Aur. Let the Cosmic Intelligence activate my spirit, my spirit activate my mind, and my mind activate my body. So mote it Be."

Stamp ten times on the floor to conclude the exercise.

Use your newly forged astral tools as often as you can. You will soon find that they take on a life of their own.

# Yesod

## "The Pure or Clear Intelligence"
### SEPHIRAH 9

*H*aving worked hard in Malkuth, you can let your imagination loose in Yesod.

Here is the realm of creative fantasy, a place of refuge from the harsh "realities" of the earth sphere. By harnessing the inspired imagination in conjunction with its ability to attract the energies it represents, a worthwhile magickal operation may take place. The image of Yesod becomes the receptacle for the force of Netzach and the willed conclusion of Hod. In this Yesodic vehicle, the magician's aspirations are carried down into Malkuth, where they act as a focus for the directed Will. As we have already noted, "Fantasy is the ass that carries the Ark."

The color of Yesod in Yetzirah, Briah, and Atziluth is purple-indigo, the same color as the Akashic egg of Hindu cosmology. It suggests darkness with a tinge of light, or the realm of imagination and psychism. The Akashic egg contains the whole of creation, and all of the knowledge of all of the worlds. In Yesod, we first perceive the existence of the Akashic Records—though it may be a while before we are able to access them. The psychological equivalent to Yesod is the subconscious, in which is stored every experience we have ever undergone, arguably both individually and en masse.

It is through Yesod that our consciousness is attached to the Cosmic Whole—in the case of the Qabalah, to the rest of the Tree

of Life. Dion Fortune expresses this principle admirably in her
novel, *The Sea Priestess*, when the emotionally repressed and psychically disenfranchised Wilfred Maxwell learns to communicate
with the moon, and opens up channels of much wider communication in the process. It is significant that he must be "knocked
out" by an asthma attack in order to begin this: a state of altered
consciousness is required. Likewise, Yesod is rarely contacted when
one is in a Malkuthic frame of mind; in these instances, the closest we get to this sphere is through symbolism. Visiting a symbol-
ist or surrealist art exhibition, for example, is witnessing Yesod in
Assiah—that is, from the work-a-day standpoint of Malkuth—but
in order to "get into" the pictures, a willing suspension of disbelief
is required. On the verge of sleep, we might run our mind over a
particular image from the exhibition and see into it, beyond it,
experience it in an entirely new way. This is Yesod in action on its
own level, Briah.

It stands to reason that the godforms attributed to Yesod should
be lunar, reflected in the aspects of Diana or Artemis, Selene, Isis,
Thoth, Hecate, Rama-Chandra, to name but a few. The specific
implications of each are very different, but as the moon has many
phases, so does Yesod have many facets. Yesod may been likened to
a spectrum, breaking consciousness into a rainbow dreamworld. I
often think of the rainbow as a symbol of Yesod because the astral
worlds accessed through this Sephirah are so pristine and colorful,
the higher ones at least. The rainbow symbol also recalls Iris,
ancient Greek messenger of the gods, a tactful intermediary and,
significantly, one of those able to "cut the cord" connecting the
spirit to the body. This role is deeply relevant to Yesod, which is
approached by the thirty-second path, *Tau*, the same path travelled after death.

The traditional scent attributed to Yesod is jasmine. Indian
visionaries often experience their saints in the higher spheres as
perfumed, and the chosen aroma is usually jasmine or sandalwood.

Jasmine has mystical connotations suitable to the sphere of Yesod, and its whiteness and sweet scent seem to represent purity. At night, the jasmine looks a ghostly indigo, the color of Yesod. Reminiscent of paradisiacal gardens such as the Eden—now reachable only through the Gate of Death—the lovely jasmine evokes emotions of pleasure, nostalgia, and sensuality, all of which are native to Yesod.

However, all these perfumes are tools of this sphere, and anything evocative and dreamy will do, any scent that lifts your spirit out of the mundane world of Malkuth and into the spiritual empyrean.

Burning a miniature fire of Azrael will help attune you to the "Moon Sephirah." To do this, gather sandalwood, juniper, and cedar wood chips (all available from New Age shops) and mix them together on a charcoal disc. Alternately, you could employ essential oils for their scent. In an ideal, ecologically stable world, one would use proper logs on an open fire (as does Morgan Le Fey in *The Sea Priestess*), a combination reputed to bring prophetic visions. Wonderful if you have the resources, but rare! Still, merely smelling these redolent ingredients in their diminutive version, as oils or even joss sticks, will provide you with a suitable frame of mind.

Another powerful moon-inducing scent is rosemary. Most moon incenses contain large dosages of this herb, as well as relevant aromatic gums, so burning one of these will help. Do not overdo it though—you don't want to choke on the smoke (charcoal discs in themselves can produce a great deal of fallout). A *hint* is better than an overdose. You want to feel ethereal, after all, not asthmatic.

Incenses are very good for producing a sense of ritual and import, but a dab of oil on the wrists can often produce the right effect with a lot less mess and smoke. Personally, I find it best to extinguish charcoal discs before meditating: they have an alarming habit of crackling and spitting sparks, and one should be aware that they can represent a fire hazard. A good compromise is to burn the incense on a disc about an hour before the operation, leaving the door shut in between. This should allow for just the right amount of scent without smoke. (Sometimes smoke is required, of course, and this method would be unsuitable; for the purposes of this book, however, the technique is apt.)

# Getting from Malkuth to Yesod
## "The Administrative Intelligence"
### PATH 32

To get from Malkuth to Yesod one must travel the thirty-second path of the Tree, symbolized by the Tarot card the World. There is a line in *The Lost Book of Paradise* that describes the realization of the thirty-second path to perfection: "life is not a beginning and death not an end." It is worth meditating on this before you begin.

Sometimes, due to prolonged pressure and/or distress, this path is travelled spontaneously, just as the world of sleep takes us up without ceremony. This is the same route we travel at death and, conversely, at birth. Essentially, this path connects us with the astral plane.

When Persephone was gathering narcissus, in the myth perhaps most central to occult lore, she was in Malkuth (though also, technically speaking, on the island of Crete). Pluto snatched her and dragged her into the chasm, and as she fell she travelled the thirty-second path. She ended up in Hades, here symbolic of a region of Yesod.

Her experience was far from pleasant, but eventually she assimilated and became Queen of the Dead as well as a powerful priestess. Temporarily stripped of power and plunged into an environment alien to her, Persephone opened up areas of her psyche hitherto undiscovered, and became conversant in both realms. Living part of the year with Demeter above ground, the other part in Hades, the bipolar Persephone, as well as being obvious choice for the

High Priestess card, exemplifies the combination of skills symbolized by the the World in Tarot.

The World card usually depicts a naked androgyne or female dancing in space, framed by either a laurel wreath or a snake eating its own tail (the *ouroboros*). The figure is traditionally a virgin, denoting one who has not yet reproduced. Instead of being externalized, the figure's potential is in a state of gestation.

The laurel tree and its branches have long been sacred, and were used extensively in the Greek mysteries. For example, the oracular Pythia at Delphi burned and sometimes chewed laurel leaves to induce a stupor through which Apollo might speak. Like the figure in the World card, she was a virgin, though here it represented naïveté, lack of any precocity which could threaten the authenticity of her utterances. The Pythia was intended to be a simple soul. The woman/androgyne in the World card is also a simple figure, but not through lack of internal complexity. Her experience runs deep, but it has been assimilated and brought under control. She is the mistress of her Malkuthic body and its neurone reactions. She has thrown off the shackles of slavery to the senses, and is cosmically liberated.

In the corners of the card the four Kerubs of the elements are represented, figures which also reflect the Tarot suits and the levels of the Qabalah: a lion, man's head, an eagle, and a bull. The facets of each have been perfectly combined and enhanced in the figure at the center, which represents the fifth element of Akasha, or spirit. The legs of the figure form a cross-shape at lower-leg level, representing Malkuth, whose Hebrew letter is *Tau* (ת), meaning "cross."

To ascend to Yesod (though it often feels more of a descent, like "falling" asleep), you need to be aware of all your faculties, physical, intellectual, creative, and spiritual, as you were when playing the Magician in Malkuth. Imagine your powers in all their fullness, integrated into a perfect, progressive whole and at the height of their potential. Having gathered up the skills and knowledge gleaned in Malkuth, you are ready to progress to a higher level of understanding. The World card represents just such a cosmic voyage as you are about to undertake, one that leads beyond the bounds of your present realm of experience.

Take several deep, cleansing breaths, and stand with your feet together, your arms outstretched.

Imagine that you are travelling with speed up a tunnel of flashing blue, black, and indigo fractals. These patterns of light fill up the space between conduits of darkness, impelling you in a manner that seems vaguely familiar, their bruiselike colors reminiscent of a moment before some age-old amnesia. If you lower your arms, you travel faster; raise them, and the colors pulsate and clot around you, slowing you down.

All of a sudden you come to a stop. Standing with your arms comfortably at your sides, your inner eye scans the vicinity for a clue as to your whereabouts. It is very dark.

A faint rustle above you alerts you to the presence of trees. You dimly perceive them to be ash. As your eye grows accustomed to the demilight, you notice tangled thickets of deadly nightshade flowering in the dark. Your pupils expand in response, revealing more of the path's inhabitants.

A gray-backed crocodile lolls not far from you, but his presence is not alarming. Rather, he seems so slow and heavy that you wonder whether he is mobile at all. The gray matter is probably dust; the air does not move much here; in fact, it is rather stifling. The unpleasant stink of blocked drains and pubic toilets permeates the area. Raise your arms to the T shape again in order to travel higher.

You push yourself through more tubes of flashing fractals, feeling as if you are in an elevator whose roof space is getting smaller and smaller, until you arrive at the next level.

Here, a purplish light illuminates the faces of four figures, all of their gazes bent upon a globe of what looks like quartz crystal. Something tells you, however, that it is in fact rock salt.

Many scenes are being enacted in the center of this sphere of salt. The four figures watch the play intently, calmly planning some strategic coup. Their heads are those of a bull, an eagle, a man, and a lion.

As you watch, the ball of salt begins to grow. The four figures stand back, and the salt continues to shimmer into a tower of vast, female proportions. The figure reminds you of the Tarot card the World, with its pronounced procreative capacity and cosmic femininity.

She introduces herself to you as Gaea. Blue streams form her hair; her robes are as green as Beltane, her aura is both protective and dynamic. She is, of course, the embodiment of the planet on which we are based, and her strong, clean energy is all that you need to get you through the final part of the journey.

If she smiles on you, you will be propelled with great velocity towards a purple door on which a silver crescent shines.

If she does not offer you graceful encouragement, then you may be crossed by Saturn's influence at present, and it is best not to continue pathworking until the planets are more favorably aligned.

If you decide to continue, lie down to visualize the journey to Yesod.

Allow yourself to feel drowsy as you lie flat on your back, center-ing your attention on the top of the bridge of your nose, between the eyebrows.

Imagine streams of purple light gathering and then descending through this point in your skull, and being soaked up by your brain like a sponge absorbing fluorescent purple wine. The drug mixes well with your thoughts, inducing pleasant visions and a sense of drunken irresponsibility. Here, in your world, you can do and think and look and feel however you wish. Better still, you can create your surroundings to fit your purpose.

Spend a little time while creating in your mind's eye what you consider to be your ideal environment. Do not censor yourself. Even if your thoughts are absurd, let them be—indulge your imagination. If they are tranquil, do not consider them boring, but grab the opportunity to take a break. Your mind will soon let you know how it would like to be occupied.

## Encountering the In-House Divinities

In Yesod, the God-name is *Shaddai El Chai*. This is the first authority to whom we must apply for admittance to Yesod, so muster up your energies, ready to visualize and, more importantly, perceive this aspect of the godhead.

Shaddai El Chai is the aspect of God that is called (continually) upon in the Torah (first five books of the Old Testament, a.k.a. the Hebrew Bible) to grant fertility and tribal increase. The aged Abraham and Sarai, for example, are granted a child well beyond the normal physical capacity to reproduce. This is Shaddai El Chai representing God's abundant side. As Yesod lies directly beneath Tiphareth and Kether, it is well placed to receive a direct divine infusion. Indeed, it is in Yesod that the godhead/bride Shekhinah (dwelling in Malkuth) is purported to be reunited with the Messiah (dwelling in Tiphareth), every week at midnight on Friday, the Sabbath eve. Thus we see Yesod's function as the Sephirah of reunion and reproduction.

Shaddai El Chai is almost entirely feminine, fierce of countenance and liquid in form. Its towering green-yellow waves of energy are crowned by scarlet fire. Within it the intuitive, imaginative powers of Water are tempered by the will of Fire. This is an aspect of godhead that is swift, impulsive, and acts responsively to other energies (as do all the Sephiroth, though some react more obviously than others). The name translates as "Almighty, Living God," reflecting its swift reactive qualities.

Yesod is a highly receptive sphere, and much is redoubled in its subtle, fluid energies. Its particular affiliations are with Hod, Netzach, and Tiphareth. Through these we understand more of the nature of this aspect of Deity. For example, though Yesod as a sphere is imaginative and controlled by the emotions, the godforce here is informed by intellect and logic, as represented by Hod, thus justifying Yesod's title "the Purifying Intelligence." We also perceive the qualities of redemption through sex and the elemental forces of nature, gifts of the gods bestowed in such spiritual disciplines as Paganism, Tantra, and astral exploration. Art and imagination belong to this sphere, as do uplifting dreams and psychic experiences or interest in the magickal arts.

Holding the image of a face of radiant flame and a body of brilliant emerald and flashing sunlight, speak the name Shaddai El Chai out loud, and ask permission to explore Yesod. Try to concentrate on the resonance of the name as you envisage the living colors and formidable powers of this oceanic expression of God.

Of course, the aspect of God rules the roost in any Sephirah, but you would show yourself to be polite and desirous of a good experience to introduce yourself to the deputy authorities before entering (at least, when the entrance is deliberate; if spontaneous, one may conclude that spiritual passport control has already approved the visit).

The Archangel of Yesod is Gabriel. The most commonly known myth about Gabriel is again a reproductive one. It was he who delivered the message to Mary that she was to conceive a Christ (Tiphareth) by the Holy Spirit (Kether). Thus, like his Sephirah, he acts as the intermediary between higher spheres and Malkuth, and as herald of fertility.

Facing west, envisage this sacred being framed by cascades of falling water. It must be remembered that although one name for Gabriel is "the strong man of God," the element ruled is Water and the planetary correspondence is the moon, giving rise to a distinctly feminine set of characteristics. Though some of Gabriel's attributes

are masculine, the predominant features are feminine. However, as
Yesod lies on the Middle Pillar and is thus of a balanced nature, we
may conclude that its Archangel is androgynous, i.e., female.

The face is beautiful, reflective, a silver spiritual moon as change-
able as the human emotions. It is full and round, ever-watchful. A
slight breeze disturbs the silver-blue hair wafting around Gabriel's
throat.

Wings of brilliant blue are folded behind slender shoulders,
sweeping down to feet clad in silver sandals. The body is strong and
athletic as Artemis', very fluid but full of force. It glows purple, like
Yesod itself. The torrential energy of this deity is extremely versatile,
capable of penetrating every nook and cranny of the human psyche
and the cosmos at large, just as a universal deluge would leave no
place dry, however small the entrance or huge the chasm.

Gabriel's arms are soft as a mother's, indicating the quality of
compassion, but in the right hand a sword of glowing silver is held
aloft. Just as a mother's love is the strongest, so too is Gabriel
strong both in force and protection. Water looks like an easy
medium, but its tides can drown the strongest of swimmers. Complex tides and currents are active in Yesod. Likewise, Gabriel's
sword can act with apparently merciless swiftness, but the motives
are based in compassion and a "rightness of flowing." The expression "go with the flow" applies perfectly to this Sephirah, as it is
only by giving oneself up to the currents of life that the ocean of
spirituality may be encountered. Cloistered and regimented minds
have little hope of experiencing or even perceiving the celestial
wonders that tower above Malkuth.

The glowing set of scales standing before Gabriel echo his affiliation to cosmic justice, represented in its entirety by the Sephirah
Chesed in conjunction with Geburah. It is to Yesod that we first fly
once the silver cord that binds us to life has been cut, there to
receive the initiation into the karmic portion of our next stage.
Often this is a blessing, though our loved ones on Malkuth may see

it differently. In dreams we are frequently scooped from earthly plight by the ministrations of the angelic forces of this Sephirah, underlining their compassionate nature.

Gabriel's legs are strong and the feet winged, indicating swift action when required, and again, a continual adaptation to circumstance. The feet are balanced between worlds, just as Yesod itself lies between the material world of Malkuth and the spiritual world of the rest of the Qabalah.

What strikes us most, however, along with the overall luminosity of this divine being, are his eyes. They glow a deep, aquatic green, clear and beautiful and in dramatic contrast to the soft silvery mauve of his aura. They are eyes that know infinite depths of love, and which, long ago, knew great pain, still unforgotten. The impression we derive of Gabriel is thus one of great spiritual strength, vast creative compassion, and superb equipoise.

Once you have established Gabriel's image firmly in your mind's eye, enter into his shimmering electric aura and request that you be guided and protected in the Yesodic world of *aethyrs* to which you are about to gain access.

When Gabriel has added his loving assent to that of Shaddai El Chai, you are ready to envisage the final authority of the sphere of Yesod: the Kerubim.

This group of angels is predominantly male, with an upper aura of purple and amber and a lower body of gray-green. They are headstrong dreamers, compassionate and related mentally to Chesed, sphere of love and mercy. They are proud and strong, more cerebral than physical, yet capable of shouldering a great deal of responsibility. Their mercurial bodies mean that they are very swift to act and able to convey a great deal through visceral sensation. Their feet are planted in the greenish waters of Yesod, representing their essentially tactile, intuitive natures.

Encountering these deities will have given you a vivid insight into the realm of Yesod.

Presuming that your request was granted, it is now time for you to progress into Yesod itself.

## The Temple of Yesod

The floor of the Temple of Yesod is tiled in black and white like that of Malkuth, but this chamber has no roof. It is beautifully perfumed, with several silver censers emitting clouds of ethereal vapor and smoke. The atmosphere is alive with possibility. Over the Temple hangs a sky of pinks and purples, full of yellow stars and fat silver moons.

You intuitively perceive that the Temple has nine sides, though several of these are clouded in dreamlike mist. Distant mountains of purple and mauve capped by silvery-white snows rise up before you, and when you look at them, the very air around you seems to thin out and become clearer. Are you imagining it, or is that the sound of chanting at the edge of your mind? In this pristine, yogic atmosphere you know that you could hear the whispers of the Gods, and they yours.

In another direction lies a green wood, and as you look the silver mist that veils it clears, and the scent of pine and fresh earth delights your nostrils. Many animals are visible here: a baby rabbit peeks from the undergrowth . . . birds such as we never see on earth flit from tree to tree . . . a stag runs past. In hot pursuit comes swift-footed Artemis, her golden arrow pulled back in the silver bow. She is so lithe and light-footed that we barely hear her until she is upon us. Her gaze, however, is fixed solely on her quarry.

You suffer a moment of horror on the stag's behalf. It seems terrible that such a beautiful creature should be slain for sport, but as you think it, the goddess shoots and laughs. The stag crumples to the forest floor, a single drop of blood coursing down his side. The goddess glances at her kill, tilts her head listening, and quiet as a snake moves on to the next conquest.

Standing in shock at the apparent pointlessness of this act, you witness the body of the stag vanishing into thin air. As it does so, the drop of blood begins to take form, and a new, identical deer appears in its place. It arises, looks about and, if you are not entirely mistaken, seems to laugh. When it is quite sure it has tracked Artemis, it runs off in her direction.

In another darker swirl of Temple mist there looms an enormous three-headed statue of a woman, one of her faces young, the second maternal, the third old. At her feet lie the bodies of three dogs, their throats slit, and her image seems surprisingly dark for such a bright place as this. In fact, now that you look properly, there is no light but that of the distant stars, and the statue is the only marker on the crossroads at which you find yourself. Three crows fly overhead, cawing loudly.

The crows make you wonder what it is like to be a bird, and even as you think it, you become one, flying with graceful ease over fields of green bathed in silver, following sparkling ley lines to tors and rings of stones and ancient chapels on faery hilltops. The air filling your feathers delights you, and you send a bird-brained pulsation of thanks to Paralda, king of the Air element. Now seas span out beneath you, glittering at one moment in moonlight, the next shining beneath the sun.

Soon you again behold the black and white tiles of the Temple of Yesod below you, and descend through the open roof. By now the semiveiled images have shifted into others, and you long to chase each one to its ultimate conclusion, but that would take longer than forever.

As you stand on the cool marble floor enjoying the scent of jasmine coming from a nearby Indian garden (isn't that Radha walking in the moonlight? Her silver-white sari is just the same color as the night-blooming jasmine . . . mmmm, that fragrance!), you are approached by a beautiful being of lilac and silver hue, made of light: it is the Archangel Gabriel. He smiles, his emerald eyes refreshing your very soul. As he does so, he touches you on the third eye area of your forehead, and you feel the energies rising in your spine.

You are ready to explore Yesod in your body of light.

## Entering the Sephirah

Taking several deep breaths of silvery-purple light, envisage a door of purple embossed with a pearlescent moon, and knock at it nine times.

Nine is the number of this Sephirah, as well as being the ultimate number of the Moon Goddess, expressing her threefold aspect of maiden (new moon), mother (full moon) and crone (waning and dark moon). All moon goddesses are ascribed to this sphere, for obvious reasons. The Tarot cards are the four Nines, particularly the Nine of Cups, sometimes referred to as the "wish card," as the mind has every hope of influencing matter when this card appears. This, of course, is a concept eminently suited to Yesod, where thought directly creates matter. The card particularly refers to affairs of the heart. However, there are only nine out of ten of the cups present, representing the continued need to strive.

Enter the gateway to Yesod when you feel ready.

What you find on the other side will depend greatly upon your own state of being at the time, as well as your location and other arbitrary circumstances. However, a few features will remain constant, such as the texture of the atmosphere, which is very subtle and conductive, crackling with electromagnetic activity. There is a multidimensional blanket of etheric energy spreading out across the sphere like a thick spider's web, and those who move around do so in a variety of astral forms: animal, vegetable, mineral, and human alike, all very bright in their imaginatively sculpted bodies of light.

This is where all dreams, fantasies, and moods—however fleeting—are embodied, hence the occultist's awareness of the maxim

"Think no evil . . ." All that we emanate finds a form on the astral plane, on one side or another. The flip side of Yesod are the "Astral Hells," regions of which are easily accessed from Malkuth. Yesod and Malkuth share the same etheric aura, and are very much part of a pair (bear in mind, though, that most Sephiroth operate in threes). Many cases of psychosis and wanton evil are caused by beings from the infernal regions of Yesod which merge with Malkuth. As Blake put it in his *Proverbs of Hell*, "Everything Possible to be Believed is an Image of Truth." Certainly this statement may be taken quite literally in Yesod.

One of the titles of Yesod is "the pure and clear intelligence," and one of its experiences is the uplifting of understanding as one rises up by a plane, out of the spiritual straightjacket of Malkuth and into the loose robes of Yesod. With freedom to move, speculate, and imagine, the visitor to Yesod finds their senses freed and an exciting new perspective gained. Yesod also filters the preceding planes and Sephiroth into a form permissible in Malkuth, so that we might understand rather than be blown away by it. Yesod, for example, manifests as the physical moon, and Tiphareth as the sun. We have material symbols rather than raw forces in Malkuth. However, in ascending the tree it is possible to experience the energies in something closer to their original form.

What you experience in the realm of Yesod will be highly subjective. Enjoy it for as long as you like, and try to write it down (even just as lists of symbols encountered, if you do not feel up to an in-depth description/interpretation). In all cases it will aid your progress immensely if you keep a written record of your jaunts into the wonderful realms of the Qabalah, much the same as maintaining a dream journal enhances one's oneiric exploration.

Often, particularly in Yesod, it will prove difficult to keep the thoughts coherent and to formulate a clear inner journey. This is, of course, a state quite natural to the dream sphere. A visualization could be concocted to keep the attention on track, but such very focused pathworking is anathema to Yesod. Instead, I have decided to offer the reader some of my personal experiences of Yesod—or aspects of them, for its patterns are as various as those of a kaleidoscope. The best way to experience this sphere is to daydream as ritualistically as possible, tapping into universal symbols and interpreting them on a personal, psycho-spiritual level, and, as mentioned, recording these impressions for later interpretation.

## Personal Encounters with Yesod

As a guide, here are some thoughts of my own. They are unchronological, which is a normal state for Yesod, where emotion is the prime mover and time as we know it does not exist. The individual personality and circumstances of incarnation are highly relevant on this lower level, and their repercussions are unavoidable in Yesod.

Contemplate your own childhood and adolescence as you read these snippets of mine. Think of why we appear where we do, when we do, as children and siblings of our particular parents. There is more to our lives, our relations, and our life experience, than mere genetics and chance: that much is sure.

Where have you been before? Where do you think you might go next? Try to focus on these questions as you feel yourself entering the radiant sphere of violet-silver Yesod.

While attempting to formulate a visualization for Yesod—one that might evoke both the nature of the Sephirah and its most useful qualities—I found myself drifting into inner space, daydreaming, and reading poetry. Coleridge and Poe appealed greatly, and I felt almost opium-drugged as I absorbed their verse:

> A damsel with a dulcimer
> In a vision once I saw:
> It was an Abyssinian maid,
> And on her dulcimer she play'd,
> Singing of Mount Abora.

*Could I revive within me*
*Her symphony and song,*
*To such a deep delight 'twould win me*
*That with music loud and long,*
*I would build that dome in air,*
*That sunny dome! Those caves of ice!*
*And all who heard should see him there,*
*And all should cry, Beware! Beware!*
*His flashing eyes, his floating hair!*
*Weave a circle around him thrice,*
*And close your eyes with holy dread,*
*For he on honey-dew hath fed,*
*And drunk the milk of Paradise.*

That the Romantic poets, Coleridge especially, knew their way to Yesod is beyond all doubt. The "honey-dew"—*ambrosia* of the Greeks and *amrita* to the Hindus—is the key to eternal life, the bliss of communion with godhead which can be sampled via Yesod. The "milk of Paradise" is the firm knowledge of Cosmic Beneficence—without this appreciative element, the dugs of the Universal Mother run dry.

"Beauty is in the eye of the beholder" in more ways then one: faith can bridge the gap between the manifest and the unmanifest, and bring rewards according to its own expectations.

Coleridge's character has become formidable in his knowledge, and his power must be contained, hence the weaving of the protective circle. Three, however, is the number of the Goddess, a close relation to the "Abyssinian maid" of his astral vision, and having a circle woven about him thrice will only serve to enhance his power.

His hair floats in eerie disrespect of gravity, for he has discovered the path out of the illusion of Malkuth and into the illusion of Yesod. The difference is that in Malkuth, objects are real on the outer plane and delusions on the inner; in Yesod they are delusions on the outer plane and real on the inner. Maya loops-the-loop between these two spheres, inverse in the realm of symbols, Yesod.

Coleridge's character has been empowered by his re-assimilation of the "music loud and long" of the astral planes, the vibrational key to the existence of all things. This is the true "music of the spheres," akin to the Hindu sacred syllable OM. He has regained the knowledge with which we are all born, but are rarely allowed to access except in times of great emotional stress, or under the influence of drugs or love.

In "Kubla Khan," Coleridge has visited a more pleasant region of Poe's "Dreamland":

> From a wild, weird clime, that lieth sublime,
> Out of SPACE, out of TIME;
> Bottomless vales and boundless floods,
> And chasms and caves, and Titan woods,
> With forms that no man can discover
> For the dews that drip all over;
> Mountains toppling evermore
> Into seas without a shore;
> Seas that restlessly aspire,
> Surging, into skies of fire;
> Lakes that endlessly outspread
> Their lone waters—lone and dead—
> Their still waters—still and chilly
> With the snows of the lolling lily.

Yesod is indeed the realm of poets, artists, and dreamers, where the Muse roams free in whatever environs our psychology creates for her. Yesod is a pool of the Collective Unconscious, and myth is enacted here. As to the genesis of myth—that is another story.

The characters created by the joining of minds have certainly taken on a life all of their own since their conception.

I floated on Poe's deathly pool awhile, my mind caught like one of his lilies, in lolling stasis, then drifted back to the more stimulating imagery of the "flashing eyes" and "floating hair." It was like drowning in a pool with two currents: one sinister, weed-entangled, and Gothic, the other colorful, hallucinogenic, and beguiling.

Dozing upright, my mind reaching upward and outward, but finding little of substance to attach itself to, thoughts of my parents and brothers crept into my mind, and I felt the presence of the Real Family around me, the network of souls interlinked to all eternity. Some of these are blood ties in this incarnation, others not. Either way these figures are among those who serve as constant reference points to one another, beings which meet and interact from life to life and plane to plane.

## In the House of the Tarot Kings

I lived for a while with three Tarot Kings, whom I considered my brothers. One was dark and earthy, with blinkered vision and a heart like a hearth at which I warmed my Hades-frozen hands. He was not gifted with wings, but had a soul of good salt. He flavored our house with humor and stability.

Another was the King of Swords, strong in his judgment, often cutting and merciless to the less gifted. He did not suffer fools gladly and was slave to a pretty face. His cynicism kept me from leaving this plane; he tempered my trance with grounding realisms. Cold as steel, yet loved by us all for what we deduced lie underneath: a little boy playing with a big knife.

Up in his attic of dreams lived the noble King of Wands, ever-creative, his den packed with relics of the natural world. He helped me invoke the Unicorn, never guessing it would lead to my downfall, and for hours we would sit prophesying the beginning of the end of the world like a two-person cult: I scripting our thoughts in runes, and he divining for comic truths among strewn-about sticks and bones, a tall skinny shaman lost in the modern world. We both felt more attuned to the Yesod sphere, I think, than this one, though he was more firmly based in Malkuth than I was. I had no roots, and was wind-swept by a thousand emotional and psychic currents.

And so the four of us shared a space, I playing the part of Persephone, obliviously gathering flowers as if born again, and vaguely remembering what came next, but compelled to reenact the myth all the same. I wrapped my mysteries about me like a big cloak and thought as Dion Fortune's Morgan Le Fay would have, had she been utterly neurotic and without a clue who she really was.

We lived in the country. The place was vibrant with elementals, and everyone could sense them. Mushrooms abounded in autumn and brought with them Hecate and her lunar trickster gnomes. Godforms walked disguised as humble humans. Archetypes were being channeled thick and fast, don't ask me why. Lots of us seemed connected from other lives, even other stars. The power of the land gathered up and threw us into Faery. We lived on the brink, all of us, not just those who were aware. We were dwellers at the threshold, and all of us were touched. It was in the air, the water, the sodden emerald earth, and in the fiery leaves blazing on the trees in autumn. In the bonfires we lit, the incense we burned.

We sat back and relished the shadow-play. The music was enchanted, the images inspired, the feelings entertainment in themselves. Anubis and Odin and Loki and Isis and Seth partied together. Ishtar was rising, Tammuz prevailing, Hapi lurking. Hecate was billowing, all the elementals were dancing.

Then the air currents reversed, with no warning. A whirlwind was about to carry Persephone through a chasm in the earth, and she fell into it willingly, predestined in this. The flickerings in the enchanted ones' eyes were too much to resist. Memories flooded in, covens of the past paraded past the windows, spirit-forms abounded, myths reworked themselves in the microcosm of our daily lives. With no grounding in Malkuth, I could offer no resistance. My soul was like a kite with a broken string, and there was no one left to reel me in. I'd grown addicted to enchanted fruit, and now the others seemed like citizens of the will-o'-the-wisp-lit shadowlands to me. My own reality became something much more solid, one infinitely darker.

## Coming Back to the Surface

The path out of Yesod is not an easy one unless you are well versed in Malkuth. I had been glamoured: it takes good salt to counteract the sickly sweet taste of faery fruit, and I had none in my soul. "Beware, beware!" Don't enter this sphere unless you are able to stand four square in the face of glamour. The magnetism of Yesod is what makes you want to return to a beautiful dream, the vision utterly absorbing while dreamed but fragile when revisited in the daylight. It is much the same when visiting this sphere—a soporific feeling, drugging the will, yet wonderful, a Muse-haunted mirror-pool. But do not fall in love with a reflection: when you try to embrace it, it will drown you.

All through this life we encounter those we knew before, some way or another, bound together by the links forged in our previous experiences. This is not unusual—as the Buddha said, "Everyone in the world has once been your mother or your brother." (Of course, he may not have meant it literally—more as a point illustrative of the unity of all life/consciousness.) Many people are linked like this, whether they realize it or not. What makes the experience unique is the use of memory, our facility to remember. And—unlike the Midwich Cuckoos with whom many of us have one or two points in common—the idea latent in these associations and points of psychic contact is not to rule the world or dominate others' minds; rather, this gift of relations should be used to understand and integrate with them, looking for our unique place in the universe, utilizing each spirit as memory-prompts and mnemonic signposts.

Or are we just sad, deluded strangers? Well, I myself have most certainly suffered from mystical delirium at times. Yet, I would rather suffer this kind of madness than the dead/alive limbo in which most people spend their entire lives.

In the case of some of these long-term acquaintances, friends and lovers, the full import of their position in my lives, and vice versa, took many years to come to light, until which time they were merely people I liked (or even disliked) from a distance. Some still have not been identified as such—but the soul-bonds are still there, indubitably. Unfortunately, in my Tarot King days the psychic concentration, and various arbitrary factors attracted by this bright psychic beacon, acted as superstimuli on my teenage brain, and stewed that organ in its own juices. I became overexcited, having no base in Malkuth. At the time, I lived in Yesod and had interests in every other Sephirah—but Malkuth was anathema to me.

## Dwelling in Yesod

As an adolescent, my bedroom was a sphere of Yesod attached to the grim Malkuth/Abyss of the rest of the house, "where an Eidolon, named NIGHT/on a black throne reigns upright." (The Eidolon, in this case, was my irrepressible Victorian of a stepfather.)

In my bedroom, one of its windows opened directly onto the outstretched branches of an overgrown pine tree, and the other enjoyed a full view of the moon as she sailed her nightly course. This was my dream-sanctuary, the ever-full "treasure house of images."

And in this small room appeared arches of moons, waxing, full, and waning; angular angels invoked from the Qabalah; a violet-eyed, white-bearded Mage who lived in a cave by the sea; and countless entities of less-pleasant aspect. My own vampire self made a guest appearance one night, looking exactly like me but with heavily slanting eyebrows and eyes glowing phosphorescent green in the dark. Having been reared as a Christian I was very superstitious and had no concept of *daimos*, the Greek duality of nature, both good and bad. I spent entire weekends attempting to astrally project, living in my bubble of psychic dreams and hormones. I listened to music all the time, letting it feed my malnourished soul, letting the sound and rhythm sculpt my inner landscape.

I invoked various godforms, often inappropriately, as repressed beings are prone to do. Every morning I performed a sun-hailing ritual as prescribed in one of my metaphysical books. At dawn I perambulated the tiny floor space of my room with a lit joss stick, invoking: "Hail, Ra! Hail, Mithras! Hail, Apollo!" Perhaps not the best course of action for a little girl with an overbearing Leo stepfather: the male was already an overwhelming force in my life. I was eulogizing these powerful solar deities without the least understanding of their history or nature. All very melodramatic, but then the teen years tend to be, even at the best of times.

I was much better when working with the strong lunar currents that focused on my Yesod sphere. I developed, from the age of fifteen or so, a strong relationship with Diana/Artemis, and with it a streak of unmitigating arrogance, a necessary antidote to the constant dampening of my tender ego by those surrounding me. The more I attempted to escape, to project outwards, the stronger my Dianic streak became until I was relentlessly strong in certain areas.

Girls at school took one step back. My "feminist" approach disturbed them, as did my support of bi- and homosexuality. The belief that it is the soul within that is of relevance, rather than the physical vehicle, seemed anathema to them. Had they spent a little more time in Yesod and a little less in church or experiencing Malkuth in Assiah, they would have been capable of assimilating these so-called "radical" ideas proposed by me. After all, when you know you're male or female by turns, and that the body is merely a shell, why would same-gender attraction confound the senses? Yesod helps with accepting relationships that operate outside the norm. In Yesod, we appear as spirits, not as finite bodies. And the majority of spirits are bipolar.

One of the best Yesodic experiences I had in that hothouse of psychic growth was, I believe, the result of magickal training in other lives, combined with a fairly long time spent conscious between my last death and subsequent rebirth.

Partly the influence of rampaging hormones, partly the result of the latent psychism that broke the dams of my consciousness around this time, I had the experience of total energy exchange with someone: and to say it blew me away is no exaggeration. I was fifteen at the time.

## Initiation in Yesod

I went to bed.

Quite naturally, I felt myself ascending, and began to look around. I was flying in perfect lotus posture, as I had become accustomed to doing in the night, but instead of the usual trees, streets and houses, I beheld below me a sparkling ocean of deep indigo, each wavelet clearly defined, even though I was flying way, way above it. I was travelling at speed, which I perceived more through innate knowledge than sense perception, for there was nothing in the unchanging scenery by which to gauge my progress. I simply enjoyed the sensation of motion, and the spectacular color.

The sky was also purple: a paler, slightly pinker shade than the sea. In some respect I felt that the salt in the air, rising from the water, was helping me levitate. I felt deeply exhilarated and spiritually as light as a feather, yet I had perfect control. With one flick of the switch of will I could bring myself closer to the surface of the sea, or rise at as steep a gradient as I desired.

Eventually I saw before me an arch entirely comprised of yellow harvest moons. The one at the very apogee was full, while those on either side were waxing and waning respectively. On each side were six spheres gradually slicing down to sickles, one new, one old. The progression was very regular, thirteen yellow moons in every stage . . . and I found myself flying straight through the middle of them.

On the other side of the arch of moons hung in purple space a radiant being, not cross-legged like me but full-length, suspended at its leisure. I approached and looked into its eyes. They were those of someone I knew, and they transmitted such a bolt of empathy and love that I felt my astral body unfurl as I drew closer, palms open to face those of the other soul. With the most infinitesimally small gestures we communicated a vast amount of information and emotional energy, accompanied by a feeling of such elevation as is rarely encountered while incarnate.

In the purest, clearest realms of Yesod, then, I received my first full initiation. It marked the beginning of a quantum leap of consciousness for me, and the end of the childhood of pleasant or painful oblivion.

We hung here for what might have been aeons, charging one another with energy, swapping atoms which became molecules of infinite power in the exchange. Whole universes appeared in our pupils, spinning out of concepts too abstract to describe in the human tongue. The air and the water were alive in a way they are not, perceptibly, on the earth plane. The true music of the spheres, which holds all life together, was played so finely that it was not audible but more a sensation of the spinal cord and blood. It was a truly mystical experience, perfect, beautiful, and resonant throughout the planes and ages. There are some adherents of Aquarian philosophy who believe that, eventually, this sort of experience will occur on all conceivable, individual levels, for each being—until at last all souls will undergo such an initiation, en masse. It will happen, if we but will it so. This was recognized by the mythic Atlanteans—but they blew it. I perceived this wisdom, and much more information, intuitively as I levitated there.

## Under an Indigo Moon

This is what Yesod does: it gives you an overview . . . shows you things that cannot be perceived by the gross senses alone . . . takes you astral travelling, even when you don't mean to . . . introduces you to your spirit guides, without whom we would be nightly fodder for hungry Qlipoth. This sphere makes you think, occasionally, that you are going mad, as when others do you attempt to tell them your experiences. Best only to talk of such things to others on the same path; it is hard enough clinging to your sanity without the children of earth disparaging you. You either understand it or you don't. There are beings on other spheres who laugh at the suggestion of life on earth, and cannot get their essences around it, for physicality, god-ignorance, and obliviousness to the true cosmic sources and energies are very difficult states to envisage—if you are accustomed to greater, or different, clarity.

Play with these images, these ideas. They belong to all of us, and are part of our race consciousness. They are ours to explore at our leisure. Yesod is a delicious sphere full of truth and wonders as well as the home of delusions and hormonal moonshine. It is easily accessible to the repressed, which is one reason I give thanks for my childhood, locked in a sterile housing estate in the middle of nowhere.

There are former cynics and materialists in Yesod now—just imagine! The same beings who would have locked up the visionary when alive are floating on astral seas and sailing the clouds of astral skies at this moment. Thus it will always be: the state of earth is a state of incredulity. And the state of Yesod, in the little sleep as well as the longer one, is one of liberation and vision. Especially with practice.

So, practice as you doze off, and soon you will find yourself going on trips like this one, into a reality perfectly compatible with our normal one, if only we would admit it. It is the craft of the occultist to mingle the levels, the two manifestations of Maya. Which reality is the "real" reality? To find out, we need to penetrate further, to the heart of the matter.

Come with me, then, further up the Tree, where we will find our experiences defined and qualified, or disqualified. The ascent is a great learning process, after all.

# Hod

## "The Absolute or Perfect Intelligence"
### SEPHIRAH 8

On reaching Hod, it is time to pull oneself together again. The images and inspirations of Yesod are useless without the qualifications of Hod and Netzach.

The best way to prepare yourself to experience this sphere is to read something with a philosophical bent, or anything you find mentally challenging but not completely confounding. The ultimate guide to the subject, Dion Fortune's *The Mystical Qabalah*, might be an appropriate place to begin. Alternately, do some mental arithmetic.

A shower will help brace you in a manner suitable to Hod: make it cool and citrus-scented. The morning is a good time to contemplate Hod, especially sunrise, so long as you are fully alert. The afternoon presents the best alternative.

One of the names of Hod is "the Water Temple." This may seem surprising, as Yesod, sphere of flux and reflux, seems more appropriately affiliated with this most moon-influenced of elements. However, water does not have fluidity as its sole attribute: it is also highly reflective.

Hod reflects the higher ethical principals of the Qabalah, symbolized as a whole by Chesed. Hod represents the highest aspects of the personality of man, our reflections unperturbed by the truth-ruffling emotions of Yesod. It is intellectual rather than mystical, and is the source of civilizing forces in Malkuth. When a good soul is unable to perceive God, it remains a compassionate atheist rooted in Hod. The intelligence of this sphere is "Absolute" or "Perfect" because it originates in Chesed and has not yet reached Yesod's distorting zone of subjectivity and subconscious (thus insidious) influence.

Precision and logic are the essences of Hod. Meticulous detail, applied effort, and all scholarly qualities are represented by this Sephirah. It is the sphere of thaumaturgy because of its combination of will, ritual, and attention to detail. The force of Netzach is contained by the form of Hod, its parallel Sephirah: the two must always work in conjunction, and imbalance is the instant result of failure to achieve harmony between these spheres. Hod is a Sephirah associated with the transformation of force into the communication of ideas, an alchemist of deeds into expression.

The Tarot cards connected with Hod are the four Eights, particularly the Eight of Cups. The latter presents us with the image of a man with his back turned on the chalices of his former emotional experience; he is walking away from what has been established, staff in hand. His cloak is red, denoting a degree of pain in the process.

Nostalgia is often a cause of anguish in abandoning what has become obsolete or an obstacle to our advancement, and nostalgia derives from sentiment: both are Yesodic qualities. To override these traits it takes the combined qualities of intellect and will—Hod and Netzach, respectively. Thus, the card represents the ascent of mind and body alike—the character is physically walking away, using his Malkuthic abilities—out of the emotional quagmire, and onto something higher. It appears in a reading when the querent is either mentally initiating or physically embarking upon a change for the better, usually abandoning a relationship. The process is often filled with anguish, but is necessary all the same.

Water lies between the chalices of love lost and the departing querent, understood here as Yesod/Hod, while he has now proceeded further, stepping onto the terra firma of Hod/Netzach.

The moon, or Yesod, looks down on the character in the card with a sad expression, eyes shut. It is all a dream, an illusion, she seems to whisper. The situation the querent is abandoning becomes consigned to Yesod, the sphere of Memory, and the traveller journeys on.

The Eight of Swords is also relevant because this suit denotes the powers of mind and intellect, both native to Hod. Here we have the distressing image of a woman standing blindfold, her hands tied behind her back, her body like another stake in a fence of swords. At first glance she appears to be bound and trapped, but closer inspection reveals that the cloth bindings are fairly loose and her feet are free. The swords are stuck into the ground around her in a deliberate manner, true, but they do not surround her entirely. A little initiative would free the victim in no time.

"Victim," however, is the operative word when this card appears. The querent, represented by the unhappy woman, is the subject of circumstances she thinks she cannot alter. One of the best examples of this is provided by *The Mythic Tarot*, which depicts Orestes trapped between the command of Apollo to kill his mother (to avenge his father), and the Furies, who punish matricide with hideous torment; Orestes finds himself in an apparently impossible situation. Similarly, the character in the *Rider-Waite* pack feels pretty sorry for herself, and so she stands there like a martyr, half-hoping that somebody will drop by and rescue her. She longs for sympathy and a shoulder to cry on, and until she can finds these, feels little impetus to move.

This is a state of Yesod in the negative. Surrounded by the inertia-pricking swords of Hod, she could easily slice through her dream-stupor, but emotion holds her back. In this sense, the Orestes allusion does not work. Athena will rescue the hero eventually, but he is truly in the hands of the gods. He does not have available the options of positive action which are hinted at in the more traditional Tarot image.

In the latter, each of the eight swords is a reason the character
has for staying put—she is masochistic, and on a deep-rooted level
is rather enjoying the melodrama. Who put the swords there, and
bound the girl up? She did, though she would doubtless protest this
assumption. Indeed, the fundamental reasons for her state are not
her own fault—nobody reared sanely would choose misery over
freedom—but she needs help to see how she has inflicted her
predicament on herself. Thus, the querent who receives this card
needs to be brought out of what is actually the thirty-second
path—the state of death-in-life, the adoption of the psyche of the
stricken rather than the resurrected Persephone—and into the
clarifying influence of Hod. The mercy of Chesed, which we recall
is reflected in Hod, includes compassion for the self. The energies
of Hod help cut through neuroses and break old emotional habits.
The benefits of analytical psychology and cognitive therapy are
obvious examples of Hod operating in this capacity.

The Eight of Pentacles is relevant to Hod only in that this card
represents the qualities of all the lower Sephiroth working in unison to induce industry. Hard work is creating a future in which
leisure time might enable the character (here, a metal smith) to
think beyond the immediate and physical, though this is an implication, not a definite.

The Eight of Wands, however, relates to another facet of Hod,
that of communication. Unexpressed intellect might amuse its
host, but it is sterile until shared. Hod is the sphere of Mercury, and
as such its qualities include communication skills, debate, and the
exchange and cross-fertilization of ideas. The Tarot image of eight
wands on display as if the celestial Magician is brandishing them
and saying "Pick a straw, any straw," represents communications of
all sorts, from traditional letters to ultramodern faxes and e-mails.
And at the end of each line of communication, who knows what
opportunities lie in wait? True, one might be a short straw, but
there are still other choices. There is a great deal of creative poten-

tial when this card arises, always involving the influence of other people. Discussion, debate, and mediation: all classically Mercurial functions. I particularly like the image in the *Tarot of the Old Path*, in which eight broomsticks are flying through the air. The querent can metaphorically mount any one, and ride it to its destination. Thus we also see the hidden potential inherent in the eighth Sephirah. This echoes the fact that much of the "thought" of Hod is in the abstract. How will these concepts influence our lives? We can tell only by following them to their ultimate conclusions.

In the abstract, these flashing ideas indicate the root of Hod's experience, that of the "Vision of Splendor." Having glimpsed the "Holy Guardian Angel" of spiritual potential in Malkuth, and begun to perceive the enormity and synchronicity of the "Machinery of the Universe" in Yesod, we are now party to the inspiration of sublime messages received from higher up the Tree. This insight is a presentiment of Netzach, whose influence is naturally always flowing directly into Hod. We may not be able to pin these concepts down, but we can certainly conjecture about them and enjoy the debate thus engendered. Just as Mercury is the messenger through whom the gods convey their communications, so too is Hod the point at which concepts are exchanged.

One of the symbols of Hod is the caduceus, indicative of its Mercurial attribution and reflecting the healing properties of Tiphareth, to which it is connected by the twenty-sixth path. The caduceus is comprised of a basilisk superimposed on a staff or wand. The crowned entwined serpents of the basilisk represent, among other things, the dangers of knowledge used incorrectly. The basilisk, like Medusa, is said to kill at a glance, yet it represents wisdom. Hod is a good example of the idea that "a little knowledge is a dangerous thing," as many of its initiates are prone to arrogance. When certain goals in life are attained—particularly feats of the intellect— it is easy to fall into the falsehood of believing oneself superior to others.

The two serpents of the caduceus could be construed as representing light and darkness, Yin and Yang, the Pillars of Mercy and Severity—intertwined and counterbalanced. They are winged, reminding us that they emanate from a higher sphere. The qualities they represent are transcendent.

The elements are represented at the points at which the serpents cross the rod. The Qabalistic caduceus, or "Wand of Hermes," includes the Hebrew letters *Shin* (ש), *Aleph* (א), and *Mem* (מ), representing Fire, Air, and Water, respectively. (Earth is not counted as an individual element in Hebrew teaching; it is deemed a combination of the other three.) In the case of the Wand of Hermes, the staff itself, particularly the base, represents Earth.

Hermes, the celestial trickster and odd-job man to the Olympians (see "Getting from Binah to Kether," the twelfth Path), is also a great magician capable of bringing sudden luck and fortune, and equally likely to withdraw these gifts. He certainly seems to exude these qualities himself, as we learn when he steals Apollo's cattle for a lark, then sacrifices two of them and combines their remains with the shell of a passing tortoise to create the lyre. His ingenuity and the stroke of luck that brings these factors together get him off the hook with Apollo, who is so enchanted by the musical instrument that he begins to bargain with Hermes for it. The word for windfall in ancient Greece was *"hermaion"* in respect for this connection.

The trickster figure closely resembles the folklorist's Fool, the representative of the eleventh path, *Aleph*, the spirit of aethyr. It also recalls Loki, one of the Norse Aesir, who is either mildly or entirely malevolent, and always a fool unto himself. The concept of the wily court jester is perhaps the flavor of fool most befitting Hermes and the concept of Hod (see "Getting from Chokmah to Kether" for more on the Fool).

In addition to the golden wand that Apollo swapped Hermes for the lyre, Hermes received the ability to divine from pebbles, a trait that sets him in parallel with the Norse god Odin. Hermes' roadside shrines probably looked like diminutive scarp-slopes built up around a small pillar, on which was mounted an image of the god's head, as each devotee would place a small stone there in honor of this gift from the god of prophecy, Apollo. I imagine that his worshipers also removed them from the shrines and used them like runestones once they had been sufficiently charged by the presence of the god. Indeed, it would befit Hermes' nature perfectly if people snuck back in the dead of night and stole the devotional pebbles for their own divinations.

Hermes is also connected with magickal activity by having shown to Odysseus the herb that could counteract the sorceress Circe's spells. Without "the giver of good, Hermes," Odysseus might well have spent the rest of his existence on Circe's enchanted isle. Not such a bad fate, one might think, but the hero preferred and was destined for a more active life of trouble and strife, as a mortal. In a similar manner is Hod, sphere of ritual magick, the Sephirah in which talismans are constructed and magickal antidotes formulated. The caduceus, symbol of the medical profession, aligns itself with this aspect of the Craft.

Hermes is also capable of passing through a keyhole like a breeze, a trait that associates him to Aleph, air, with which he assumes a closer relationship further up the Tree. Light and air are two ways in which spirit is made manifest. Similarly, he can become invisible by donning "the Cap of Hades," also worn by Perseus (to whom he bears some resemblance) and, on occasion, Athena. The idea of a Cap of Hades suggests specifically a kind of death-in-life, a living ghosthood, if you will. It recalls the Hindu mystic's ability to separate spirit from body and wander with impunity even among crowds, a feature amply demonstrated in Paramahansa Yogananda's *Autobiography of a Yogi*. Being the cap of Hades, it suggests that the body is undergoing a deathlike state while the spirit roams free. This sounds distinctly like astral projection as practiced by many on the magickal paths.

The rod or wand about which the serpents of the caduceus weave represents the tool of the Magician, whose ritual is intimately connected to Hod. It reminds us of the alchemical implications inherent in Hod, the "first stop" in the quest for Hermetic wisdom. The symbol of the caduceus is omnipresent in medieval alchemical diagrams, and relates to the transformative qualities of eloquent Mercury, whose skills of translation can turn the base metal of the soul into the gold of the well-versed initiate.

Hod is also the sphere of Thoth, Egyptian equivalent of Hermes, Lord of Learning and Keeper of the Records. Like many Egyptian deities Thoth is chimerical in form, having the body of a man and the head of either an ibis or a baboon. He was associated with science and arts magickal, and like the Grecian Apollo was connected with the art of prophecy. The priests of Thoth would sit in the dark and bark like baboons in a manner not dissimilar to Apollo's Delphic Pythias, though sometimes the representative of Thoth would really be a baboon. In both cases, the will of the Divine was purported to inform the oracle; what sense was derived from it depended largely on the intuition of the supplicant and the help of professional interpreters.

Many of Thoth's functions were scientific and practical. It was said that he created the first eight deities by the vibrational power of his voice. This is strongly reminiscent of the principle of creative sound prevalent in Hinduism, and parallels him with Brahma, creator-god, and Sarasvati, goddess of sound, wisdom, and creator of the Sanskrit alphabet. All three of these deities bring order to disorder through applied intelligence, exactly as Hod illuminates Malkuth, Yesod and Netzach. The physical, the fantastical, and the purely energetic are tempered by organized thinking.

The Twins provide another symbol for Hod, partly because Gemini is ruled by Mercury, and partly because this Sephirah's other major symbol is the hermaphrodite. It would seem appropriate for these to be male-female twins. However, as the twins are often purported to be Castor and Pollux (as in the path between Malkuth and Netzach), this might seem strange—two males representing an androgynous state—until one recalls that they were asexual babies, and Pollux half-divine swan at that. Pollux is born (or hatched) along with Helen, the children of Leda and Zeus. Castor and Clytemnestra emerge simultaneously, but their father is Tyndareus, Leda's husband. So, one "twin" is fully mortal, the other half-divine, a suitable mixture for this level of the Tree. However, both were known as the *Dioscuri*, divine children of Zeus, and their relationship was always harmonious. No doubt the features of their mother Leda are just as pronounced as those of the shape-shifting Zeus or cuckolded Tyndareus, and thus they are suitable emblems for the hermaphroditic Sephirah.

The story of Hod is that of Cybele tamed. Originally the fierce hermaphroditic monster Agdistis, the great nature goddess (here representing Netzach and Binah) was controlled only when Bacchus-Dionysus caused it to become intoxicated on wine. Exactly the same trick is used to quell Hathor when she becomes bloodthirsty Sekhmet. Both of these scenarios are reminiscent of the Indian accounts of Kali reeling drunkenly across the battlefield: the goddess is halted in her tracks by the prostrate body of her husband, Siva; in her case, love is the civilizing influence. The Egyptian goddess is saved from her own fury by the soporific influence of drink, as is the Greek Cybele. In all cases, natural momentum is quelled by the forethought of others.

Forethought as a civilizing quality is not to be underestimated, and it plays a considerable part in the mythology of many peoples. In both the *Iliad* and the *Odyssey*, Odysseus is referred to as "Peer of Zeus in forethought," explaining his expert tactical skills and the position of Zeus as most powerful among the gods. Likewise is Zeus' daughter Athena an exponent of thinking before acting. This forethought is a quality absolutely relevant to Hod.

Cybele in most of her forms is inimical to Hod, as are Sekhmet and Kali when roused; the eunuch priests of Cybele do, however, recall the hermaphroditic aspect of this Sephirah. Perhaps the idea of Sallust, the Roman historian of the first century B.C.E, is of relevance here: that the myth of Cybele is illustrative of the trials undergone by the soul in search of God. In her primal form as Terrible Mother, akin to Kali, she belongs to Binah, the Sephirah at which force is constricted by form, that is, the point where conception takes place. The castration of the original Cybele/Agdistis reminds us that the animal within must be tamed in order to aspire to the sanity and order represented by Hod, and that, once this has been attained, both the male and female aspects of the psyche may be put to good use.

In Hod, we combine the anima and animus, male and female properties, and emerge with the best of both worlds.

## Entering the Sephirah

Envisage yourself surrounded by orange light. The tiny ball of radiance begins in your brain and spreads outwards, gradually encompassing your brow, head, neck, and a larger and larger portion of the room and your own anatomy. Before long it is the size of the room.

The walls of the sphere shimmer, indicating a liminal state between realities. Despite this, you feel quite normal and well earthed as you sit in meditation, and mentally ready for anything. You fancy a challenge, something mentally bracing like a difficult crossword or the cracking of some kind of code.

As you contemplate Hod, you become aware of the seat of your intelligence resting in your cranium, and feel your intellectual capacities rising to the occasion.

## Getting from Yesod to Hod
### "The Collecting Intelligence"
#### PATH 30

Sitting up, take several deep breaths of fresh air, and imagine it vibrating with light-filled prana. Drawing the light up from your lungs, concentrate it on your skull. Gradually the light sinks into your head, until it is glowing with bright solar energy.

The path from Yesod up into Hod is dominated by the sun, and its colors reflect this. Its Hebrew letter is *Resh* (ר), meaning head. Just as the sun rules the solar system, so too does the head rule the system of consciousness made physical, the body. Here, baser instincts are filtered out and overriding intelligence given reign. The emotions of Yesod are refined to core fact. Travelling the other way, thoughts are given form in Hod (their energy coming from Netzach), and brought to birth in Yesod.

One deity who befits this path is Athena. Her owl identifies her with lunar Yesod, while her nativity ties her to the cranial imagery of Resh. She is the daughter of Metis, "wise council" personified. Zeus, fearing a prophecy that this goddess' child would usurp him, devoured Metis, live and pregnant. When she gave birth, the new child rose up into his head, giving him the world's first *hemikranios aigros*: a migraine headache. Finally, when he could stand the pain no longer, Hephaestus the smith god came and split his skull with a chisel. From the wound sprang Athena, grown and fully armed, screaming a fierce war cry. Her qualities as military tactician and promoter of reasonable behavior (not as unrelated as one might think!) make her an excellent guide on this path. Its features are regal and stately, just like Athena's gifts. Also, the sword-wielding goddess is compatible with Michael, Archangel of Hod, whose sword cauterizes personal faults. We are reminded of Athena's intervention between Achilles and Agamemnon in the *Iliad*, when she tells the furious Achilles, "Let him have a lashing with words, instead." Her cool gray eyes quench the fire of the hero's wrath, and save him from the ignominy of rash action. This is precisely the civilizing influence of Hod represented by Michael.

As you push yourself mentally up and to the left, fractals of amber, red, orange, gold, and yellow pass you by in rapid succession, seeming to warm you in different ways according to their hue. The amber makes you feel the benefit of past experiences, including harsh ones—and in the sublimation of pain, energy is gained for the present. By following the sun, you are releasing yourself from past cycles and becoming resurrected into a joyous new mode of being. The thick warm amber, its texture dearly gained, conveys these thoughts to you. The orange is like the brilliant robe of a Buddhist monk, making you think of salvation through renunciation. The color warms you on its own, with its determined hue, and this sensation is redoubled by thoughts of messianic intervention. All of the solar deities spring to mind: Jesus Christ, Apollo, Osiris, Horus, and the latter-day incarnation of Vishnu, the Kalki avatar.

As you work this path, you perceive three royal figures walking ahead of you. You know they are royal because of their stately bearing, not to mention their golden crown chakras and trailing scarlet cloaks, also embroidered in gold. They walk in procession, and heavenly music accompanies them, a celestial choir singing in joy.

Following them, you glimpse the gifts that they are bearing: frankincense, gold, and myrrh. The smell of the frankincense wafts around you as you walk, bringing to mind images of great prosperity. You have a sensation of imminent celestial celebration.

Moving up further still you encounter pockets of leonine yellow conveying a sense of confidence in your abilities both as intrepid explorer and analyst of your adventures. All the time, the heat increases, but rather than stifling you, it seems to add to your energy.

Finally, you emerge in a beautiful green meadow, the sun shining directly above your head, and seeming to merge with it. Raise your arms to the life-giving star and feel its energy filling up your entire body.

Give thanks to the source of light and warmth and growth, and feel your youth in comparison with its ancient yet ever-powerful status. In our cosmos the sun is the king of kings, a physical expression of Tiphareth, and through it Kether, on the material planes.

See and feel how powerful it is? Imagine, then, the intensity of spiritual heat and light of these higher Sephiroth. No wonder the body must be left behind when we visit them.

Finally, you ascend through a tunnel of brilliant orange, a similar color to that of having the eyes closed in bright direct sunlight. At the end of it is a door of orange with the symbol of Mercury embossed onto it.

You are now ready to approach Hod.

## Encountering the In-House Divinities

The relevant godform here is *Elohim Tzabaoth*, the God of Hosts. Although visualizing aspects of God is necessarily a limited technique, you may perceive some of the energy of this eighth emanation of supreme Deity by considering an entity of blinding brilliance, golden wings raised above the head and outstretched, the lower stratum of their light swooping down to the being's knee-level. If this deity could be embodied, its limbs would be scarlet, the rest of the body a green, blue, and yellow pulsar of radiance.

Repeat the name "Elohim Tzabaoth" until you feel you have attained rapport with this Atziluthic entity, and request that you be guarded in your adventures in his sphere.

Once this has been affirmed, the Archangel of Hod may be approached: Michael, "like unto God."

Michael represents the element of Fire, but is often confused with the Archangel of Air. The eponymous saint became mixed up with him somewhere along the line, and as many places dedicated to the latter are on airy mounts, the synthesis of the two came about. However, the altitude may be perceived as light-casting rather than airy, making it more appropriate to fire. As a luminary, this attribution is more appropriate to Saint Michael also.

As to the Archangel, he is predominantly of orange-fringed blue, and framed by tongues of fire the color of a flame's epicenter or of the water of Hod. His body is strong and muscular, full of force. In his right hand he holds a flaming blue sword, and the scales of justice stand before him, glowing in brilliant blue. Here, again, he displays some of the attributes of Air, and it is easy to see why some feel he is more appropriately assigned to this element, or even to that of Water. Indeed, with Hod as the Water Temple, it is logical to won- der what an Archangel—arguably one of Fire—is doing there. The usual answer is that academic, intellectual Hod inspires enlight- enment, an obvious symbolic function of fire. Still, the Archangels have been occasionally reshuffled, and it is good to work with what suits you personally when working on a solitary basis, though in group work such innovations can prove more of a hindrance than a help. (It is for this reason that I have stuck to the most popular correspondences throughout out the book.)

Sometimes Michael appears as a dragon slayer, fierce and mighty as he bears down upon the symbol of uncontrolled wrath. He is a rescuer of innocents. His countenance is protective, aquamarine, shimmering as in a heat haze. He brings the light of compassion, of higher understanding to brutish realms, in the same way that the luminous concepts of Hod can be civilizing. His name is usually pronounced "ME-kahl." Repeat it until you feel you have gained contact with this mighty, flickering force.

The angelic forces of this Sephirah are the *Beni Elohim*, the "sons of the Gods" whose bodies are composed of fire. Their slen- der faces are framed by wings of emerald-blue, their bodies aure- oled by flame. Their feet are in water, reflecting their relationship with Yesod, sphere of intuition. Their faces are male, but their bodies predominantly feminine. Though they are extremely pow- erful throughout, there is more strength in their upper than lower bodies, representing their intellectual nature. These Angels are supremely rational, not prey to the influence of emotional appeal like the Kerubim of Yesod. They make you feel capable of inter- preting even the most surreal experiences you may have while on this journey up the Tree. The Beni Elohim are like missiles guided by the powers of the intellect. Their torsos of flame are almost impossible to look on, so brilliant is the light coming off of them. It reminds us of the sphere's relationship with Tiphareth—to which it is connected by the twenty-sixth path, that of the Devil, also known as "the Renovating Intelligence."

When all of these authorities have approved your entrance into Hod, you are ready to explore.

## The Temple of Hod

The Temple of Hod is fully walled and roofed, though there are five clearly marked exits on its right side, each bearing the sign of a Hebrew letter and a specific picture. You recognize these as the Tarot symbols of Judgement, the Sun, the Tower, the Devil (on which door there hangs a peacock feather like those of Malkuth), and the Hanged Man in turn, rotating from bottom to top. You feel good in that you know exactly where you are and what you are doing, and suddenly the hazy phantasms of Yesod seem like child's stuff. Surely this on-the-ball clarity of information is far superior?

Your feet are wet. You look down to see black water ebbing about them. The substance is in no way negative, but extremely receptive. Its conductive properties are palpable to you.

You are not shod. You wonder why this should be, and receive the mental reply that all of the Priests and Priestesses walk discalced in Hod, absorbing information through their feet as well as through their heads. It helps them forge new paths, apparently.

Tallow candles burn here, reflected both in the water and by the roof, which seems to be made of shooting flames. Yellow light fills the Temple, and despite the relaxing nature of the candles and water, you feel mentally taut. Ready for a challenge or ritual, or both.

An altar covered by a silver cloth sits beneath a gigantic caduceus, and before this altar you know that many souls have sat in intense discussion and debate. Occasional lightning flashes

shoot from the Temple roof to its floor, each one gathering and dis-
pelling something from the atmosphere, then adding its energy to
the black mirror-pool. So far, you have not been struck by one, but
you realize that if you were, it would be quite a life-changing experience. You recall smaller versions when you were at school, as a
fact suddenly makes itself clear in your mind, along with its implications. "Light has dawned!" the teacher used to exclaim.

You cannot explore this path in the same way as you did in
Yesod as you do not know the passwords yet, and here you will cer-
tainly need them. Instead, you sit in contemplation within the
Temple.

When you have finished, you feel ready to really study the sphere
of Hod.

## Entering the Sephirah

Knock eight times on the nearest surface, imagining that you are
rapping at the orange door of Hod.

Shutting your eyes, envisage a walled town of stone, a university
town something like Oxford, but caught in a timeless sphere with
no traffic or bustle, just the steady low hum of mind-cogs turning.
With each turn of the cranial wheel evolution progresses inside
this fortressed seat of learning and living and reading.

You can almost smell the vellum and aging pages of its native
tomes from here. You can almost feel the weight of learning in
your hands.

You instinctively sense that there is more to Hod than scholar-
ship, more to its denizens' pursuits than academe. What is their
secret? You will have to enter the town to find out for yourself.

The walls are strong and high, like those of any exclusive establishment. The bricks are surprisingly regular, very old and square.
They emanate a solemnity similar to that of a cathedral, with an
odor of thaumaturgy. How many rituals of High Magick have these
stones witnessed? Their molecules seem saturated with history: the

endless careful reenacting of ritual, rubric, perfected order. Not the fluid emotional magick of Yesod this, but the heavily structured magick of the pedagogue.

Hod is dogmatic. You can sense this even from the outside. To enter you must first pass through the guarded portal to your left. Tentatively, you approach.

A very ordinary man in a smart uniform is waiting at the window of the porter's lodge. He reminds you somewhat of a butler or a chauffeur, and you sense that he is one of those who "knows his place," as well as everyone else's.

You ask to be admitted into the sphere of Hod, and the porter looks patiently through his papers to see whether this is permissible. He checks and double-checks the information, and then rejects you without further ado. You are not on this year's list, and evidently not of a suitable caliber.

You return to base—wherever it is you are meditating—to contemplate your next move.

It strikes you that there should be no such restrictions on the astral plane, and that you are as good as whatever privileged souls are to be found inside the sphere of Hod. What is the basis for their bias? Are they classist, sexist, racist, ageist? You take stock of your own form. How do you travel? As a human, a man, a woman, or gender unspecified? Form unspecified? You look at yourself and realize that you are travelling pretty much as is, forgetting to modify yourself for the subtler standards of the Inner Planes.

Right, then: we'll give that porter what for. How can he distinguish you from a denizen of Hod if you disguise yourself as one? The problem is, you are unsure what these beings look like. You ponder further.

They are academic types, unlikely to be greatly concerned about appearance. Utility will be the key to their form. Yet, fed by brilliant ideas, they are likely to exhibit an inner radiance which, of course, will be externally visible here.

The mind itself is not fettered by gender—intellect and sexuality are poles apart—so chances are these beings will be asexual; or, to put it more accurately, hermaphroditic.

Create for yourself a radiant astral body of ambivalent gender. Really concentrate on building up your form, starting at the feet and working upward through legs, genitals, torso, shoulders, arms, neck, and head. If you are female, imagine you inhabit a male body, but superimpose your own features on it. As a male, endow yourself with the soft fulsome lines of the feminine form but keep the strength and dynamism of your own earthly shell.

Now use your will to return to the fortressed seat of learning.

To your surprise, you find that on reappearing you do not even need to apply for permission to enter: the walls simply melt away before you.

You find yourself in a library crammed full of books shelved so high up that your gaze cannot penetrate to the ceiling of the building, though you feel that it is probably domed. The overriding color is pale orange-yellow, and the thick, thought-infested air smells slightly ferrous.

On closer inspection, you notice that all of the books are ordered into sections, arranged alphabetically within their categories. Despite their differing sizes and shades they exude a peculiar conformity, reminding you of the bricks on the outside of this university town. The architecture of Hod is probably amazing, but it is too big for you to get a perspective on it now. You notice some fine Doric pillars and leaded windows and sense that the area has been formulated in accordance with very specific regulations. It is like a mental arena in which one might encounter wild beasts under the strictest safety laws, exercising the gladiatorial skills with impunity, and providing a spectacle for analysis without running the risk of chaos.

Dionysian revelry is far from this place, and Apollonian learning and logic is the order of the day.

Hanging above the library is a bright golden plaque embossed with the motto: "As Above, So Below." The phrase, an axiom for the whole of your venture up the Qabalistic tree, strikes a chord with you. You recall that you are here not just to explore and admire the scenery, but in an attempt to draw closer to the god-head and channel some of its perpetual cosmic power into your life and those around you. You recall also that everything natural is the image of God, as it springs directly from the divine dreaming. These books are the records of our progress as a race since consciousness began. The idea of so much truth compressed into one space excites you, and you long to gain access to some of the arcane erudition on the groove-carved shelves.

At tables sitting on stone chairs are the forms of many bright beings, barely distinguishable one from the other but for the degree of their radiance. Some are successful scholars and philosophers, known on earth from ages past, or to be famed in ages to come, happy in their regular haunt, absorbed and musing. Others are temporary visitors, barely aware that they are there, or entirely oblivious to their presence here. Many are alive at this moment, sitting at their desks at home in London, Washington, Jerusalem, involuntarily projecting into Hod as their minds tap into the cosmic source of form and intellect. And you, along with several others you can perceive, are a day tripper, popping into the celestial library for a quick reference. However, now that you have discovered the way in, you can visit any time, as a particularly effective meditation prior to taking an exam or facing a mental challenge or debate.

Walk about the library, feeling the ancient stone made smooth by so many discalced feet, rather like a monastery but without the grim Gregorian monotones. This place is a symphony of learning, albeit a well-tempered and subdued one.

On each table sits a tallow candle, burning its yellowy radiance into the jaundiced atmosphere. Yet the thick air does not tire you

or bore the senses. Rather, it excites, like the discovery of an anti-
quarian book on your favorite subject at a church jumble sale.

Mages of every discipline hold conferences here at certain times
of the aeon, deciding with the greater powers on the forms most
suitable and easily assimilated by the minds of men to be introduced at each stage of their evolution. Thus we had the European
Enlightenment, in which coherent forms closer to the truth were
established and much confusion and superstition was swept away;
the Industrial Era, designed to lighten our load but—as with much
in Malkuth—backfiring somewhat; and now, the era of occidental
free-thinking. There are certainly more individual souls apparent
in Hod now than there were just a hundred years ago. Library
membership is becoming a right of the people, as was originally
willed in its creation.

Wander about this fascinating, arcane library until you reach
something that interests you. Be sure to make a note of any subjects that attract you, or words that spring to mind while you are
here: they are bound to be significant as regards your mental
development.

Something strange catches your eye.

One of the brighter beings, somewhat taller and more imposing
than the others, is tearing the pages out of one of the books. You
just have time to glimpse thick black script on the parchment
before the flame from the candle on the mage's desk licks it all up
and transforms it to ashes. As it consumes the parchment, the fire
burns blue, and—weirder still—you seem to see the words themselves leap off the page and into the ether, hang there, still quite
legible, and then slowly disappear. You think that maybe the bright
being has made a mistake, until you see the ritual quite deliberately repeated with another page, then another. On the final burning you try mentally to follow the air-borne script where it goes,
and end up back in your own room.

You realize that they are transferring knowledge to earth. With
so many books in the cosmic library, you cannot help but wonder

how much more must be to come. It is rather a daunting prospect, and reminds you of the adage, "The more you know, the more you don't know."

It has certainly renewed your own appetite for facts. Facts, that is, and not the fictions of Maya, the spirit of delusion. Contrary to popular belief, many spiritual truths are intellectually tenable and quite "scientific" (if science means following the laws of the physical, rather than simply what is perceivable by our feeble instruments and untrained brains). It is one of the delusions of Maya to make us believe that the spiritual runs contrary to sensible belief.

As great teachers of the East have always taught, religion is a science, that of detecting universal truth. Likewise, the Qabalah is a science. It takes creative vision, will, and integrity to climb the Tree of Life, and those who attribute its fruits to dreams are merely too lazy, or scared, to try and scale it themselves. For the fruits that the ignorant call unreal provide lasting health and nourishment on the Inner Planes.

# Netzach

## "The Occult Intelligence"
### SEPHIRAH 7

*N*ext comes Netzach, the cosmic orchard and abode of all powers elemental.

To get attuned with this faery sphere, take a walk in a park at twilight, preferably in spring or at the summer solstice (careful lest you stub your toe, or worse . . . an unfortunate requirement of Malkuth). Whatever the season, though, the nature *devas* are around, attracted by any natural form—or rather, by its expression on the astral plane. Plants have enchanting auras, and only a bard could adequately sing the praises of trees. There is more to hippie notions than meets the eye: encountering dryads is an intense and rewarding experience. Too bad people couldn't reach this level without LSD or other substances in years gone by—these days, many people can "turn on" through natural means, meditation, or other holistic methods.

With Venus as this Sephirah's main attribute, the illuminating lamp, erotic girdle, and resplendent rose as its symbols, and all the powers of Nature in its sphere, it follows that the experience of Netzach is the "Vision of Beauty Triumphant." This beauty, however, is far more than skin-deep; it is an appreciation of all of the higher aspects of life. It is triumphant over all former obstacles, informed by relief. Arrival at Netzach is often preceded by a psychological struggle. Deliverance into Netzach as a manifestation over a prolonged period—states and paths are, of course, far more than visualizations; they are real-life processes—frequently follows a period of blackest depression. The desolation inherent in the twenty-seventh path, that of the Tower, is an initiation in itself. A part of the personality dies a grisly death here, and with resurrection in Netzach comes a redoubled gratefulness and appreciation of life and its beauty. Entry into each Sephirah being traditionally an initiation, in Netzach a portion of the explorer may conceivably "die of a rose in aromatic pain."

The ways of Netzach are distinctly Orphic, counterbalancing the asceticism and mental discipline of Hod. Without the faculty for pleasure, particularly sexual (as rejected by the Puritans, the Victorians, and other groups to whom transcendence from animal status is of tantamount importance), suppression of natural urges short-circuits the aspiring individual. We see this problem amply demonstrated in the Greek myths, when, for example, Hippolytus scorns Aphrodite in favor of chaste Artemis. Sexual chaos results, and the price he pays for the hubris of believing himself "above" Aphrodite's gifts is disgrace and death. Likewise, the minotaur in his labyrinth is a suppressed and raging sexual beast, again the result of the anger of Aphrodite. It follows that one of the "achievements" of Netzach involves balancing the ascetic with the hedonistic and finding a workable medium between the essential stimuli of pain and pleasure. This represents control of the body and personality, those lower faculties so necessary as a foundation to build upon.

As far as the personality of the individual is concerned, Netzach represents will. Hod gives the "form" with which the magician performs his ritual magick, but it is an empty vessel without the energy of Netzach filling it. On this level, Netzach is the power, and Hod the ceremonial glory (further up, Geburah and Chesed share a similar, though loftier status). They meet both directly through the transformative twenty-seventh path and indirectly through the mediations of Yesod and Tiphareth. It is said that Tiphareth is the Higher Self—the part of us still concerned with the ego but has an informed overview—and Yesod the subconscious. The intellect of Hod and will of Netzach combine with these qualities to manifest the physical individual in Malkuth. The essence of Netzach is the victory of will over any obstacles which might stand between higher and lower selves. Each element is, of course, of equal importance, and all must be in balance for the personality to function properly.

The qualities of Netzach are apparent in the four Sevens of the Tarot. The Seven of Wands, for example, depicts a man with a staff fending off six other staffs, held by unseen assailants who are threatening him from below. He fights from a higher vantage point: the weapons of his enemies, held high, merely reach his waist-level. Though he is under siege, he is clearly dominant. The element of struggle is undoubtedly present, but it will soon be relieved by the victory indicated by the attribution of the card to Netzach.

Creativity is a core element of the green Sephirah, and it frequently results in innovative rather than conventional work. In the Seven of Swords image, a man tiptoes away from an enemy camp carrying five swords and leaving two in the ground. What his plan is for these spoils we can only imagine, but it is certainly an unconventional one. "Occult Intelligence" it is indeed—his thoughts are entirely hidden. His offbeat activities combined with his determination to succeed will lead to a sneaky victory, albeit not necessarily a moral one. Similarly, in *The Mythic Tarot*, the Seven of Swords represents Orestes stealing in the dead of night to his mother, whom he plans to kill (in order to avenge his father, whom she murdered because he sacrificed their eldest daughter—on and on it goes!). Orestes is forced to follow the dictate of Apollo despite the fact that he knows it will bring him only torture. He is driven by energies and intelligences greater than his own. Personal ethics are fairly redundant in Netzach, where force is not yet qualified by such concerns.

The Seven of Cups is a magickal image of seven chalices, each containing an entirely different symbol and implication, levitating amidst a billowing cloud of powder. In the foreground, a character resembling a stage magician seems to conjure these objects out of thin air.

The implications around this image are numerous and representative of many different attributes, but I will focus here on those relevant to Netzach.

The chalices, as receptacles of various creations, seem to appear out of nowhere, as do the raw energies of Netzach. The magician is informed by and the chalices created out of the "Occult Intelligence" of the Sephirah's title. The objects themselves are greatly diverse, as are the elemental energies of this powerful sphere. Netzach is where division and categorization in the lower Sephiroth begins. Each chalice also represents, not just an already established fabrication, but the power of creativity, a central aspect of procreative Netzach. It follows that each is pregnant with possibilities and will lead to a completely different conclusion to the problem: which is real and which is illusory? This is one of the dilemmas presented by the card. With so much energy about, it can be difficult to decide. In Netzach, impulsive action is the only reliable sort. Balancing it out with analysis would drag the energy out of its pure Netzachian state towards qualifying Hod.

Finally, the Seven of Pentacles is relevant in that it indicates potential harvest, though swift action is necessary if the fruit of the dreaming man's labors are not to rot on the vine. The symbol of the harvest is relevant to fructifying Netzach. In Tarot, the Empress—the corn-haired matriarch who is most readily identified with Demeter—bears the astrological symbol of Venus on her shield. This, of course, connects the goddess of the crops with the seventh Sephirah.

# Getting from Hod to Netzach

## "The Natural Intelligence"

### PATH 27

This is not an easy path. However, controlled visualizations are quite different to experiencing something in an apparently interminable or unpredictable manner, and they can teach us how best to deal with similar circumstances on more physical levels. So this is one to refer to when you've had the ground whipped from under your feet, and feel that you are falling into the great unknown with no control over your circumstances.

The Hebrew letter related to this path is *Peh* (פ), meaning "mouth"; and, indeed, one is likely to feel chewed up and spat out on this route. Still, nothing may be digested until it has passed through the mouth, and it is a necessary process for assimilation, however bitter the taste at the time.

The Tarot card related to this path is the Tower. The image of a lightning-struck, crumbling tower, with people falling headfirst from its windows, is never a cheery addition to one's reading. Indeed, as the image suggests, it denotes a state of crisis in which the querent's entire worldview may be destroyed, everything that kept them safe and protected suddenly going up in smoke. Even lofty overviews are struck down. In fact, the higher the tower, the more elevated the thought-processes . . . and the further there is to fall.

Does that mean this is the end of the world as the querent knows it? Yes. Which means it can only be the beginning of the next cycle, that of recovery and rebuilding in the light of new knowledge. Being struck by lightning is highly propitious in some respects: one has been singled out by the Powers-that-Be to receive the ultimate celestio-physical shock. One is being "highlighted" when the Tower crops up; old habits are being destroyed in order to herald a new mode of being. At the time, however, this comes as an almighty shock, and it is understandably difficult to see the long-term benefits from this disaster.

Standing with your feet planted in Hod, start to envisage yourself travelling right, to the parallel Sephirah of Netzach.

The tunnel between Hod and Netzach is scarlet, flecked initially with sparks of emerald green. The hues vary in brilliance, but the overall effect is as red as blood, and the air smells ferrous. The atmosphere of the tunnel is aggressive, and you feel as if you have to fight for every inch of progression.

In some areas the red burns like chili pepper; in others it is mentally maddening. From out of the vermillion a disembodied hand passes an iron chalice containing emerald green liquid to you. You sip it, and it fires your blood. You begin to feel the effects of fire as a purgative: it seems to burn away the dull outer shell and all of its clinging irrelevancies, leaving the tactile inner body free to flow like liquid along this pulsating vein. It is a strange vein, with a flow going either way. Try to get into the channel heading away from Hod, otherwise you will be swimming against the tide, and the journey will be even more exhausting.

Eventually you reach a chamber of rough-hewn ruby. There is nothing inside it but for a dancing bear bathed in red light.

At first, you smile at this apparently joyous image, but on closer inspection you perceive that it is dancing because it has metal nails in its feet. As you draw closer, its pain makes it aggressive, and its eyes grow wilder beneath the shaggy fur of its brown pelt.

It is your task to pluck the nine nails from the bear's paws. It will hurt the more as you extract them, but the long-term effects will benefit the creature. Remember this as you approach him . . . and watch out for those swiping arms! They could knock your head off like a doll's.

Spend as long as you need rescuing the bear from its plight. When you have comforted it, you may proceed.

A final pulse of orange-flecked-green, and you are delivered at the door of Netzach, a shimmering vision of hills and vales as occasionally glimpsed on Malkuth as a doorway into another dimension. The sight of so much natural beauty is a salve to your sore senses, a spiritual emollient. You feel intense relief as you exit the twenty-seventh path and knock seven times at the door, a portal bearing the symbol of Venus.

## Encountering the In-House Divinities

The expression of God in Netzach is *Jehovah Tzaboath*, meaning "The Lord of Hosts."

The main energy here is a brilliant otherworldly reddish purple, medium-pitched. As one might expect, it combines immense strength and potential fierceness with spiritual grace, and covers almost every aspect of the spectrum in its entirety—all modes of existence are bound up in it. This force appears to us towering and winged, and can best be experienced through your own contemplation. It sits on the Pillar of Mildness, and is not as saturnine as its counterpart in Hod.

The Archangel of Netzach is Haniel. This entity is predominantly feminine, tall and slender as a flower stalk, with an aura of great determination and quiet power. Blue wings sweep up from her shoulders and encircle her legs; in her strong arms she holds a sword and a set of scales vibrating in brilliant green. The angelic force is bathed in amber and emerald light, and fills you, the onlooker, with a pleasant, inquisitive energy.

The Order of Angels is the *Elohim*, the predominantly green divinities we encountered in a different form in Hod. Their beautiful bodies are made of fire, their slender faces framed by wings of emerald-blue, their lithe forms framed by living light. The presence of the Elohim is vivifying, exuding luminous excitement. They make you feel capable of doing anything, setting out on Peter Pan-like adventures and triumphing as you dwell in this sphere.

Several authorities, including Dion Fortune, claim that the name "Elohim" translates as "Gods and Goddesses." The word contains, they say, a masculine root, *El*, and a "hidden" feminine plural ending, *in*. However, none of these authorities claim to be scholars of the Hebrew language, and Fortune expressly states that she is not. This being the case, I am follow the reading given by the other camp, an opinion represented by Dr. Siegmund Hurwitz. According to this opinion, the word's true ending, *im*, is clearly *masculine* plural. This is in some senses unfortunate, as an androgynous appellation amply befits Netzach, referring to the godforms (in particular those of Nature) with whom we are so familiar in Malkuth. An androgynous being here would also be appropriate for Shekhinah-related theories elsewhere on the Tree (see *Jehovah Elohim* in Binah). However, it ill behooves us to promote inaccurate information for the sake of a theory.

To simple pagan minds of yore, these demigods—later represented in such diverse forms as Pan, Gaia, Isis, and Thor—were the very zenith of spiritual aspiration. The energy behind the concepts of divinity embodied in Hod comes from the Elohim—or, rather, this energy *is* the Elohim.

## The Temple of Netzach

Rose petals strew the winding path to the Temple of Netzach. As you enter the energetic green of the sphere, you feel at once soothed and stimulated. The atmosphere is natural and relaxed, and yet this is not nature as you know her. Things look strange here, heightened, their characteristics exaggerated. You realize that you too will become a caricature here or, euphemistically speaking, an archetype.

There are no walls, but seven trees mark the seven points of the Temple, and between and above them hangs a star so perfect it could be carved of purest crystal, each facet emitting a ray of piercingly brilliant light. Seven giant mushrooms, their gills facing skyward like satellite dishes, catch the rays, presumably dispersing the star energy into the earth.

There are two other radiant doorways here. You realize intuitively that you may travel *into* these objects. One is a hypnotic
swirling moon, the other a Ferris wheel such as you might expect
to see at a faery fair. It glows with tiny colored lights, and looks
enchanting, but you do not wish to go in any of these directions
just yet. Instead, let us concentrate on the heart of Netzach.

The altar is a simple stone placed reverently at the center of a
tall stone circle. Their atmosphere of great, silent knowledge tells
you that they have been so positioned on the luxuriant grass for
aeons, and you wonder whether they witnessed the very first rising
of the sun and moon. These stones seem to be the "hard drive" of
the earth's consciousness, retaining the patterns of life lived and
vibrated out upon it. Even the shadows here are ancient. The folk
of the kings of the Elements weave about the earth's memory like
children around a Maypole—salamanders hovering like fireflies,
softly crackling and hissing the name of Djinn, their lord and master; the sylphs undulate, sighing and caressing the stones, the blades
of grass, ruffling your hair; the water-nymphs create jewels of dew
on the vibrant flowers, and the goblins thread them together and
offer them back in the hope of pleasing the little pretties. Ghob,
their king, laughs and slaps the back of Nixsa with a splash, causing
the nymphs to jump and dissipate in a shower of silver. They re-
form in the arms of Paralda, king of Air, who lifts them a little
before returning them gently to the sweet flower stems.

On the altar sits a golden chalice, bright with gems, and a girdle
made of flowers. The symbol of graceful Venus, or of genetic
woman, is etched into the stone. Beneath it is a carving of a woman
anything but graceful: a thunder-thighed Earth Mama, her dugs
heavy with milk, her face expressing little intelligence—clearly her
mind is as dense as her limbs. As you think this, she transmutes into
the very image of slender-limbed femininity, which smiles and
winks. You blink yourself, and the old chthonic Cybele/Pacha-
mamma/Venus of Willendorf is back before your eyes.

One more item graces the altar: a Temple light which, the salamanders whisper, has never gone out. Better still, they tell you that it has never been unlit; not since the Sephirah was first "spilled," anyway. They guard it with their lives, feeding themselves into the flames to ensure that it burns forevermore.

This is certainly the most frenetic Temple you have visited so far. Adventures may be had just by being present in Netzach's antechamber. When you are ready to explore a little more, you may enter the Sephirah.

## Entering the Sephirah

Once you've taken your walk and feel attuned to the natural energies and patterns of the seasons, knock seven times as you envisage the entrance to Netzach.

Lie flat on your back, close your eyes and imagine yourself in the most enchanted land, one where it is perpetual spring and all of your germinal wishes begin to flourish into meaningful manifestations—but they are only *just* beginning. They are still like ideas, but finding form. The overriding sensation you feel is one of hope.

Wearing ribbons of green on your sleeve, you step into the glorious sphere of Netzach, feeling the energy permeating you as you do. It's like the beginning of a fresh, promising love affair, the steady thud of sap rising in accordance with the nature devas' rhythms as they enact their sorcery on the willing soil.

Netzach is like Cornwall, Devon, or Ireland . . . experienced on magic mushrooms. What seems inanimate in Malkuth is very much alive in this realm: the redolent fur-backed earth, angelica-green; the singing stones and giggling chains of undines posing as brooks, the gossiping trees. Everything here seems to represent the prototype of its kind: the spreading oak, a perfect picnic bower, the cool pine radiantly aureoled, the perky fat blackbird alert to the potential worm.

The moon and sun both hang in the sky, for mortal time is suspended here. They are equidistant, and you feel equally attracted to both. Just as the denizens of Hod were of both genders, so you feel the forces of your psyche balanced out in Netzach.

A ring of standing stones lies before you on the gently sloping lush green land, one which looks as if it has seen many a rush of energy played out at its epicenter. Shooting stars and comets, their tails eloquent blazing portents, are visible in the darker parts of the sky.

On the ground, there are secret rings of mushrooms to be found among the dewy blades. Nothing here is angled the way you feel it ought to be, and when you walk you seem suspended midstep, as if wading through water or walking on the moon.

Wander around a little and take in the uncanny scenery.

In warped thatched cottages live curdle-milk witches, half-glimpsed through cracks in twitch-curtains, at work at copper-colored fire-licked flickering cauldrons, with one cat's eye cast on a dark familiar, the other clocking you. The pitch-black witches' gardens back onto cat-filled spinneys of narrow elm and spindle-trees and tangle thickets from which briar roses shine. Their leaning broomsticks guard the threshold to herb-filled kitchens of potent spells and pungent dingy gingham.

The sound of faery steeds is a constant dim thunder on the verdant earth: there is some kind of race going on in the distance to which you are not invited—bards alone are admitted to such events.

Further on are groups of elfin folk bearing sweet-smelling pine torches glimpsed in shafts of moon and sunlight, then snatched into the shadows like dreams half-remembered. There seem to be zones dedicated to particular beings and activities, and though you try to communicate with some of the sprites you encounter, they seem very much absorbed in their group projects, like ants gathering food, or bees in a hive.

In the branches of the trees hang many lamps, the quality of light given by each visibly unique. Some have a thick, buttery aureole like Van Gogh's luminaries in his *Starry Night*, their energy strangely solid. Others give out a thinner, more refined emission, rather like a laser. Other lamps shine faery color from the trees, green interlaced with red, pearlescent and delicate, all colors at once. The overall effect is breathtaking. You feel truly blessed to be admitted to such a beautiful, joyful realm.

Continue to peruse this fascinating sphere for as long as you wish: it should certainly appeal to the Narnia lover in you.

Return to the stone circle when you are ready, and envisage your-self sitting cross-legged at its center.

As you do so, you feel a vortex of energy gathering there, its centrifugal force concentrated on your third-eye area in the center of your forehead. As it gathers you feel the vestiges of your earth-bound self being swept away, leaving you free of psychological cob-webs and ready for a new perspective on the state of Being.

With the invigorating force sweeping round you like the trans-parent veil of a rapt mystic dancer, blurring the ancient stones of the circle into one, you note that all occurs en masse here: few things seem individualized. You sense groups of clearly defined types; mineral, elemental, flora, fauna, human . . . but nothing in single units as it was in Hod. It is a pool of race types.

Thinking this, you too begin to feel your identity slipping away, and a larger sensation, a wider knowledge, steals in on you. It does not deplete your sense of self; rather, it is augmented by the race awareness.

Spend a little time involved in this sensation, particularly if it is a new one to you. Be aware of the progress of your spiritual race—whether it be Egyptian, Celtic, Norse, African, Greek—and then of the species as a whole. Reflect on how silly it is to think of ourselves as unique when our flesh-bubble on earth bursts so very swiftly, and then it's back to the cauldron to create more flesh bubbles from the same ingredients. A million of us think the same, dream the same, and are of the same stock. As such, we are released from the pressures of individual success. To strive, to do the most we can to further humanity's cause, this is good; but to selfishly pursue a personal prize is a futile full-stop to our collective progress.

Compassion is a virtue of Netzach, because it is with compassion that we learn to look beyond our blinkered selves at the greater picture, to feel ourselves as part of a larger plan. Christianity attempted to teach this, but it became caught up in self-martyrdom and the attachment of responsibility on another. In Netzach we are not compelled to subjugate ourselves, but to fulfill ourselves for the sake of something beyond our temporary, individual identities. Our actions resound on many levels: this is one of the lessons of Netzach.

The wind still sweeps around you, uplifting your senses and invoking joy in you, though when you come to think of why you feel so good, you cannot define it. There is no specific reason; it is a general sensation and one you know is permeating the entire sphere as you perceive it.

Excitement tingles in the rose-scented air, similar to that felt prior to a date with a new paramour. The goddesses of love—Hathor, Radha, and Aphrodite—are worshipped here. This is the celestial garden in which they delight in the joy of lovers; the atmosphere is light, sparky, and, of course, erotic. It also carries the promise of great futurity.

The May Day festival, Beltane, and Netzach itself, represent the irrepressible (and, indeed, necessary) urge to procreate: they are symbols and products of natural fecundity. With the motif of unselfishness, then, it is fitting that a vice to be conquered in Netzach is that of inappropriate lust.

Netzach, as you may well have noticed, is peopled by, among others, the satyrs whose lifeblood is sexual pleasure, music, and revelry. They are the embodiments of these elements. However, we, as humans (especially as humans) intending to climb the Tree of Life, have another theme on our minds, and are required to resist the faery lure of the Bacchanalia—at least, some of the time. Responsibility to others is paramount here.

Sit thinking at the center of this faery storm for as long as you wish. Allow it to blow away all of your preconceptions about life in Malkuth, for this sphere is living proof that there is a celestial agenda quite independent of that of humankind.

When you are ready, maintaining the sensation of essential union with your kind, return to your position on the bed in the realm of Malkuth. Try to nurture this sensation of being part of a greater whole, a nonspecific unit in a mass consciousness, and carry it with you into whatever actions you perform next. It can provide a proper antidote to the egotistical blues, and is the antithesis of the way we are taught to think in the ego-crazy Maya-ridden West.

Whenever you feel your personal responsibilities or circumstances becoming too much, take a trip up to Netzach. It will be different every time, but one thing is certain: the experience will always give you a reality check. Sometimes the so-called "fantastical" is the true measure of our own delusions of reality and our willing suspension of disbelief is the best way to discover truth.

By meditating on Netzach, we soon discover the constellations of truth which lie in the illusion of individual stardom.

# Tiphareth

## "The Mediating Intelligence"
SEPHIRAH 6

*T*his radiant sphere lies at the center of the tree, and is a stimulating stop indeed. Here, the promise of Netzach is carried closer to realization, the Venusian instinct satisfied.

Tiphareth benefits those suffering cosmic light depletion and the subsequent spiritual etiolation. In Tiphareth's healthful rays, the starved soul can photosynthesize until replete with the necessary light and energy.

As well as being the physical sun in Assiah and the spiritual luminary in the three worlds of Yetzirah, Briah, and Atziluth, Tiphareth is the center of the psycho-spiritual cosmos, representing individuality. Its light is refining and transformative. It is "in touch with" more Sephiroth and their diverse influences than any other sphere. Most importantly, it provides the lower Tree with a diminutive Kether, hence its titles "the Son" and "the Lesser Countenance." It follows, then, that the prophets, intended to reflect God's love (i.e., Kether) in Malkuth, emanate from this central sphere.

Tiphareth represents love on a personal level: it stands for the worthiest, most selfless feelings that we can have towards another being. It is the center of true Christian devotion, representing the sun-king, the Christ as light-bringer, a Promethean archetype. The crucified Christ-figure is the epitome of unconditional love, the link between our world of Malkuth and the spiritual world of

Kether. Through Tiphareth, Ketheric energies are channeled (via
Yesod) to Malkuth. Tiphareth conditions these energies in order to
make them digestible on the earth plane; without passing through
this process, they would be too refined for our systems, which are
accustomed to heavier energies. They would "surpass all understanding" and we should have no chance to assimilate them.

Just as the great prophets bring us God's love in ways we can
understand—embodied as parables, miracles, and feats of faith—so
too does the sphere of Tiphareth work on our behalf to transmute
the cosmic skies of fire into a microcosmic regular sun we can place
within the canopy of our own daily lives. Its title, "The Mediating
Intelligence," describes this quality.

Tiphareth relates to the solar plexus chakra and is visceral, in
that we can perceive its effects both psychically and physically. It
is the center of our physical health and well-being, and connects
us along with the heart chakra to all other living entities. It unites
us with the universal organism.

Tiphareth is a cleansing place where emotional baggage may be
sent up in purifying smoke. It is a place of forgiveness and forgetting: the bridge between the lower and upper spheres. Just as we
ought to shed petty concerns about death, so too should we shed
them at Tiphareth if we are to proceed further up the Tree. We do
not wish to be fettered by small conceits and earth ties such as
grudges, resentment, and worldly ambition: to find God we must
be able to fly free, not have our wings clipped by worry or find ourselves homing to Malkuth due to deep-ingrained training. So
when we arrive at Tiphareth, we need to offer up our heaviness
and ask that it be replaced by the refined energies of the beings of
light resident in this sphere.

One of the symbols of this Sephirah is the phoenix. With this
creature, what appears to be death is revealed as life; what was
ashen becomes vibrant flame. Such a resurrection theme is central
to Tiphareth, along with the motif of "faith rewarded." As in the

path between Netzach and Tiphareth, death loses its sting when perceived as part of a continual progression of consciousness.

Because one of its icons is Jesus as Messiah, Tiphareth has a connection to conventional Christianity and monotheistic religion on the surface. Paradoxically, the idea of a lofty, impersonal, or punishing God, such as is popularly construed, is deeply unhelpful to those wishing to unite with the positive cosmic consciousness, and of course the image of Christ on the cross is one heavily imbued with the former worldview. So much damage has been done to this spiritual icon that it is amazing it still works. Yet it does, for its god-power is far greater than the image perpetrated by confused minds, even when they work in unison. As Dion Fortune points out in The Mystical Qabalah, it is not the Calvary cross of suffering represented here, but the equilateral cross of balance and transcendence.

There are pernicious people in every walk of life, and Christianity certainly attracts its share of them. In some respects the symbol of a man in agony nailed to a cross is indicative of the cruelty and hypocrisy of our species, and seems unlikely to yield positive results on meditation. However, to completely refute Christianity (or, indeed, to deny any path to the Light emanating from the Ain Soph) is to throw the baby out with the baptismal water. Meditation on symbols of love, and reading and absorbing the works of such spiritual bridge builders as Paramahansa Yogananda and his own guru, Sri Swami Yukteswar, will reveal the transience of the negative aspects and the permanence of the positive. Viewed as an equilateral cross, one of the most important and protective symbols in the esoteric planes, the symbolism of Tiphareth loses its imposed orthodox Christian warp. Here it implies balance, the perfect poise between Kether and Yesod, and Geburah and Chesed.

Particularly important is the latter balancing act, for Christianity itself is concerned with the balance between Geburah in its positive aspects—discipline, controlled force, and power—and

Chesed—mercy, love, and the materialization of the intent of the masters in Malkuth. Tiphareth, symbolizing selfless devotion and love, perfectly exemplifies this balance.

Other messianic figures also belong to Tiphareth: Krishna, for example, along with all avatars of Truth. Krishna is one of the "Christs of the East." All of these figures are "sons" of Kether; i.e., aspects of Godhead personalized in Tiphareth, and thereby potentially redemptive denizens of Malkuth.

Ra, being regal and solar, belongs to this Sephirah, as do Apollo and radiant, innocent Baldur of Norse mythology. Apollo is the only Tiphareth deity to avoid being sacrificed for one reason or another, though even he is forced to serve his time in menial tasks on occasion. Ra is compromised by Isis to facilitate a serious power shift within the Egyptian mythic universe. The gods are almost always born to suffer in the mystical realms of Tiphareth.

Flip it over into the negative, and Tiphareth becomes overbearing and loses touch with its spiritual source, Kether (the "Crown" of the Sephiroth). This devolution engenders a heaviness of ego, false pride, and everything in fact that is typical of a Leo at their worst. Many a guru has fallen by the spiritual wayside here; it is a real stumbling block for those who talk more than they meditate. Indeed, if you are undergoing spiritual training, or are considering it, beware the teacher who takes you to Tiphareth and calls it Kether. How can one tell? They will imply that they are King, Christ Come Again, Osiris Risen. The true king and queen of heaven are humble, and the true master, though never grovelling, treats all as equal, seeing God in all and all in God. If the soul is gentle and lacking in ego, preferring meditation over any other activity, never rowdy, never overbearing, ever patient and loving, they are reflecting Kether. If they exhibit anything other than these qualities, they are more likely stuck on the dark side of Tiphareth and will probably complain of being forced down from Chesed.

They are actually emanations of Qlipoth, the shadow side of the
Tree of Life, and are to be avoided absolutely . . . if you can.

As with interaction with beings on any plane, always check that
they are "beings of good intent" before allowing them access to
your psyche/soul. Chances are you are interested in angelic, god-
like entities, not demons or dead humans (either physically or spiritually). Unfortunately, just because somebody is involved with
the spiritual does not make them good. There are plenty of vam-
pires and ill beings out there, bodiless *and* incarnate, who choose
(or are forced) to seek the absorption of others' energies.

Always say a prayer before you work, to the bright being of your
choice (the Cosmic Intelligence—visualizing its purifying radiance; the Goddess, as Isis or whichever form you personally revere;
Krishna . . . the choice is yours), and do not forget the use of the
astral armor described at the beginning of the book. Do not feel
vulnerable: you can kick up if need be, you can fight.

One of my own problems when first encountering ritual magick
was an intense reverence and misplaced awe for all involved. Many
lower forms are attracted to psychic experimentation, particularly
in its initial stages, and its practitioners can be unscrupulous. Stand
your own ground, have confidence in your abilities, all the while
maintaining a healthy sense of your own smallness in the cosmic
scheme of things. This is the type of balance represented by
Tiphareth, along with that between the physical and spiritual
realms. Tiphareth truly stands for the equibalance of all of the
aspects of our lives.

The Tarot cards representing Tiphareth are the four Sixes.

The Six of Wands depicts a man, staff in hand, riding to victory,
both he and his staff wreathed by laurel. As already discussed, laurel is associated with the Pythia and the art of oracular utterance.
Thus we may conclude that the querent knows his or her own
future in this matter, and that victory is certain. The quest may
only be minor, but the card indicates an achievement of some

kind. In this sense it suggests the twenty-fourth path between Netzach, sphere of Victory, and Tiphareth. This path is concerned with karmic cycles and the expression of true will, and indicates that the achievements of the Six of Wands are the well-deserved result of past effort.

In the Six of Swords the querent finds that a journey across a sea of sorrow is necessary, suggestive of Binah and its qualities. This means, in mundane terms, the abandonment of the old in hope of a better future. In the picture, a man performs the Charon-like task of steering two downcast souls—a woman and her child, symbolic of what is to be—toward a distant, mist-swathed shore. Like the sphere itself, the boatman is the "mediating intelligence." In this case, between one shore (or state, understood as a Sephirah) and another. The cowled, hunched woman is too wrapped up in her own pain to be the active force; she has passed the responsibility over to another. The Tipharethian role of rescuer, of martyr even, is not difficult to discern here.

In the Six of Pentacles, we witness Tiphareth as benefactor. The qualities of healing and giving are highly pronounced in this central Sephirah. The illustration is of a philanthropic-looking man dropping coins from his right hand into the upheld palms of a kneeling mendicant. Another beggar, his cloak patched, awaits alms to his left. In the other hand the benefactor holds the scales ubiquitous among the Archangels, indicating his temperance and capacity for implementing justice.

The Six of Cups is Yesodic in that it represents nostalgia, memory, and a living connection with the past; but the innocent love inherent in its illustration of one child handing a white flower in a chalice to another reminds us of the guileless Sun card, which of course is relevant to the solar sphere, Tiphareth. It is also a card of healing, a quality of Tiphareth. The runic symbol *Gifu*, the kiss-shaped cross depicted carved on stone, represents the healing power of love relevant here. Its appearance in a reading indicates both the reemergence of someone or something from the past in a manner that is emotionally restorative, and the therapeutic qualities of love and affection with no strings attached.

## Getting from Netzach to Tiphareth
### "The Imaginative Intelligence"
#### PATH 24

The Tarot card ascribed to this path is Death.

An armored skeleton rides a white horse over a supine body, and is clearly about to continue despite the presence of two kneeling children and a praying bishop in his path. No supplication can prevent the reaper from gathering his crop when it is timely.

Like the atmosphere of Maundy Thursday, the world seems dark on this path. The light has gone out, we feel, and the powers of wrong are prevailing. Pain seems to hang in the air, taunting, snuffing out any spark of hope as it arises.

The Hebrew letter ascribed to this path is *Nun* (נ), meaning "fish." Jesus is a fisher of souls, and an acronym related to him, ιχθυς, is the ancient Greek word for "fish." The combination of this symbol of Christianity with the attribution of the Death card brings to mind the sacrificial nature of the light-bringer. One of Vishnu's avatars was also a fish, strengthening the connection with messianic symbolism. Furthermore, the Hebrew word for "priest" or "righteous teacher," *tzaddik*, clearly relates to *Tzaddi* (צ) of the twenty-eighth path, meaning "fish hook"; the letter reminds us of the object associated with it.

As you tread this bleak and bitter path, you feel as if you are being stalked. The dust rises in barren clouds as you drag yourself towards Tiphareth—though why you are bothering you barely know—and a presence behind you draws increasingly near. Occasionally you glimpse a shadow, but when you turn, there is nothing there.

Regiments of black beetles scuttle across the arid path before you, and a huge scorpion waggles its stinger threateningly in the road ahead. It takes you a moment to realize that it is stinging itself to death.

Your energy is running low fast, and the desert path seems interminable. As you think this, a heavy blow fells you from behind.

Struck down, you lie amnesiac for a while, your mind a blank. You, whoever that may be, feel no motivation to move. You may as well lie here and wait for the insects to devour you, to be absorbed into their bodies—they are as good as your own shape, after all. Why cling to one's own atoms as if they are any better than anything else's?

Your form begins to dissipate as you think this, and your mind loosens its control of individuality.

A sudden hiss shakes you from your ennui.

Startled, you look up to see an enormous serpent rearing before you, its green-blue eyes hypnotic, its will utterly beguiling. Having stared you out of your stupor, it lunges for your tailbone area.

You wait tensely, expecting at any moment the sensation of fang scraping bone.

Instead, a wonderful sensation begins to creep up your back, higher and higher, reviving, stealing toward the top of your spine, bestowing a blissful sense of relief and rightness with the world. You begin to feel attuned with your body and individual consciousness again, only now they seem enhanced to their optimum capacity. The thrilling sensation snakes its way right to the top of your spine, through the medulla oblongata and finally explodes in a fountain of brilliant light from the crown of your head.

You awake to find yourself lying before a door of blinding radiance, feeling cleansed and reborn.

## Encountering the In-House Divinities

The godforms at the lower levels are difficult to describe, but from Tiphareth upward they become all but impossible. Therefore I shall cease to attempt a description, leaving it to the reader to meditate on the impressions caused by vibrating the name and concentrating on the qualities and symbols of the Sephirah. One has to be in the right mood to do this properly; merely trying to pronounce the name authentically will not suffice.

In the case of Tiphareth, the name is *Jehovah* or *Tetragrammaton Eloah Va Daath*, referring to Tiphareth's status as "second son" (or emanation) of Chokmah and Binah, the primordial parents. Their first offspring is Daath, which operates on a different level to the rest of the Tree.

The traditional Archangel of Tiphareth is Raphael, but, as Lord of Fire, Michael also deserves acknowledgement at this juncture. Both of these Archangels rule over an aspect of Tiphareth, Raphael's being the light-bringing, warmth-emitting, basic solar properties, and Michael's relating to the spiritual manifestations and embodiments of these qualities. Both emanate healing properties applicable to all levels: Raphael's are of Air (mental problems, breathing difficulties, claustrophobia/agoraphobia, lancing a canker, and mystical delirium would all fall into his domain), and Michael's of Fire (cauterization of an infection, either physical or spiritual, astral "laser treatment," lassitude, depression, and so forth). Michael, of course, also rules over Hod, and many Qabalists tend to think of Tiphareth more as Raphael's domain.

Dominating the central Pillar of the Tree, Raphael spreads his healing sky-blue wings over the lower Sephiroth, his face shining like the sun, his resolute body emanating mercy and protection. His body burns like a flame, yellow at the top, through oranges and red to blue from the torso down. His feet are planted in Chesed, but he is no stranger to the tides of Geburah; in his hands he holds a sword of brilliant blue which is not only for decorative purposes. A set of scales confirms his balanced outlook: justice is of essence here. He heals, but often by cutting or burning away cankers intimately attached to the sick body or psyche, a process painful and seemingly dangerous at the time it is performed. Raphael's whole body shines with cauterizing, cleansing light.

The Angels of this sphere are the *Melekim*, a regal host clothed in shimmering green flame, flashing purple and blue. They operate mainly on the planes perpendicular to ours, but Tiphareth is a cross-junction of levels. From their colors and tone we perceive that they are divinely programmed to be self-sacrificing, merciful like Raphael, and prepared to take risks of their own volition. They are in touch with our spiritual dreams and fantasies (as opposed to the psycho-physical emanations of Yesod), and can provide great emotional healing in times of stress, though often by pulling the mind up a plane or two, causing perceptions and visions which others will most likely reject as the hallucinatory effects of fever.

The essential message of all the divinities of this sphere is sublimation through suffering, light at the end of the tunnel, a new dawn after the dark night of the soul—hence one of its attributes, the "Vision of the Harmony of Things."

On a mundane level, we can appreciate the message of Tiphareth by waiting for the sun to rise.

I once spent the night in a flimsy tent on a moor in Yorkshire waiting for the solstice dawn. It was hot when my friend and I set off (you have already met this friend as the King of Wands in the chapter on Yesod), and I did not bother to take a sleeping bag or even a jumper. In our spontaneity we forgot to pack several other essentials, including food and a flashlight. As I mentioned previously, I was extremely out of touch with Malkuth at the time; besides which, when we departed on the long trek up to the desolate moors, my companion and I were quite happily warm and fed.

Once we arrived at our destination, however, I soon cooled down in my thin Indian skirt and vest top, and then the wind kicked up. Evening fell, and our resilience began to wane. Never mind, we kept saying, we're only here for a few hours, until dawn.

Our efforts to light a fire were thwarted by the rapidly increasing gusts and, before very long, we were freezing.

We kept one another entertained, of course, with sparky conversation, but the elements were definitely winning the battle against our resolve. It was more like winter than summer. Our hands were numb. Had we stood any chance of catching a last train out of the nearest village (which was miles away), we would have, but we had definitely missed it by now.

Night settled in and we kept vigil, shivering—just us, the bleak moor, and the dismal stone circle. Far be it from me to deny a stone circle its natural mystique, but when you are cold, hungry, and exposed, creature comforts are all that counts. I felt utterly unspiritual as I sat there. The experience was not at all as we had envisaged. Eventually, my companion dropped off to sleep.

That night seemed to drag on forever. I could not help but sympathize with primitive man before he felt entirely sure that the golden orb actually *would* rise in the morning. The uncertainty must have been terrifying.

I dearly wished for some of the intoxicants attributed to Tiphareth: a bit of Dionysian revelry would have warmed body and soul. Sobriety and vigil are grim companions.

Stones and heather beneath me, black cloudy night above me, cold air creeping in between every hair in my body, I wished to the Goddess that I had stayed at home, enjoying the Sabbat eve in the warmth of my own bed.

The first rays of sunlight at dawn, however, gave me a primal thrill that would have been denied had I spent the evening in cosier circumstances. The relief! The promise of warmth, and light, and comfort! This is what Tiphareth represents, its expression in Assiah (the World of Action) being the physical sun.

I had never been so glad to see the dawn in my life, and, though it was far from physically spectacular (sunrise on the moors seeps through the sky like gray paint rather than in anticipated radiance), I was grateful. No wonder northern man sacrificed so vehemently to the sun in his pagan rites.

# The Temple of Tiphareth

The Temple of Tiphareth is at the very center of this sphere, its altar the cell's glowing nucleus. Because of its position at the middle of the macrocosm, it might be said that the Temple of Tiphareth is the point from which life grows up and down the entire length of the Tree.

The air is rich with frankincense. Here the Melekim process in purple robes, taut and regal. Their auras show great pain, carefully controlled. They know that it is for a greater good that it is so.

Choirs of Angels sing a high, pained, beautiful sound, as cold as frost on Christmas Eve. To those unaccustomed to opera it is a shock to hear them, like very high mathematics presented to those still learning to count. To those familiar with classical music, the sound is less foreign, but still octaves and concepts above our terrestrial version, even at its most sublime. The music of the Sephiroth could blow our souls to smithereens with the resonance of its pure, concentrated symmetry.

The altar itself is made of gold, and on it burn ten candles, one for each color of the Sephiroth as psychically visible on the level of Yetzirah. The gold is so lustrous that it is difficult to look at, and you instinctively shield your astral eyes. Looking down, you notice that the floor is covered in a warm flood of brilliant red liquid. Where is it coming from?

The outer *temenos* surrounding the structure has eight gates, each marked with the Hebrew letter of the path to which it pertains. Inside, golden mist surrounds the Temple like the aureole of a candle, and through the glowing air you can see yet more archways, leading to the inner sanctum itself. Blood appears to be dripping from each of these arches in turn.

The first is decked with oak, holly, mistletoe, and ivy, and in amongst the leaves and branches can be seen the face of a young, happy god, a flaxen-haired goddess, and an old, sorrowful god. It is the latter who is bleeding in this array, his face growing ever more ashen. The goddess, on closer inspection, has three faces, and though the one she turns to us is pleasant and the one turned to her left loving, the third visage, which she presents to the old god, is chilling.

This seems a very odd illustration to find in a Temple whose key note is transcendent compassion and love. What can it mean?

Slightly perturbed, secretly sorry for the sad-looking god, and, albeit guiltily, thinking this goddess something of a bitch, you search for further clues in the picture. As you do so, you realize that it is not flat, but a rotating wheel rather like those that once used to grind corn. It is moving even as you watch. In response to your questioning thoughts, the wheel begins to move faster. As it does, something strange happens. The man's face on the left begins to cloud, and that on the right lightens up. All three of the goddess's faces become neutral. The wheel turns more, and her features express love for the god she formerly cold-shouldered, and disdain for the one she formerly smiled upon. They too have exchanged expressions. Now it is the previously happy god-priest-king who is dripping his ruby-red blood onto the floor of the Temple of Tiphareth. *To everything its season*, is the whisper on the breeze.

The next archway is equally slick with spilling life-force. Here, a beautiful youth is depicted above the passage, his blonde hair and bright blue eyes distinctly Norse, his muscular body the envy of every man and desire of every woman. *Except not*, you hear sighed. He was so well loved that none envied him, and so respected that all love borne towards him was pure . . . except for that of Loki. As you hear the sighed words, you witness again the penetration of the mistletoe arrow of spite, set to flight by an innocent archer, into the unguarded body of beauty. The scarlet blood cascades to the floor as the god is sacrificed once more, this time for your instruction. You realize that so too does jealousy extinguish the light of the world, and resolve to eradicate it and the spawn of envy from your soul.

The picture above the next archway is of Christ crucified.

This image is so well-known that it barely needs reiteration: between two thieves, the mocked king hangs in transcendent pain. Roman soldiers jab at him with sticks of thorn, their eyes glazed with boredom, their real sin that of being grounded too well in Malkuth, a vice considered by many a virtue. "Keep your feet on the ground!" we are taught. "Don't believe all that stuff and nonsense the madmen and so-called prophets preach: believe only in the established order. Be logical." And so the soldiers prance about the foot of the cross on Calvary while the most symbolic act of the next two thousand years is enacted before them, wondering what they'll be having for dinner.

The blood of Jesus Christ gushes onto the floor of the Temple of Tiphareth, strengthening it.

The next archway's imagery brings no relief. Here, we witness Prometheus tied to a boulder, a sharp-eyed vulture digging into his liver. Day after day Prometheus suffers his fate as *plat du jour* to the carrion hunters, enduring every peck, every wrench and tear of living organ in the knowledge that it will never end, yet happy in his fate because he has brought fire to man—and no quantity of vultures or nocturnally regenerated livers can turn back the clock, or eradicate this fact. He has delivered fire unto earth, he has initiated evolution. He has brought consciousness of higher things to mankind! Even as the hooked beak penetrates the soft, sentient tissue of his body, he smiles, knowing that at the very moment of his suffering, light is dawning in the minds of others. Thus the blood bubbling from the wound that is his perpetual punishment becomes a fountain of life, spurting joyfully into the pool of protoplasmic red in the Temple of Tiphareth.

In the fifth archway we behold a blue-skinned god, quite different to those so far encountered, yet strangely alike. He too is beautiful, with an aura of cleanliness, of transcendent goodness. Yet the scene is incongruous: he is encouraging a prince to go into battle against his fellow men. The prince, Arjuna, protests, but graceful Krishna encourages him to kill. How can this be?

Blood drips from both blue-skinned Krishna and pale Arjuna onto the floor of the gaudy Temple of Tiphareth. Does it really seem gaudy? Arjuna thinks so, at this moment. He does not crave glory or power or religious quest; he desires only to live in harmony with his fellow men. Krishna, however, wishes to test the prince's faith, for the legions of innocent and beloved have only illusory lives of flesh, and if Arjuna is true to his spiritual insight, he will slay them without a qualm, knowing their spirits to be eternal. Thus, all the higher human instincts—love, compassion, empathy—even these must be overcome in the search for *Samadhi* or union with God.

The sixth archway is a blank: not void, but a living, breathing gap of formulating potential. This is the space reserved for the messiahs to come, the little portion of Tiphareth in which their great sacrifices will be enacted. The blood flowing from this archway is transcendent, the most brilliant red imaginable. Heat makes it evaporate into particles of living light. This light is what makes Tiphareth the major luminary of the Tree.

## Entering the Sephirah

This operation is particularly effective when worked on a sunny spring morning. However, intention is everything in magick, and any time of year will do if your mood is right. For Tiphareth, try to perform the visualization when there is natural light around: you will find it much easier.

First, open the windows of the room you plan to work in. As you do, be aware of the prana flooding in; these are tiny particles of life energy, the breath of God. Even in the heart of the city there is plenty of prana around, albeit grubbier than its country cousins. It is partly through prana that atmospheres are transmitted, and it is part of what knits us into the dream-texture of our existence.

If it is a cold day, put on plenty of clothes or get under your duvet. Either way, lie flat on your back and take huge, steady lungfuls of this prana-filled air. Feel yourself becoming consciously attuned to the organism of which you are part. Try to feel the unity of all things. We are all dream projections in God's mind, all made of the same substance: light and electricity. Feel the walls of your flesh and personality melting as your mind rises and becomes a small sphere of light like a miniature sun floating just above your body, then ascending.

Envisage a central door of solar yellow, and rap at it six times.

Become aware of the brilliant true spiritual sun blazing above you, so large that it fills up all the space in the sky; not painful or scorching, but welcoming and calming. On its surface are dim outlines of beings with outstretched arms, many of which seem familiar.

Start to send your ball of light up towards the expansive blaze above you, releasing your perceptions, releasing your earth memories until you begin to loose track of where your consciousness begins and ends. You are becoming infused with a power much greater than your individual status, saturated in a light whose fundament is unconditional love and mercy. Feel these qualities becoming absorbed into you, feel your heart and solar plexus opening up without fear, in this place where there are no shadows; the light is so great that shadows cannot be supported on this side. Here the structures of all that is wrong or warped are absorbed into an unconditional embrace of acceptance. Thus does base metal become gold.

In the center of the refulgence you behold an equilateral cross, and before it a figure not pinned, but with his arms outstretched in a gesture of all-greeting. There is no pain on his face, and no odor of sanctimony or martyrdom, though there has been a sacrifice of animals performed here. The unrefined senses and addictions of the animal self have been burned in the cleansing fires of Tiphareth.

TIPHARETH                                135

Resolve to sacrifice your own animal by forgoing the animal instincts of pride, lust, greed, sloth, or whatever your particular concoction of venal sins might be. Then, in the smoke of this sacrifice, the shape of the true self might materialize.

Converse with the Christ-figure. The results of this conversation cannot be predicted here, as it is personal experience for each of us. Note that the symbol dominating this scene is not the property of the established Christian churches, but a product and element of the universal collective conscious, and that one is free to work with it, whatever one's creed. The Christ-figure himself appears, perhaps, as Baldur, Krishna, or even Osiris, depending on your spiritual frame of reference. The original Christ embraced all and everyone, and is no relation of the manmade, bitter Christs of thorn and whip available to less-expansive souls. The being we encounter on this journey is a direct expression of God, infinite in his mercy.

A gateway appears with the equilateral cross starting from its surface, a livid black in stark contrast to the brilliant yellow-white of the door itself. Send your ball of energy along with your consciousness through the gate.

On the other side you are confronted by two thick, powerful rivers of light.

### The River of Personal Glory

The river to your left is a dark, lustrous torrent, its surface fascinating, hypnotic. It is flanked by thorn trees in whose pointed spindle branches enemy spirits flap in the wind like torn rags waiting to be collected, unpicked and remade into whatever design pleases their gatherer. Bizarre plants like alien cacti flourish along its black wave-lapped banks.

Music drifts in intense pockets of scented emotion about this dark place. The aroma is something like frankincense, reviving and sharp. Some of the snippets you hear are gritty and thumping, like really good thrash metal, a welcome antidote to all that is sickly and confining in the world. The earthiness and sweat of it makes you feel grounded and powerful. Other musical genres float through the air with an energy that is complex and sophisticated, harmonies interlacing with the perfected melodrama of opera. These induce a feeling of transcendence of the mundane, petty problems and concerns of others, a sensation of elevation, superiority. Your mental skills seem particularly acute, and you long for the recognition your unique personality deserves.

Other pockets of sound are rhythmical, reminiscent of Netzach. You find yourself thinking of people you admire and aspire to emulate, perhaps those you desire. You think of the faults of those who are a part of your life, and the brilliance of other people, the pick of the crop. You see yourself surrounded by beautiful people, all of whom consider you the apex of perfection. This can apply to any walk of life. The praise might come from work mates, friends, or family; the emotion of being bolstered by admiring support is the relevant factor.

Then comes nostalgia, breezing into you on the wings of melodic sentiment. The lyrics and soul-moving music of memory move you out of this era and into another time and space. This is especially powerful if it involves one loved and lost.

Each kind of music evokes a certain ambience, full of longing, full of desire. You find yourself craving what these melodies and atmospheres represent: beauty, power, seduction, and more: pure adrenal excitement, sexual and emotional satiety.

The river itself seems to promise all this. Look into it: in the patterns of light and liquid darkness you see faces from the past, cast in obscure roles; glimpses of terrible, powerful civilizations and cities; images of yourself ascending through the aeons to power and glory.

While contemplating this fascinating stream of black light, consider what it would be like to have everything you have ever wanted, to be truly powerful. Imagine how it would feel to be able to manipulate people and things to your own will, to have dominion over all you survey. To have everything you desire, to be worshipped, feared, and adored. Imagine your enemies cowering in terror at the very thought of you, being made to repay you for past wrongs. Imagine total revenge on all who've stood in your way. Allow the intoxication to steal into your blood.

When you have satisfied your imagination and feel fired up with an uncensored determination to succeed, turn to contemplate the right-hand river of life.

## The River of Personal Humility

The shores of this river are lusher by far than the other, but seem more conformed, less touched by the skilled hand of personality. Flowers of entrancing scent and exquisite appearance flourish here, and the power of nature is undeniably present. It seems less tampered with, and you find this refreshing.

At first you experience an uncomfortable sensation of . . . what is it? The word "inferiority" springs to mind. Amidst the emerald green verdure, you feel rather insignificant. By the other river, where nothing flourished, you felt like a success story. Now that you have turned to the other river, you must share your glory with that of others, and with other species. Well, you'll give it a whirl, but can't promise anything as yet.

In this stream too you see images, but subtler, more delicate ones, and the faces glimmering in its surface are gentle and seem to irradiate love and compassion.

Music floats here too, but it has a mantric geometry designed to pacify your soul, so that the images you perceive are larger and more abstract than before. Indeed, they seem to bear no relation to you as an individual at all, but paint for you a larger mental picture in which you are but an element. An essential element, but one which shares its significance with others.

With this release from the ego, though, comes a great sense of freedom. Ironically, it seems as if your potential, rather than being diminished, has grown. The stars do not seem so very distant now. Unlike the other river, your blood is not filled with impatience here; rather, it is a relief, like a cool shower after a scorching day, to visualize this pleasant flow of positive light.

## The Choice

Consider what the long-term rewards would be if your former cravings were granted.

To be king or queen for even one day would be a burden of vast responsibility, with every action capable of affecting the lives of others in incalculable ways. Opportunities missed would be just as incriminating as those grasped; the accumulation of bad karma would be unavoidable.

The only way to counter the impending negativity of such a position would be to go into the service of your fellow souls, acting always in their best interest and being ever merciful.

Imagine the attitudes of others to us if we were all-powerful, even on a minor scale such as being cast in the role of "office tyrant." Sycophantic flattery would be the height of their commitment, for fear would lurk behind their every interaction with us. A black, misguided mood on our behalf could cause irreparable damage to our standing. Think of all the times you've said or done things you've regretted. Imagine what a fit of all-powerful pique could do in those circumstances; history is littered with tyrants and their temper tantrums . . . they are usually surrounded with the bodies of those they executed in their momentary rage. Carry these contemplations as far as you can, countering every image you held earlier with its consequence, until you honestly feel that you would rather pay your respects to beings of greater discrimination and self-control, the masters and benevolent deities, by allowing *them* to guide you, than attempt to handle these formidable energies in ignorance. You would not, after all, allow a child to handle a chain saw, however much it pleaded and thought it wanted to. There are reasons for the limitations of our power as human beings.

Reflectively reconsidering the first river, you psychically perceive that it leads to a dark, stagnant cave, its walls decorated with skulls in states of foul decay. It emits an unpleasant atmosphere you had not noticed before, being too busy riding the rapids in the raft of your own ego.

Ponder what lies at the end of the other river.

When you are ready, expand your auric bubble and allow this glowing river to flow through it, carrying away the debris of unclean thoughts on its steady currents.

Now decide which river you would rather follow on a permanent basis, and resolve to do so. Bear in mind that at this progressed stage it doesn't matter which one you chose, since both will carry you along faster than sitting on the fence (or riverbank). But whichever you chose, you must dedicate yourself entirely to it. There can be no wavering between the two, or you will drown in the crosscurrents. Only remember—one is a finite stream, the other the river of immortal life. The work you devote yourself to can be either paltry or great: we have the choice. You do not need to be an initiate to work out which is which.

# Geburah

## "The Radical Intelligence"

### SEPHIRAH 5

*G*eburah is the first stop in the final stage of the journey up the Tree of Life. In these spheres we experience the more-refined aspects side of Creation and, microcosmically, of the psyche, having left our egos in the Qlipothic dustbin of Tiphareth.

Those familiar with the imagery of the Tarot can visualize Geburah as the homestead of the forward-forging Charioteer.

Remember the earthy thrash metal music we encountered in the dark river at Tiphareth? Here, this music is everywhere, but it is sanctified. It befits its purpose, filling the blood with strength and the urge to forge forward. It represents resolve, with no room for sentiment or fence sitting.

This dissonant, chaotic music is necessary for earthbound spirits, and its success in Malkuth is an undeniable comment on and reaction to orthodox socio-religion and the artificiality it engenders. Divorced from the visceral impulses of nature, we seek an antidote to the excessive sterility brought on by dogma and those who enforce it. In teenagers—especially boys—the impulse to revolt against orthodoxy is particularly strong, hence their love of metal-based "death music" genres, and the proliferation of (so-called) Satanism among teenage populations across the Bible Belts of America and in some of the more parochial parts of Great Britain. Similarly, Gothic music and style counteract the "health and wealth" mentality that places matters of prestige and physicality above those of emotion and spirituality. Essentially, they re-invoke *Pachad*, the fear that is in fact healthy awe of the processes of life and death, without which we become complacent and stagnant. Both are overt reactions against the repressive conditions of mundane community consensus. Where is the warrior-spirit to go, and where the psychic discharge of the fact of mortality, once our constant companion? Is socialization really supposed to make us forget what we are doing here?

Geburah redresses the balance between meekness and spiritual strength as manifested on the physical planes. Geburah is resistance, attack, and defense. It destroys to preserve, making Siva an appropriate godform. It kills to protect its own, and is the defense of the positive against those bellicose alien forces that seek to swamp us (evil, in this case, being that which is unfamiliar and dangerous to our standards in our set time and space). Its icons are all of the gods of war and force: Ares, Mars, the Norse god Thor, and others. Zeus too could be attributed here, furiously smiting the earth with his thunderbolts. All of the repressed energy of mankind might be said to manifest itself here, and its modes of expression are forceful in the extreme.

However, far from being destructive, the energies of Geburah are ultimately profoundly positive. Geburah clears away the old to make room for the new. The sense of desolation caused by the termination of an old form is but an illusion, for in its place will arise a new, improved version. It is akin to the energies of revolution and mutiny that are bloody and brutal in the present, but look forward to an enlightened, nonoppressive "New Régime." Of course, in our terrestrial enactment of cosmic principles the effects and causes are inevitably tarnished, and the New Régime becomes as tyrannical as the old, as do the "progressive" pigs in *Animal Farm*. Still, the principle remains the same. What may appear as destruction is really progress, the necessary decomposition prior to recomposition. This is the reality of Geburah, whose wars are fought not for love of death but for love of life.

The four Fives of the Tarot each reflect an aspect of Geburah.

The most obvious is perhaps the Five of Swords, a card whose atmosphere is so spiky that even the clouds in the background are dark and jagged. A smirking man stands in the foreground clutching three swords; the other two lie near his feet. His enemies, their backs turned, slope away towards the sea. Sorrow and bitterness are their lot, and the victor is glad.

Like the character in the Seven of Swords, this man's expression is inscrutable, but we know he is plotting something. The battle might be over, but the war is not yet won. He seems be visualizing daggers in the backs of his retreating fellow men, and further strife and discord are inevitable. The emotions driving man's belligerence are ingrained into the imagery of this card: envy, spite, superiority complexes. Further sorrow is certain to the querent who cannot lay down the swords of his anger.

The figures in the Five of Wands seem also to be in turmoil: a knot of men brandishing staffs in an ineffective, confused manner. They may be fired up by Geburan energies, but they need discipline to help them express it in a less-chaotic form. Are they building a pyre, or having a mock battle, or really fighting one another? It is difficult to tell. The image makes me think of drunk morris men trying to form their batons into a pentacle, but unable to work out how. Indeed, if they acted in synch, they could perform any number of useful or enjoyable feats.

Here, the Geburan instinct has gone awry. Being fired up by emotion is all very well, but the energy needs to be channeled in the right direction if it is to have any positive effect. So, instead of having a working team, we have a shambles, a mock battle. When this card appears in a reading I often find the "mock" element to be of relevance, representing emotional habits rather than intelligent action. It frequently occurs with reference to stormy relationships in which bad emotional habits and expectations have formed. Mental discipline is required, and possibly some kind of mentor or guide. Certainly in the case of the men in the card, leadership is essential. Likewise, a legion of soldiers, however inspired by their cause they might be, will deteriorate into chaos without the guidance of an officer or centurion.

Finally, the Five of Wands shows the importance of working in a team. Clearly this is relevant to Geburah, in whose martial grounds all are consigned to one "side" or another, as is the nature of conflict.

The Five of Pentacles indicates this element of teamwork: two beggars hobble along together with an air of companionship in their plight, but they are certainly not happy. The Geburan trait of enforced "economy" takes its toll at their financial expense. These poor souls have been cast out into the snow, both literally (in the card) and metaphorically. Behind them shines a stained glass window depicting five coins, well out of their reach. Warmth and light lie behind the wall, but they have no chance of attaining them.

Of course, when this card appears in a reading its implications are not always so dire—I used to get it all the time when still a poverty-stricken student—but it certainly indicates a time of discomfort in which the beneficence of the universe seems to be flowing in the opposite direction from the querent. Disappointment in some matter is almost inevitable, and cherished schemes may fall into ruin due to lack of physical clout or mental discipline. Financially it is self-explanatory; belts are tightened, old clothes are patched rather than replaced. Hardship is implicit in Geburah, the Sephirah of strife.

The Five of Cups is a melancholy image: a black-cloaked man stands with his back to us, gazing downcast at three overturned chalices, their contents seeping into the arid ground. Two remain standing behind him, but he is more interested in bemoaning the loss of the three than in preserving and being grateful for the other two.

This represents the part of ourselves that will not make the effort to salvage or improve a situation; the sensation of loss and depression is too enjoyable to forsake. In other words, the querent is happy feeling sorry for themselves. This stubbornness is relevant to Geburah, in which the warrior-instinct can easily be replaced by pig-headedness. We need only observe the fundamentalist from this, that, or the other belief system to see how blinkered an individual can be who believes in the exclusive rectitude of their creed.

So we see how the vision of power inherent in Geburah might lapse into cruelty and wanton destruction. One of its symbols is the scourge, which as the Wiccan reader knows is a symbol not of punishment, but of purification. The energies of Geburah, when used correctly, can act as a purgative, both as an antidote to aggressive political philosophies (as in the case of actual war) and on the personal level by which we "suffer to learn."

## Getting from Tiphareth to Geburah
### "The Faithful Intelligence"
#### PATH 22

To get from Tiphareth to Geburah, one must work the twenty-second path, that of justice.

The Hebrew letter ascribed to this path is *Lamed* (ל), meaning "ox whip."

Imagine yourself moving rapidly up through a tunnel of green and blue fractals. At the beginning the colors are pale, like the first buds of spring, but rapidly they deepen to rich marine colors, flashing and vibrant.

As you ascend, consider the Archangels so far encountered, and the fact that many of them hold a sword and a set of scales. Force and equilibrium are equally important. Sometimes a little force is needed to perpetuate a motion that might otherwise grind to a halt. Take the ox, for example, traditionally used to plough fields and drive carts. This great beast would have little incentive to direct its steady, powerful plod in any direction other than the nearest lush grass or cow were it not for the skillfully handled goad of its owner. Conversely, overusing the whip would drive the bull to madness, and it might then trample the fields rather than help tend them. Balance is needed to control force, and force is needed to preserve balance.

Soon you arrive in a chamber bathed in blue light. An elephant and a spider are here, sitting in opposite pans of a set of scales. Despite the obvious difference in their weight and body-mass, the scales are held in perfect balance. Contemplate this image before progressing.

Next you pass through a tube of emerald green, and arrive at the red door of Geburah. You know which Sephirah it is because it radiates heat and power and has the symbol of Mars branded onto its surface.

## Encountering the In-House Divinities

The expression of God in Geburah is known as *Elohim Gibor*.

The Archangel is *Kamael*, also known as "the Burner of God." Kamael is very large and strong, with a body predominantly composed of searing blue flame. He breaks down what has become obsolete to us, and thus is both reflective—able to see the consequences and ramifications of particular facets—and resolute. Kamael is something of a nemesis for those he meets: he brings about the karma of the bully and the tyrant, initiating the inevitable processes within the consciousness of those who have taken Geburan qualities too far. Like most of the Archangels, he carries the sword and scales, the weapons of justice. In his case, they are of a brilliant cerulean blue.

The choir of Angels is the *Seraphim*. Their energy has an upper body of fire, shimmering into green lower down. Known also as "the Fiery Serpents," we may envisage them as seething with precise, sharp fury. These are the Angels concerned with matters between enemies and rival factions. However, their knowledge and potential for healing is formidable. These are some of the fiercest angelic forces on the Tree, and possibly justify some of the terrible

imagery of the Old Testament. As avenging Angels, the residents of
Geburah are unsurpassed.

## The Temple of Geburah

This is a five-sided Temple, heavily draped with curtains and veils
of red. Behind some of these are chasms of black, mini-abysses that
exude their own hypnotic charm. On noticing them, part of you
yearns to catapult yourself into the open arms of Binah which are
waiting behind. Your form seems small, a flesh bubble that might
pop at any moment, and you long to evaporate through the Gates
of Fire back into the melting, brewing, cradled energies of the cauldron of life. You know, however, that you cannot do so yet.

The music of this Temple is the clank of metal on metal, the
sound of gunshot, slingshot, and cannon blast booming. Behind
the latter you briefly perceive the "OM" of the universal motor, and
it fortifies your structure.

You are aware of yourself as flesh strung up on bone, pumped
through with blood, a physical force to be reckoned with. The
aethyrs of Yesod seem fleeting fancies to you now. Here, in this
stolid Temple of red and iron and five sure sides, you feel yourself
begin to exude a certain power. For many of us reared in Christian
households, this is a new experience, even a shock. No longer victims, we become active in the Temple of Geburah, empowered.

A gong chimes five times, tiny bolts of lightning flash in your
mind in time to the rhythm of the sound. How long have we
strived to reach this point, straining, breathing, bearing up—sur-
viving, merely. Here now to prove a point, a fact of life. To do
brave combat as an automaton might, devoid of thought.

The smell of many men invades the air, with their strange noises,
their hostile stare. Their tongue is a chaotic Babel in our sacrosanct
space. We will not suffer them to push themselves into this, our
familiar place.

Two giant basilisks hang above the altar, spitting fire. Their very
glance could turn a man to stone. The Angels are on our side . . .

these men before us are only apes. We scorn them without dis-
cernment, completely. We will not suffer more them to be born:
they offend the very air they breathe! Our weapons cleave to our
sides, then find our hands: "For land, for love, for family we fight;
to put the encroaching enemy to flight. Fall to, fierce warriors of
Might, knights of Geburah, to fight for what is Right!"

## Entering the Sephirah

Drink a glass of red wine to prepare yourself for this visualization
(if you are not averse to alcohol or on medication), and, as you do
so, imagine that it is transferring to your soul the same qualities as
a glass of bull's blood would to your body. If you are not able to use
actual red wine, any red beverage (such as beet juice) will suffice.
Feel the iron, the life force and strength flowing into your bloodstream, the creative powers of the forces of former destruction.
Feel the ruby-redness of the drink imbuing your body, vivifying it.
Allow your resolve to be enhanced by the alcohol—but do not
exceed one glass. Will power is all-important in this sphere.

When you have finished the wine, sit bolt upright in a slightly
uncomfortable chair (cushionless, of course), rest your forearms
on your legs in an Egyptian pose, and shut your eyes.

Think of the red of the wine you have just consumed glowing
throughout your body and rising to your head. Concentrate on
this until you see the red all around you, a Martian auric landscape enveloping you. If you are a naturally timid person, gather
your courage and resolve to make this a successful visualization,
no matter what you might encounter. If you are of a naturally
courageous, fiery, or hotheaded temperament, use your will to
define your reactions; resolve not to fly off the handle or become
emotional about the images you observe. And if you are naturally
placid and stoic, determine to really *feel* the images you
encounter, abandoning your habitually detached standpoint in
favor of a more visceral experience.

Concentrate on the fact that you are entering Geburah in order to prove yourself. If you are not feeling astrally focussed, or if you are shaky emotionally, do not attempt this exercise. Only do it if you are feeling capable and determined, well grounded, and not easily spooked. Not that Geburah itself is spooky in the least, but it is important that you be able to withstand the forces you are going to encounter. Don't forget that astral armor: you need it here more than anywhere else on the Tree.

Now see yourself knocking at a vast door of oak and iron, with the symbol of the primal male scorched into its surface. You rap at it five times, then force it open. As you do you hear alarm signals thudded out on drums, their skins those of freshly hunted quarry, and know that you are being screened by those within as a possible impostor.

Large men like Vikings are running towards you, their heavy forms thumping on the arid ground, sending up clouds of reddish dust, the horns on their shaggy heads glinting in the sharp light.

Clearly you need to act in order to avoid being forcibly ejected.

You have three choices: you can explain your reason for being here and hope they will accept it; or you can adopt a similar form and *become* them; or you can fight them. It is up to you whether you use your astral-physical strength to do battle with them, your powers of sympathetic magic to emulate them, or whether you employ reason to explain your motives. All come down to the same essential soul element, courageous determination, and the sons of Thor will respect this . . . you hope.

Whatever your means of entrance, you are struck by the strong smell of male pheromones within the walls of this strange city. Geburah emanates strength and force, and a magnetic vitality like that of a Roman arena during a gladiatorial conflict.

There are warrior-like beings everywhere, most of them going about their business now that your presence here has been sanctioned. One or two give you the hairy eyeball, but your gaze reciprocates theirs with the astral metallic clink of a protective sword rising to meet the challenge of their own weapon. *Touché*, you think.

Some of the eyes you encounter glint like the guillotine, giving
you a foretaste of your own eventual death. However, far from finding this disturbing, you find it a strange comfort, a perspective-bring-
ing glimpse of your short sally on the stage of human life, and so a
blessing in disguise.

Spend a moment considering your own mortality, the certainty
of physical death, your transition into the purifying fires between
lives. Though taboo in the West for its morbidity, awareness of
one's mortality is as intensely important as the knowledge of one's
potential in this life; indeed, the two go hand in hand. An understanding of death is a great stimulus: there is no time to waste in
readying ourselves for this certain fact of life.

In Geburah, what seems horrific to us—battle, death, despotic
force, destruction—is sanctified in that it is entirely necessary in
the much greater scheme of things. Geburah breaks down, transforming matter into energy ready to be recycled.

Feel the fact of the eventual corruption of your physical body,
and imagine what you will have to say for yourself when assessment time comes. What have you done to further the evolution of
humankind? Have you fought for your good? What have you done
to benefit other species on earth? Are you progressing in your particular spiritual quests? If you are making absolutely no progress on
these fronts, or are in the throes of particular karma, it is Geburah
that will strike you down. Sudden, violent death and death by
battle all come from Geburah. It is also Hiroshima, terrible destruction in the name of greater balance. It counteracts the efferves-
cence of merciful of Chesed as it destroys the restrictions imposed
by form-bringing Binah. Geburah removes the obsolete, however
painful this may be at the time. It is the Geburah instinct that compels us to crush the skull of an injured animal rather than watch it
die in prolonged pain. Geburah, with all its sound and fury and letting of blood, is the ultimate bringer of euthanasia.

Look around Geburah and absorb its atmosphere. Make the most of it, for you do not know whether you will experience it in tranquility again. You are going to confront the symbol of your fears in the arena, and should you not conquer them, you will be unable to proceed with the ascent of the Tree.

Find the arena. It shouldn't be difficult: there are bloodthirsty crowds gathered outside it, along with cold groups of voyeurs, entirely objective in their stance. They remind you of politicians blithely sanctioning mass destruction, allowing no break in their daily schedules. Others of the audience seem wise, above such considerations, like Arjuna when Krishna finally explained to him the reasons that he had to go into battle. It was all an illusion, as is every stage of God-divorced death-in-life. At the moment, however, your adrenaline prevents you from entirely appreciating this point.

As you approach the central focus of the citizens of Geburah, use the opportunity to consider what you most fear. In every personality's case this will carry its own tincture. For example, fear of being out of control is often symbolized by an apparently irrational phobia on which all of our terror is focussed. *We will be all right*, we tell ourselves, *as long as we never encounter this particular object, animal, or situation*. Phobias I know personally range from the fear of being buried alive to the less-explicable fear of butterflies; terror of water, fear of birds, and the ubiquitous spiders and snakes. In all cases it is not really the object or situation that is feared, but the idea of being unable to protect oneself. If you harbor a strong phobia, try to embody it mentally and resolve to fight it in the Geburan arena.

The idea of standing up in public and giving a speech may be your personal bugbear, or maybe it is the thought of being ignored or ridiculed by all around you. Perhaps you most fear the loss of a partner or loved one, or the demise of your own physical faculties. Public humiliation is often dreaded by those who have hitherto lead successful lives. Whatever your fear might be—perhaps an amalgam of some of the above, or something entirely different—resolve to confront it here.

Once you have reached the arena, you enter a short tunnel and have a moment or two to gather your wits. Remember the ruby-red wine you have imbibed, a symbol of life, strength and courage, and allow it to work its magick on your senses.

Gather your armor tightly about your astral frame, and think of all in your personality and life that is worth fighting for. Do not attempt to avoid confrontation; it comes to us all, whether we wish for it or not. Better by far to confront it in the time and place of our choosing than to be taken by surprise.

As you emerge from the tunnel you hear rapturous applause. The arena is smaller than you had expected. The fight will be swift and decisive.

Taking stock of your astral armor, making sure it shields you all round, you hear the gate shut behind you with an indubitable clank.

Although you feel fear in your blood, you also perceive the respect emanating from the crowd because you have *chosen* this challenge. The crowd is behind you, you know that. Nervously you eye the gate opposite, a strange exhilaration swelling in you. You feel your weapons primed and ready to work your bidding. This is an exciting challenge indeed. Here is your opportunity to slay your personal dragon and progress in your journey unhindered.

Before you know it, your opponent is in the ring with you. Its form exudes all the terrors you personally know so well; its surface seethes with your darkest fears. You take a step forward, reflecting that your opponent is made of the same matter as you are, and that conflict is one of life's necessary paradoxes, especially when you wish to lead a progressive life.

Do not wait for your opponent to strike: cast the first blow yourself. Be careful not to fall into sympathetic rapport with your adversary, as it is essential that you pit your strength against it. You must: your own evolution is at stake.

As you send the first bolt of energy, your opponent reels and the crowd screams and jeers. Waves of animal instinct flood from the onlookers, and you are reminded that nature herself is merciless, survival of the fittest being key to life in this existence. Those without courage are neither of any use nor ornament, while one strong and just can work in a truly worthwhile manner for his or her kind.

Quick as a flash you gird yourself against the inevitable retaliation. No sooner have you remembered your astral armor than a ray of spiky black light comes at you like a chain saw and attempts to penetrate your protective layers. Feel it deflected like a ray of light by a mirror. It bounces back, straight onto the sender, cutting into its torso and causing its energy to start leaking.

Do not become complacent yet: like a baited bull its fury is redoubled by its pain, and suddenly you are beset by a thousand discs of razor-light, each one intent on severing and destroying your confident astral stance. Meet those you can with your own discs of bright spinning light, dissolving the others midair. Those that reach you are absorbed into your armor and—strangely—seem to fortify it. Make a mental note to be empowered by your own fears in future. For example, fear of being attacked could be utilized in a very positive way as precaution, and the overriding instinct for self-preservation can be harnessed so as to make it an accurate psychic alarm. Fear of an object can help you empathize with others' apparently bizarre aversions, so that you can offer them support without being dragged into participation in their phobia. If you have actually been attacked and injured, you will know, like Chiron of Greek Myth, what it is to transcend the physical preciousness/egocentricity that stands in the way of spiritual progression. Likewise, the bolts of hateful energy sent by your psychic doppelganger, your reverse soul twin, are introducing you to new wavelengths, making you competent in them.

Your armor has thickened now, thanks to the onslaught of your opponent. Draw energy from the crown of your head, focus it onto the surface of your armor, and shoot. A thick blast of red-hot energy issues from your aura, not scalding you because it is of your own essence, but a hellfire blast to your shadow self.

(It is worth remembering here the philosophy that our enemies in this life are preordained, and are as much friends to us as those we think we love. These characters are elected to bring about certain responses in us, as we are in them. It is a difficult truth to get one's instinct around, as every fiber of our spiritual, moral, and personal sense will inevitably cry out against it. Still, there it is. Many religions state that life is a test, and it certainly would not be much of one were all and sundry our avowed friends. Without conflict, this life would, unfortunately, serve no purpose at all.)

The crowd positively shrieks with glee as your partner gathers up the last of its hateful concentrate and prepares to send you screaming into the abyss. Use every ounce of your energy to flank yourself with sure strength; apply it to every atom of your being. Send each individual atom back, redoubled in power. Meet your nemesis on your own terms. You invited it here, after all; it is your prerogative. You have caught your own fears on the hop, and the advantage is yours. So, exterminate them now. Prove yourself. Allow all your hurts and the frustrations of the past to invigorate the venom of your retaliation.

See the form opposite you crumple and unravel like a disintegrating mummy as your energy accosts it. The debris is blown away, but tiny worms of light are left suspended in the air, and these you draw to yourself and absorb. They are the astral medals of your achievement, and quickly become part of your own will-directed essence.

The crowd leaves you in no doubt as to whom has been victorious; but best of all, you have a sense of personal victory that could never be bestowed by objective praise.

Within yourself, you *know* that you have been successful.

# The Meaning of Geburah

The lessons and processes of Geburah are not always pleasant, and may seem superficially incongruous to one's peaceful worldview, but on the contrary they are both positive and essential. Without the forces of destruction, the whole cosmos would be entirely unbalanced. Just as the serene and beautiful Indian goddess Parvati becomes the terrible Kali when demons run amok, so is discipline and control necessary to prevent universal anarchy. Without the severity of martial Geburah, the innocent would be perpetual victims to manipulative entities. There must be the faculty of resistance and attack, and this is what Geburah represents.

You can employ its qualities within your own life without scruple, for it will only respond to a balancing cause. Attempting to employ Geburan qualities for wrongful action, as many have in the past, is signing one's own warrant of death by force. Equally pernicious is the urge to refute Geburah as undesirable. It should not be shunned or ignored, for it is the force that checks and counteracts other energies that would, if unhindered, become our evil themselves.

Geburah may seem immediate in that it is intensely physical and instinctual, but it is worthy of concentrated meditation. When you have completed this mortal combat with your own inhibitions, sit for a while and contemplate the ironic nature of Geburah. It will reward you as much intellectually as it did psychologically, and should aid in achieving equanimity.

Without shadow, this life would appear very one-dimensional indeed, and the peaks and troughs of experience would be so faint as to be almost undefinable.

Geburah's darkness defines, and its blood gives rise to new life.

This does not, however, make it any easier at the time of the battle. There can be no doubt about it: Geburah is difficult for the compassionate to swallow. Every news report bespeaks some feat of Geburah, and complacency is not the answer in these cases. Neither, however, is hand-wringing and railing against the specific or unseen causal parties. Only activity in the sphere to which we are assigned can bring balance to the world, and to our own psyches. For example, actively helping to counter a problem is a positive move, *even if we believe that problem to be cosmically ordained*. Likewise, we may not feel any celestial influence on a particular event or situation, and it may seem to us so much futile pain or slaughter. But action will help remedy these outrages, even if this action takes the form of sending comfort and love to those affected. Railing against the Maker will help not one jot, nor will blaming any who are not like us.

There are all sorts of powers at work in this world: some exist to make it more interesting, others are present without invitation. In Geburah we learn to pitch our strength against those that might be pernicious to us, and to suspend judgment on those we do not understand.

It is all part of the challenge that makes the ascent worthwhile.

# Chesed

## "The Receptive Intelligence"
### SEPHIRAH 4

The upsurge of energy from Geburah is stabilized by its opposite Sephirah, Chesed. In occult terminology the pair are often referred to as Geburah and Gedulah, these appellations being utilized in such operations as performing the Qabalistic Cross, a stabilizing ritual in which the body of the magician becomes a microcosmic Tree of Life. The top of the head (or over and above it) is in Kether, the lower body in Malkuth, the right shoulder abides in Geburah, the left in Gedulah, or Chesed.

Chesed is a paternal sphere, its magical image that of a mature throned king, crook and scepter in hand. He is the Emperor as found in the Tarot, sitting foursquare, strong in his domain. In the positive, this represents a just ruler whose love of his people informs his creative, authoritative output. He sees the potential of his kingdom and its inhabitants, and is blessed with the ability to make accurate long-term assessments. He is beneficent, his sphere opulent. All that seemed lacking in Geburah—effusive, nurturing landscapes, a sense of safety and peace—exists in abundance here. The inhabitant of Chesed is familiar with the concept of mercy (unlike his neighbor in Geburah), and is skilled in the art of transcendental love.

One of the deities attributed to Chesed is Jove, expressing the expansive, hearty nature of its king, especially when warmed by the fermented grain sacred to him. Chesed is welcoming, nourishing, and generous (in a "pat-on-the-back-old-chap" sort of way). It follows that when imbalanced, this Sephirah is despotic, just as an upstanding character can turn negative under the influence of alcohol or other negative distractions.

Chesed is described as the "Receptive Intelligence" because it receives the energies of the Supernal Triad (Kether, Chokmah, and Binah), accepting their energies as a synthesis from Binah, and moving these forces from the conceptual towards the concrete. Of course it may be argued that all Sephiroth are receptive intelligences, as indeed they are. However, Chesed is receptive in an additional sense: being the sphere of mercy and love, it is open to all, without discrimination, and is receptive to all supplicants. Its compassion is unlimited, its mode of self-sacrifice similar to that of Tiphareth. From Chesed, however, enlightened ones send forth guidance instead of following their own paths to the light. Sometimes they incarnate in order to help mankind, sacrificing themselves, as William Gray points out, to the cradle rather than the cross. This is why Chesed is also known as "the Sphere of Saints."

As the first brother of Binah, Chesed evinces her capacity for reception but without the restrictions typical of the Left Pillar. The compassion of Chesed is both informed and unlimited. Being placed upon the Right Pillar, the danger here is one of overdoing generosity, a feature just as capable of causing harm as emotional overstringency.

Paradoxically, abundance is great in moderation. An overprotective parent smothers its child, and may create an emotional imbecile through this excess of love. An inattentive parent creates equally dire results. Poverty is undesirable, but excess wealth can induce mental and spiritual lethargy. As Baudelaire puts it, boredom *ferait volontiers de la terre un débris, Et dans un bâillement avalerait le monde*—"would willingly lay the earth to waste, and swallow the world in a yawn." This is one of the dangers of Chesed, where abundance is so great that effort might be replaced with ennui.

Likewise, an excess of clemency, the key trait of Chesed, could lead to increased criminal activity. This is why we require Geburah to counteract the side effects of love and mercy. The strictures of Geburah perfectly balance the abundance of Chesed.

In Tarot, the Fours of the Minor Arcana are attributed to Chesed. Of these, the Four of Wands is the most classically jovial, depicting a joyful scene in which two bouquet-bearing characters appear to be welcoming the viewer into their homestead. Opulence is suggested by the castle in the background, and the four rods forming a doorway are garlanded. Other revellers are glimpsed in the background. The pleasures of friendship and hospitality are certain when this card appears.

The Four of Pentacles shows a dour man sitting face-on, a pentacle beneath each foot, one as a crown and one held as a shield. This is an image of establishment: the character has laid his foundations, and is determined to use them to succeed. He looks the querent in the eye, daring us to doubt him. In the tradition of the patriarchal values represented by Chesed, he is absolutely certain of himself.

It follows, then, that he is not one of the world's most adventurous characters. His jaw is set in determined stoicism; he will not be tempted to stray. The lack of lust for life (or wilful abeyance thereof) is not Jovial, but the element of stability and stolidity is. It is also typical of the Pentacle suit. This is the Taurean (and, indeed, Virgoan) at their most earth-sign avaricious, clinging to form, unable to flow with the tides of life. Still, it is on such solid characters that empires are founded, and the appearance of this card in a reading bodes well materially, demonstrating intense focus and long-term success.

The Four of Cups on the other hand depicts a dreamer; a man sits dozing beneath a tree, three chalices upright before him and another being handed to him out of thin air. One of the features of Chesed is the pursuit of the "True Spiritual Will" . . . except this man seems to have forgotten that's what he set out on. A golden opportunity hovers before him, but he is too lethargic to notice, never mind to grab it. Obedience to his higher inner dictate would doubtless cure him, but can he be bothered?

The Four of Swords represents Chesed's curative properties. One of the paths to Chesed (from Tiphareth) is that of the Hermit, and of course the key factor of this discipline is solitude. The character in the card lies supine; indeed, the querent is represented by a figure reclining across a stone tomb. Sometimes health problems and hospitalization can be indicated here, or an operation suggested by the three swords hovering above him, but more often it means a time of recuperation is necessary. The querent requires a retreat from the outside world in order to hear the "still, small voice within," as represented by the chapel of rest in the card. Meditation, pathworking and a little asceticism are the order of the day.

Another facet of Chesed is trust in one's instinct and higher nature. "Be true unto yourself" is a phrase that might be applied to this sphere, especially as one of its vices is hypocrisy. From this quality arises tyranny, another vice to be found here, for Chesed is the sphere of both the true ascended master, and of the false guru.

As discussed in the section on Tiphareth's messianic aspect, the true spiritual guru offers advice, and does not issue rules. Like the Hermit, he or she lights the way but does not compel one to follow it. Those who claim that they are suffering for the sake of others, or inflict pain for supposedly mystical reasons, are manifesting the cruelty inherent in Chesed. They are leading their followers up the garden path of their insecurities, and themselves into the abyss of their own ego delusions. There is a big difference between the enlightened master (usually—if not always—disembodied or semi-incarnate) who inflicts a short, sharp shock on the potential disciple in order to illustrate or manifest a pertinent quality, and one (usually all too physical) who abuses his or her charge. Sexual interaction or innuendo in such circumstances is highly suspect; such behavior within a system of teaching is almost always a warning sign that true spiritual integrity is lacking. At the same time, strict chastity—though entirely appropriate between teacher and pupil —can be equally pernicious. Asceticism is difficult to maintain in the West, and is anathema to the occidental psyche. It also goes against the nature of Chesed, which tends toward hedonism when it comes to drinking and making merry.

So we see that, though we are getting closer to the Truth in which there can be no fault or vice, we are not quite there yet. We are still dealing with the mind, and the mind is intricate, and fallible. Maya creepers still cling to the branches of the Tree, and parasitic entities suck at the sap of our integrity. We need to employ all our qualities of discrimination gleaned from Malkuth throughout all the spheres, but particularly in Chesed, where its evils are more carefully hidden than elsewhere. This Sephirah naturally gains our confidence, and its adepts are capable of doing the same. It is not yet the time for blind faith on our journey.

It is worth taking stock of the jovial aspect of this sphere. Chesed is not the place to take oneself too seriously. As man is made in the image of God—and one of the features peculiar to the species is a sense of humor—so is Chesed the epitome of levity within the godhead. We as mortals might hope that we are at the very least entertaining—to some extent, there is little else to recommend us. Chesed might be said to represent the amused and fun-loving aspect of God. The solemnity of the Church in the West makes no room for this essential element of divinity. Rather, Chesed's jollity is perhaps best encompassed by the Hindu festival of Holi, during which colored powder is thrown at every passerby (even the reserved onlooker), and ghee (bright yellow clarified butter) is rubbed over the heads of the revellers. Intoxication and fun are as important in Hindu belief as order and serious endeavor. I believe this to be a far better representation of the human/divine relationship than dour chanting, pleading, grovelling, and upright behavior alone.

The nature of Chesed presents a metaphysical riddle. You will, like a seasoned traveller, learn the language with repeated meditation and, after a while, begin to understand its innuendoes. Indeed, this may be safely said of the entire Qabalah: the more familiar one is with the regional patois—that is, the symbols and correspondences of each Sephirah—the greater one's understanding of what lies behind and within it.

The visualizations described here are an example of the extrapolation possible on the themes found in Chesed. Doubly powerful will be the formulation of your own images, either along these lines or completely different. Play with these ideas, improvise when you feel the inclination. And most importantly, enjoy them and make them real. The art of creative visualization is to know that, although events take place in the imagination, they are not imaginary, and neither are their results.

## Getting from Geburah to Chesed
### PATH 19

The path from Geburah to Chesed is that of strength. In the *Rider-Waite* Tarot, the card representing this quality shows a white-robed woman standing over a lion, whose jaws she holds with her hands. She is not fighting the beast; they appear to be familiar companions. There exists between the two a mutual understanding and respect of one another's strength.

The lion represents, among other things, the ego. Ego is required in the lower Sephiroth; in many ways it is the motivating force par excellence. Without an ego, we would end up as doormats to everyone else, and progress would be unlikely. Inertia, the vice of the earth sphere, might set in. Yet this state of separation from the universal consciousness is a harsh condition, and the delusion of individuality is a heavy cross to bear when one truly understands it. That cross belongs to Geburah, on the Pillar of Severity.

The opposite of ego is an acute sense of the reality of others, which overrules the illusion of one's individuality. The result of perceiving others as real—really real, that is, sentient—would be total compassion. This applies to the most godforsaken beings, even the Qlipoth. This quality of compassion is, of course, the balancing and merciful force of Chesed.

The nineteenth path, lying between Geburah and Chesed, represents the balance between might and mercy. Chesed is the beneficence of a summer's day, but when the heat becomes oppressive Geburah's thunder and lightning will shatter it. It is the second of three reciprocal paths, with the energy flowing in both directions.

The Hebrew letter assigned to this path is *Teth* (ט), meaning "serpent." As well as being the infamous seducer in the Garden of Eden, the serpent is renowned for its agility. Look at the phrase "as slippery as a snake": the serpent can wriggle its way out of any situation. Because the snake is typically vilified, its slippery quality is usually represented as a negative, but tactility is often a useful feature. Combined with the path's other attribution of strength, we can perceive the virtue of mental flexibility. It pays, especially in magick, to keep a "willing suspension of disbelief" in conjunction with informed intuition. This allows for a maximum of mind expansion with minimum gullibility. If we want to learn, we must admit concepts peculiar to us into our consideration—but we should avoid being swept away with them (as I, for one, often was when first encountering magick and its masters). The serpent of this path perfectly represents these dual qualities.

Visualize yourself riding a lion along a tunnel whose colors start as solar, then pulsate gradually into violets and blues. Concentrate on maintaining the balance between the "conflicting" forces of your psyche, those of preservation and destruction, submission and aggression, love and antipathy. Decide whether you would rather follow the sun of spiritual transcendence or be bitten and dragged down by the serpent of transitory sense gratification.

Continue on your feline steed until you reach a blue door marked
with the sigil of astrological Jupiter.

## Encountering the In-House Divinities

The name of God in Chesed is *El*. You may have noticed that many
of the names of the Archangels end in *-el* (or *-al*), allying them with
the God, particularly to the expression of God in Chesed. Chesed
and Geburah together represent mercy and might, power and temperance, the two most important elements of effective rulership.
There is no point in being a just ruler with no power; conversely, a
powerful ruler with no temperance will wreak havoc in his domain.

The symbols reflecting these facets are the sword and the scales.
The Angels that bear them represent their allegiance to the balanced energies of Chesed, those of immense might tempered by
sublime mercy. If we are spared the sword, it will be to the ultimate
betterment of ourselves and mankind. If the sword strikes, then it
is with good reason. Just as the Reaper—symbolized by the Death
card—fells us when regeneration is necessary, so too do the powers
of Chesed and Geburah work in unison to produce the right effect
at the right time. Too much mercy might keep the suffering creature alive, or preserve one to the detriment of many; and we all
know the results of excess force.

The Holocaust provides an extreme example of Geburah gone
mad, of force without mercy. Hitler is believed to have dabbled in
the occult, as exemplified by his adoption of an aspect of the
swastika (symbol of Kether, long an important symbol in the East).
The pacifists who fought against him both on an occult level (as in
the magickal Battle of Britain) and on the outer planes were the
Chesed to his Geburah. The sword of the Angels is not just a symbol of force itself, but also a counterforce to excess.

The Archangel of Chesed is Tzadqiel, the patient restorer of order
in a necessarily unbalanced cosmos (without imbalance we would
have no motion, no progression, and, indeed, no Qabalah).

Tzadqiel's name is translated as "Righteous," "Benevolent," or "of God." The root of the word recalls *Tzaddik*, the Hebrew word for a sainted person or rabbi, a "fisher of men." Tzadqiel is thoughtful, intellectual, and very beautiful. She is mostly sky blue, flashing occasionally with silvery white. Sturdy and graceful, her movements are measured in immaculate time with the celestial clock. She is conversant below, and above. Her quiet soul never falters.

The *Chasmalim*, the Angelic order of Chesed, are a little more feisty than their overlords, fiercer and brighter, definitely less patient. Their counterparts, the Seraphim, have caused this emphasis of energy in the lower stratum of Chesed. Such a dynamic is necessary in order to preserve balance. Tzadqiel and the Chasmalim are the Angels who answer appeals to the cause of friendship; they are influential in healing rifts, deepening bonds, and so on. We should concentrate on Chesed when mental and spiritual leeway is required. The shining choirs of Chesed are russet and scarlet in the upper regions, phasing into brilliant olive green lower down. They are said to have the power of speech, connecting them to Hod, which in turn is said to "reflect and cleave to" Chesed.

## The Temple of Chesed

The Temple of Chesed has four walls, each wall pierced by an archway. The structure is pale blue and minimalistic inside, very "zen."

Behind this plain façade lies a cornucopia of effervescent energy, symbolized here by the abundant greenery growing behind the veils of the Temple. Indeed, on closer inspection, it resembles nothing so much as a hothouse, with all sorts of life-forms flourishing within its apparent simplicity.

On the wall above the altar—itself flashing in purple, azure, and violet—is a picture of a unicorn, its coat silver, its horn radiant white. A saddle of gold-embroidered purple sits on its back, but it seems to have no rider. If you are pure of heart, the unicorn will let you ride it. Try, and see where it takes you. All interactive experiences in this sphere will be unique for each participant.

On the wall opposite the unicorn a set of scales is depicted. A constant promise in Qabalistic imagery is the force of justice. You may rest assured that El, Tzadkiel, and the Chasmalim will effect this justice even unto a minuscule degree. Nothing here is lost, nothing neglected. Even the Qlipoth of Chesed display an incredible attention to detail.

The air smells of wheat, the grain that will become bread in the ripening oven, and fermenting ale; both make you think of hearth and home. A place of belonging, of familiarity. Above all, this Temple makes you contemplate the Creative Intelligence that abides in the True Homestead, the celestial palace of Belonging. You resolve to do all in your power to follow the dictate of the divine within yourself. This strength is the true atmosphere of the Temple of Chesed.

## Entering the Sephirah

When you have introduced yourself to the celestial powers of Chesed and feel that you have been accepted by them as a protected visitor, you are ready to encounter the Sephirah itself.

The following visualization is an example of Chesed in Assiah. It depicts the sort of experience one might have on the earth plane that activates Chesedic functions.

Of course, every Sephirah has many aspects. The faculty of mercy is perhaps the most obvious in Chesed, and it would be possible to construct a visualization around the idea of clemency and its various effects. From any position of power—such as being a parent or employer or the dominant party in a relationship—we are able to experience Chesed every day when we grant the child or employee leeway, or lovingly guide the partner/friend. Chesed is active when we have a choice between being generous, particularly emotionally, and refusing to give.

Because the latter aspect of Chesed is quite commonplace, I chose to concentrate instead on one of the Sephirah's less-travelled roads, that of the potential disciple seeking his or her guru.

You will visualize yourself as a spiritual pilgrim in a land strange to you. For the Westerner this is usually India, Tibet, or South America, but feel free to use your own imagination.

Take some time to plan what you wish to achieve from your trip. You will be looking for self-realization, God-realization, an answer to your metaphysical conjectures; perhaps a technique such as some form of yoga or meditation that will lead you to the light, to a psychic experience, or simply a sense of belonging.

There is little doubt that we have guides and internal gurus; the issue, though, is how to access them. They are more than the individual Higher Self, or even the consciousness of our group-mind or archetype: they are the points of connection between us and the Ultimate, and they act as translators and interpreters. It is said that such souls choose sometimes to incarnate on earth for the sake of humanity. It is in Chesed that they make the decision to do so.

Decide what you would ask, if you could have any single question answered truthfully by an enlightened being.

It should be possible at this level to get a good overview of your incarnation and its progress (or lack thereof), also to make long-term plans from germinal ideas.

During this meditation you will be able to intuitively assess the future implications of any concept you might have, any plans you are considering. Business-wise, this is of particular relevance: trust your perceptions at this juncture. If, for example, you are considering an investment and the scenery you visualize is opulent, you will know you are onto a good thing (other ramifications may also become evident). If, however, you receive negative imagery, the symbolism should speak for itself. In either case, as you sit on your Chesedic throne, details should become apparent which are unique to your particular set of circumstances.

Similarly, if you are considering a romantic liaison—particularly of a potentially procreative nature—you should get some sense of what your genetic future might be. The magickal image for Chesed is, as mentioned, very similar to that of the Emperor in the Tarot: a mature man, enthroned and surveying his lands. He is satisfied, but his quest is far from over. He is merely taking stock. Experience has taught him, and he is an accurate assessor of projects, a reliable governor and authority. You can adopt his informed sensibilities while you are here.

Think all of this through before taking the journey of Chesed.

## Visualization

Imagine that you have arrived in the country of your choice, rested a while, and are excitedly setting out on a walk.

You look forward to exploring this fascinating environment, and as you take your first step outside, the atmosphere accosts you from every conceivable angle. The air is like soup, assaulting your body with liquid humidity. The sounds that fill it are a medley of the strange, the blaring and the familiar—a distant call to prayer, the klaxon's blare, the chattering of humanity going about its daily business. Small hands tug at the hems of your garments. Already you are attracting more attention than you would like.

Before long you are surrounded by excitable children, shifty-eyed "guides" and hawkers, and anyone else who fancies alleviating their boredom by gawking at you.

Look around. What do you reckon are your chances of escape from this place?

See how you interact with the crowd, and then make your bid for freedom.

In the distance there are mountains—surreal and serene, just as you imagined—but what you had not bargained for is the seething mass of activity between you and them. Make the effort to approach the site of your grail, the goal of your quest.

Despite the appearance of your destination, you begin to grow irascible in the mosquito-ridden heat. Plodding onward and upward, swatting at the bloodsuckers to no avail, you find yourself reaching pitches of irritation no mantra, however sincerely performed, can quell. Feeling not in the least bit spiritual now, you forge ahead with grim determination.

How swiftly you reach your goal will tell you a lot about yourself at the time of the visualization, and how effective your will power is at present. Take all the time you need and confront each obstacle as it crops up.

Eventually, you reach the foot of the luminous mountain. Its slopes are verdant, a quality which could cause you problems. Ascend it by whatever means you wish. Levitation is always a handy technique in visualizations, but there are others; use what seems most appropriate to you.

Remember that you are aiming for the abode of your *gurudeva*, your divine guide and bringer of wisdom, and feel the anticipation that such a significant encounter engenders.

In the blue-purple sky above the mountain the sun and the moon hang in the sky, suspended at equal distances from the mountain's peak.

With relief, you reach the mouth of a cave. From within you perceive a light—not so much physical as an atmosphere of illumination. Good, you think, that's what I'm here for. You step into the cave.

The atmosphere is electrifying. Power permeates your body as you step into the center of Chesed. The sound of chanting comes from somewhere in its recesses. You sense instantly that many have visited this place; indeed, there are many recent offerings laid before its various altars. Leaf-plates of offertory rice dishes, garlands, bunches of spices and bright saffron, whorls of prayerful incense, fruits and flowers of dedication.

There is a feeling both of reverence and protection. The cave holds you like loving arms. You are free to wander, but not to fall.

Over the backdrop of the mantras you suddenly hear a woman's incongruous voice. You are unable to decipher her exact words, which seem to be in a language foreign to you, but she sounds rapt. A pause, and then a similar sound, this time issuing from a group. There is a sinister overtone to the vibration that makes you glad for the protection you perceive in this Sephirah. It is difficult to tell from exactly which direction the noises of adulation are issuing.

Suddenly, they reach a crescendo and stop. The air slackens, as with relief.

Look around. On the left-hand wall, on close inspection, are painted stick figures of great antiquity, the red-brown figures skilfully hunting large beasts like the ancient Apis bulls of Egypt, and circling, lithe antelopes by the herd.

Facing you at the back of the shallow cave entrance are alchemical formulae drawn as red roses, crosses, and strange chimerae . . . triangles and dragons, circles divided into quarters, the human body and its humors and correspondences . . . all seems to be sign and symbol, the secret language of transforming base metal into gold.

Beneath these images is a stone ledge hollowed into a kind of seat. From it the sitter might survey the cave entrance, and through this an impressive view of the lands beneath. Try it.

Feeling like a king enthroned above his domain you sit and observe the scenery. To your right, the cave wall is blank.

Sitting in the suffused light of the primitive abode, you begin to meditate upon the course of mankind's evolution. Could the primal inhabitants of the cave ever have anticipated even a fraction of what their progeny has achieved? One life alone is difficult to overview, never mind an entire species.

Where is your incarnation going? What are your goals? What do you need to achieve before you die?

Such thoughts rise unbidden in your mind as you consider the blank wall to your right. Of course, your true aim—the reason you are here—is spiritual enlightenment. You want to find that reliable guide and cling to the hem of their robe until they drag you up with them. Well, in more desperate moments it can seem that way.

Alternately, you could go for a more equitable approach, asking an enlightened one to come to you when you are ready to progress, as ordained by whichever expression of Benevolent Cosmic Intelligence you prefer.

To do this, concentrate on your throat, the center of communications with higher sources, and on your third eye and heart chakras. The throat center spins in sky-blue, your forehead is a disc of purple light, your heart chakra glows a healthy emerald green worthy of the Netzach planes.

Chakras blazing with resolution, request your potential guide to reveal itself, either as a sign or a visitation.

Once again, it is not possible to predict what happens here: the manifestation will be different for each individual.

Your throat still bathed in active blue light, your forehead purple and your heart a brilliant green, you cast out into the ether with these thoughts playing on your mind.

Pay attention to any perceptions that come to you at this point. You may receive an image of your guide, or thoughts of significance, or just a hunch. It really depends on how timely the experience is, and how ready you are to take it in.

When you wish to stop, cease your auric activities and sit for a moment quietly in the cave. If you feel you have interacted with the energies of Chesed, a word of thanks would not be inappropriate here.

Before you leave, you notice those strange vibrations again from the inside of the cave. Staring into the darkness it is just possible to make out the stalagmite-like forms of arms raised in worship, and—do your eyes deceive you?—at the center of them, a fat man playing the role of avatar. From your individual standpoint you are able to perceive the innate wrongness of this scenario: the acolytes seem imprisoned by their own will to believe. Looking at them more closely as your eyes adjust to the demilight, you notice that their feet are stuck in the clay of the cave floor. So intent are they on the boasting man at the center of their circle that they emit no vibration of their own, but rather the group seems comprised of husks.

Turn from this collective and mentally place a symbol of your individuality before one of the altars. Higher up the Tree we may hope to merge with some powerful forces, but the personality force of another mortal, even if they claim to be channelling much higher energies, should never be allowed precedence.

Cradled in the atmosphere of loving kindness particular to Chesed, finish your own reflections as you wish.

When you are ready, return to your home base in Malkuth, hopefully with a sense of futurity and perspective, and obey your Inner Dictate on the matters you took to the realms of Chesed. The wise, experienced king, sitting foursquare in his established domain, is usually right about such matters.

# Binah

## "The Sanctifying Intelligence"

### SEPHIRAH 3

*W*e are now entering the Supernal Triad, the collaboration of three Sephiroth from which all life-forces emanate. The world's religions and mythologies are replete with creative triads: Father, Son, and Holy Ghost; or Osiris, Isis, and Horus, to name but two. Here we have the equivalent, in which Kether represents the godhead, Chokmah the active male principal, and Binah the female "sanctifying intelligence" and bringer of form.

Thus the ineffable concepts of Kether are channeled down through the Sephiroth, where they gradually acquire the qualifying features necessary for manifestation and comprehension at lower levels. Binah is the beginning of restriction, metaphysically the primal soup of evolutionary conception, the womb in which life is lost . . . and found. Binah's dual nature is explained by this paradox, for she is at once fertile and barren: in giving life to be manifested in Malkuth, she is stealing the soul from spiritual freedom. In much the same way, Binah initiates archetypes, thus beginning the process of differentiation which has in so many ways been the bane of lower levels.

Binah symbolizes the aspect of the godhead known in Jewish lore as the Shekhinah. Essentially, this is the female side of the deity, one traditionally sidelined in mainstream Judaism. To put it in more mundane terms, she is perceived as the "wife" of God. Layer upon layer of myth—ranging from the arcane to the medieval to the contemporary—surrounds this tempting concept, whose import may have been hidden in order to differentiate the Jewish way from their neighbors'. Many pagans worshipped female deities, and it may have been easier to define these practices as "Other" by subordinating the feminine aspect of the godhead within Judaism. She is not removed from the tradition altogether—the feminine side of God is far too important in all faiths for it to be erased utterly. Instead, the Shekhinah is cast within a limited number of roles. One of these is that of the Community of Israel itself, though often she is seen as the wailing mother, mourning the exile of her people both from the Kingdoms of Heaven and from the City of the Just, or the true Jerusalem. Essentially, she represents the divorce of created from creator, particularly when she manifests in Malkuth. This, of course, is the most primal of sorrows, and fundamental to us all, represented microcosmically by divorce from the mother at birth and by the numerous pathologies that spring up in our relations with the life-giving mother figure.

The story of Adam and Eve in Eden—and indeed of Lilith and Adam—provides a clear analogy for the change in states from paradisiacal unity of male and female elements to their separation. In the case of Lilith, it was (in later interpretations, at least) her refusal to subordinate herself to Adam that caused a rift; the problem of who, in a duality, should be necessarily "greater" and who "lesser." In the imaginatively reconstituted *Sefer Gan Eden*, the "Book of the Garden of Eden," the difficulty lay simply in Lilith's character. She, like Eve's first consort Samael, was "the wrong sort"; that is, not the partner intended by God. Still, the sun and moon myths of many cultures reflect the dichotomy of power between male and female.

In Eve's case it was wisdom that broke the vessel of perfection, splitting the consciousness in two. Plato's idea of androgynous superbeings echoes the same myth, leaving the two personalities, once rent asunder, in a state of permanent searching for one another, the grail in this case being the uniting of male and female energies in a harmonious, spiritually elevating manner. So too, perhaps, has the creator "lost" his creation, and now wishes to reclaim it. The suffering caused by this whole process is incalculable, but Binah provides a repository for some of it. Certainly in Malkuth the world of creation is exiled, the Bride of God analogously banished from the divine conjugal home.

In Malkuth the Shekhinah requires elevation, transformation, but in Binah she *exists as* these qualities. Likewise, the Virgin Mary suffered during the Passion while in Malkuth, but when elevated to Binah (the feminine aspect of the Trinity), she became intercessor and comforter of the condemned. The concept of the Black Madonna, particularly prevalent in South America, may reflect the influence of Judaic thought on Roman Catholic conceit. Of course, Black Isis is another ancient counterpart. All three feminine figures show a bright and a dark side to the feminine aspect of the creative source. Binah, encompassing all possible ramifications of this concept, does not discriminate; she reabsorbs all just as she, the Great Mother Goddess, gave form to all in the beginning.

The idea of the exiled feminine deity makes much sense in the context of Judaism, with its pronounced patriarchal bias. It also emphasizes the psychological necessity that is central to the Qabalistic and magickal practice of developing and unifying both male and female forces within the psyche; mildness and severity, being conversant in each but enslaved by neither. The Pillars each contain Sephiroth of male and female assignation, and the energy perpetually fluctuates between the two. Like our own psyches it can never be fixed in one extremity if it is to be progressive. Only thus may we tread the Middle Path, that of Equilibrium.

Deities ascribed to Binah include Kali and Cronos. One of the names of Cronos is "Old Father Time," and Kali, the black mother, embodies the deceptive nature of mortality. Both consume the flesh: Cronos swallows his own children in an attempt to halt the inevitable future, and Kali's vampirism is her best-known feature. Not only does she use the blood of her victims to fortify herself, but she dismembers them and wears their heads as a necklace, their limbs as a skirt. She entirely deconstructs the complex human body. Cronos, likewise, attempts to assail its very genesis.

Kali and Cronos demonstrate the effects of physical time on our flesh-lives. Kali's message, however, is one of transcendent life, for her worshippers know they will still live once they have passed into the mouth of the terrible mask of death. It is fear that makes the process seem terrible, not the process itself, which, at least when Kali is implementing it, only takes seconds. It is merely a process of transformation.

Cronos' attempt to halt progress turns out to be his downfall, and he is inevitably superseded by his own children. Thus his message is similar to that of Kali: you cannot escape the fact of mortality. Forms are made to last only so long, and it is in Binah that they are conceived.

Binah receives the fertilizing power of Chokmah and makes it finite. Silent, solipsistic as a sorceress, she creates the form to contain and thus entrap the spirit.

The saturnine nature of Binah is reflected in at least two of the four Threes of the Tarot's Minor Arcana. The first, the Three of Swords, is a card of restriction, loss, and sorrow. A heart pierced by three swords—reminiscent of Marian images of the Virgén de los Dolores, or of the "sacred heart" of Christ himself—hangs before a background of gray cloud and pouring rain. Pain is to be expected when this image appears in a reading. Those approaching Binah by the Path of the Lovers (from Tiphareth) may anticipate disappointment, sterility, and possibly abortion or miscarriage—or at least, should take precautions to avoid such an outcome.

Another aspect of this image is betrayal, of all sorts, but it occurs particularly where a "love triangle" has been established. Intentions may have been good or at least relatively innocent initially, but now the situation had deteriorated into one of deception and guilt. Despite, or perhaps partly due to, attempted secrecy, it is too emotionally volatile to be maintained. Sooner or later, all three participants will end up injured.

No life is complete without a little pain, of course, and the implications may sound dire, but these are just a part of the lessons inflicted on us by the state of being incarnate, a process initiated in Binah. The sensation of being trapped by one's own form is thus another of the afflictions indicated by the Three of Swords.

The Three of Pentacles also deals with form, but here the implications are more positive. The work of an apprentice stonemason is appreciated and constructively criticized (one imagines) by two older men, one of them a monk. The work itself is three pentacles carved into a stone arch. Here, the apprentice is literally carving his future in stone, adopting a form of expression that will see him through the best part of his life. It will prove not only a material cornerstone for the foundation of his future, but also a spiritual building block, as indicated by the presence of the man of the cloth. Creativity can, of course, be a deeply spiritual process. Thus the appearance of this card in a reading bodes well for those initiating projects and learning a new skill or craft. There is still a long way to go, but hard work and steady application will ensure eventual success.

In the Three of Wands the intrepid merchant is dipping into the sea of possibilities that is Binah. Again, this is on quite a material level—he is sending his ship out to foreign climes and hoping that it will return laden with exotic wares. The sea looks golden from his optimistic vantage point; little does he think of what lurks beneath its sun-molten surface. This indicates man's potential mastery of form; the character is taking charge of his incarnation, joyfully playing the game of life. He is not avaricious like the pentacle hog in the Four of Pentacles, but playful. He is the alchemist of Binah's attributes, using the Will of the Magician to transmute the circumstances of form, or Binah, into gold.

The Three of Cups depicts three flower-crowned maidens holding aloft their chalices in a toast of celebration. Marriage, birth, and initiation are all indicated here, all of them relevant to the positive side of Binah. As the Superior Mother, she is initiating long-term spiritual ventures, establishing patterns. These are made manifest in the realms of Malkuth, the Inferior Mother. Three being also a key Goddess number, the dancing women may be conceived of as symbols of the threefold Goddess, the qualities of maiden, mother, and crone combined. Thus feminine spirituality is highlighted by the appearance of this card in a reading.

Though Binah is a mournful, mysterious sphere, the path that leads from it to Chokmah, Sephirah of wisdom, belongs to the Empress, or Demeter of growth and abundance. The Hebrew letter assigned to this path is *Daleth* (ד), meaning "door." The plight of the imprisoned Persephone, relevant both to the thirty-second path between Malkuth and Yesod and to the Sephirah Binah, is left behind in Binah, which, exited via the Three of Cups, leads to the renewal of equilibrium and happiness. Binah, as Demeter, is concerned with cycles, not just fixed states.

## Getting from Geburah to Binah
### "The House of Influence"
#### PATH 18

There is no established direct route from Chesed to Binah, so you will have to imagine yourself back in Geburah prior to this ascent.

The Hebrew letter ascribed to this path is *Ches* (ח), meaning "fence." This is appropriate to the bringer of enclosures, Binah, which envelops the raw energy of Chokmah in form, and hems it in.

The eighteenth path is that of the Chariot.

The Tarot card the Chariot is drawn by two sphinxes, Daimos and Phobos. These represent the conflicting sides of the psyche, the warring sides of our inner selves, here controlled by the reins of will. Fear has been harnessed, made positive, as has all compulsive behavior. Much of the power behind this transmutation is caused by anger, which has the ability to make us forget more trifling emotions. Love (Venus/Netzach) and anger (Mars/Geburah) are capable of overriding any neuroses. In the Chariot, the negative aversion has been translated into positive action.

The most logical way to mentally travel this path is to imagine yourself driving the Chariot. In myth it is Ares, god of war, who drives it, and this can be relevant when one is driven by anger over past wrongs, often a strong motivating force. Some occidental philosophies condemn anger as a futile waste of energy, and, indeed, as evoking the equivalent of "bad karma," but I am not sure this is applicable in the West, so long as one does not go overboard.

For example, anger at centuries of patriarchal abuse caused women in the West not only to change the social environment for the better—ensuring equal rights for their daughters in the future —but also to produce vast amounts of creative work, from feminist tracts to art to music: not quite the bloodbath some traditional authorities might have envisaged. That the chariot of Feminism was driven in anger there can be no doubt, but rather than riding roughshod over society at large (as, perhaps, is the eastern suspicion), conditions were improved for everyone.

So, riding your chariot through the path whose name is Ches, resolve to break through any "fences" holding you in, and to reformat yourself in the sphere of Binah, where force meets form.

Allow the midnight sun of your secret ambitions to shine as you travel; let its heat blaze in your blood. In your wheeled throne you travel with intoxicating speed, yet always maintaining perfect control. Above you, the starry canopy of Egyptian Nuit beckons. Further up into the alluring darkness you travel, forging your way with the force of will. Every emotion you have ever encountered seems to be present in your consciousness, each adding its input to the force of your ascent.

Ahead of you, the constellation of Cancer spans the sky. The feeling of elevation, of divine inebriation increases as you pass right through it.

On the other side is a spiralling vortex with the symbol of Saturn blazing in silver over it.

Bring your sphinxes to a halt here.

## Encountering the In-House Divinities

The God-name of Binah is *Jehovah Elohim*. As was noted in the Netzach chapter in relation to the Elohim, the Choir of Angels, the word *Elohim* is frequently misconstrued as being a masculine root with a feminine plural ending. I have chosen to take the opposite view and accept the word as entirely masculine despite the feminine nature of the Sephirah to which it pertains.

However, that Binah represents the feminine side of the deity there can be no doubt. In Daath, which emanates from the combined energies of Binah and Chokmah, we find the primordial mother, *Ama*, and the primordial father, *Abba*, exactly balanced and procreative. The same may be said of Yesod, where "the Father and Mother are perpetually conjoined," and of Tiphareth, the "second son" of Binah and Chokmah.

Malkuth, the Inferior Mother, is a more God-divorced, matter-wed version of the Shekhinah which is Binah.

The Archangel is Tzaphkiel, the "Eye of God." He is Lord of Archetypes, and has his finger on the prototypical pulse. As Binah is the primordial ocean from which all form evolves, the spiritual-genetic information of each species would be contained here. This includes not only the obvious physical and mental criteria, but also the potential paths for spiritual development, the "racial types." This does not necessarily mean race in a literal sense, although in some cases it might. We tend to reincarnate in the environment that will provide optimum experience in the field we seek, and all areas are different. The soul looking for strict discipline, for example, would be far better suited to the environment of orthodox Judaism which being born in Israel might provide, than to the self-expression of, say, Voodoo, which incarnating in Haiti could engender. However, one could, especially in modern circumstances, become deeply involved in Judaica in an apparently incongruous environment (a London apartment, for example), or get into Voodoo in New Orleans despite being white and of Christian upbringing, so the "racial" types are not as relevant as they once were. Tzaphkiel, in league with Sandalphon, rules over all of these types, their ramifications and properties. This includes the records of the sum of human knowledge and experience, the collective conscious or Akashic Records. Like Binah itself, this is frequently construed as being an ocean or, in the Hindu *Tattvas*, a purple egg (allying it to both Binah and Yesod).

As far as "appearance" is concerned, Tzaphkiel is one of the more intimidating Angels. His aura, indeed, is almost black, and his countenance is stern. I say "he," but as with all angelic entities the overall effect is androgynous. In fact, most of Tzaphkiel's characteristics are feminine, but the severity he emanates makes him seem masculine. Binah is, of course, stationed at the head of the Pillar of Severity.

The only parts of Tzaphkiel's body that shine are his head and neck, which carry both lunar qualities—reflective, intellectual; and solar-fierce, resolute. He carries the scales and sword of justice, both of them gray. They seem to be crafted of pearlescent stone. He is a suitably lugubrious counterpart to Raziel, bright Angel of Chokmah, the one representing the dark side of creation, the other the light. Both, however, are contained within one another, just as Binah itself is at once dark and bright, depriving and giving.

Ruled by Tzaphkiel are the *Aralim*, whose name means "thrones," these strong, slender Angels are supremely flexible, yet stable. They emanate from a throne of stone, an established foundation. Their name links them with Isis, whose glyph is a throne, and who is of course intimately connected with the world of Nature. They combine the qualities of the elements to perfection, containing within themselves the ingredients Earth, Air, Fire, and Water. Air is of particular importance to the Aralim, and their long blue-green hair is ever ruffled by a gentle breeze. Their aura is marine, and brings to mind ocean rollers watched from the shore.

As Tzaphkiel is the harsh side of the sea and its potential, the Aralim are the beauty of it, the exuberant power of nature. They expose us to the currents that flow when mind and body are perfectly connected. Remember, in the primordial sea shapes are formed whose aim is to ideally suit the inhabitant and its aspirations.

Binah is a good sphere to visit when the body seems incongruous to the inhabiting spirit within. This covers every eventuality, from thinking that one's nose is too big through eating disorders, to the effect of disease on the spirit. In all cases, the spirit seems thwarted by a physical state; and it is from Binah that this prototype comes. In Binah, we are enslaved in form, or placed in the ideal vehicle for physical interaction, depending on one's mindset.

## The Temple of Binah

Unlike the other Temples, this one seems to have no dimensions—or should that be "all" dimensions at once? As we float in its blackness, not unlike that of a sensory deprivation tank, we lose all concept of time; indeed, the mind drifts so far from its usual earthbound state that all physical actions begin to seem abstract, plays played out in light, a falsity of notion, a strange elaboration of consciousness. Here, blanketed in black, obscurities are reality, yet exist only to entertain us. At other times we are blank, and simply EXIST.

In the Temple of Binah we need not strive as on the outside as we are sustained, and devoid of doubt or motive. Existing fulfills us, our solipsism eats its own tail like the ouroboros snake. Enveloped in black, sentient and damp and fertile, we are simply a spore nestling in the gills of the giant mother mushroom.

There is an impossible, uncanny vastness somewhere outside the familiar Temple, a whale of possibility rising on a tide from the deep. Will it eat us, or we it? It matters not in this eternal mandala who is the eater and who the fodder; suspended in salty water-space, we EXIST and ARE, both within and without, and neither. The rhythm guides us to the right place. When it is timely, we rotate. We circulate. Star and starchild are one and the same, of cosmic matter wrought. Consciousness flies simply to the strongest magnet.

*Ama, Marah, Maria, Maire,* and, significantly, *Maya:* names that conjure the sea, the collective consciousness in its archetypal manifestation. Repeating them (try it!) evokes images of the ocean at night, dark and salt-bitter, delusive like Maya itself, treacherous beneath its calm surface, and the stars, steadfast pulsars guiding distant sailors in their peril. Sothis, the North Star, the constellations of the zodiac, all shining out over the lulling, sighing waters, everything an eloquent analogy of our individual insignificance.

And the water, hypnotic, soporific, compelling. . . .

A sea siren seems to sing of ultimate assimilation, of rest from plight, a watery life-in-death, submergence in an element greater than the sum of all your parts: a return to the womb.

What swims in the depths of that primordial ocean?

The dreams of childhood, adolescence, as well as the dreams of a thousand million men and women initiated by the saturnine magick of the dark priestess Binah, brought into being by the touch of her tears on the earth . . . the remnants of all the personal beliefs of each who has ever existed: the personification of these concepts . . . dark strange creatures of vibrational potency . . . briny abandoned deities, their life blood extinct . . . weird whales too vast to contemplate alone, their song threatening to engulf the individual consciousness . . . all the creatures of the moon, manifest and unmanifest.

Dip your little toe into this sea, if you dare.

Never has something so three-dimensional been so multi-dimensional, so teeming with matter and antimatter, all invested with intelligence. *This* is the gift of the Dark Mother, the secret of Binah.

Time begins here.

As each energy pattern is taken from the whole and invested with individual form, it of necessity becomes finite. Divorced from cosmic sustenance, strife and the primitive urge for survival begins. Time becomes the enemy of the individual, compelled to ensure its immortality on this new level of existence. Binah, vaster than our ability to contemplate, comes personified with sorrowful visage, for we are her creations, her children, and she grieves for us. She sees ahead, and anticipates our demise. Black-cloaked and mourning, she at once denies life and gives it. In her brighter form she is like Isis, compassionate, adept, and humane; yet like Isis' shadow-sister Nephthys, she is also mistress of the unmanifest, the barren and menstrual.

In the sky of the virtual Binah you witness a similar paradox. Viewed one way, the heavens seem veiled, but not by ordinary darkness. The sky seems *layered* somehow, every conceivable shade and texture of black hanging one before the other. Though you witnessed the stars earlier, they are utterly obscured now—*absorbed, snuffed out*, you might almost say. Indeed, the overall effect is one of suffocation. Suddenly the ocean seems claustrophobic rather than vast.

Surely the tide was receding before? Well, now it is coming in thick and fast, the wind has grown warm and sounds like . . . a woman panting.

Urgh!—the water is warm! You weren't expecting that!

Alarmed, you begin to run . . . to where? The stifling blackness of the sky seems to have descended like a thousand Victorian curtains; there is no space, and little air. Behind you, the waters, hot now, are coming in black liquid walls to get you. To *get* you?

To *beget* you, to *beget you* whispers the Dark Queen Binah. *Slip in—don't resist.*

Looking at the sky another way, you experience a sensation of elevation, of potential freedom. For what can that brilliant white orb be other than Kether: so close at last!

Opposite you, you also perceive the parallel Sephirah of Chokmah, or, should I say, you *feel its force*. For that is how it reaches you as you meditate on Binah: the energy is steady and irrepressible, pushing into its receptive sister/bride, causing the motion that moves the sea. Without the input of the forcefields of this gray planet Binah would, you realize, be static, stagnant, locked in an eternal silence of forms.

Instead, with the vivifying properties of Chokmah and the light-giving elevation of Kether, station of Redemption, Hope, and Light, Binah is grandiloquent in her expression of ideas. She is the medium, the primordial mother, bridging the gap between the worlds of spirit and flesh.

Considering Kether and Chokmah from this angle, and recalling your ascent from Malkuth through astral Yesod, intellectual Hod, reviving Netzach, splendid Tiphareth, challenging Geburah, and contemplative Chesed, you begin to understand the true dynamics of the Tree.

One of the symbols of Binah is the chalice. Remember the chalice you invested with your particular energy in your visit to Malkuth? As a representative of the powers of water, it contained the properties of emotion, fluidity (i.e., flexibility), imagination and creativity, among others. The Chalice of Binah harbors some of the same properties—its association with water and creativity is obvious—but it also indicates the pure receptivity of the female biological principle. Stationed directly opposite Chokmah, the Chalice of Binah is kept topped up with the energy of her counterpart, and that male energy is harbored, given boundaries. So, rather than being simply watery, *this* chalice contains the promise of all the elements working in unison, as is necessary to engender life; the warmth and intelligence of fire, the pranic breath of air, the shape and form of earth, the gift of Akasha, the soul.

Like the elements necessary for creation, each Sephirah exists in relation to all the others; the stations are symbiotic, part of a greater whole. The Pillar of Severity, at the top of which you are now perched, exists in perfect balance with the right-hand Pillar of Mercy. In ascending order, Hod and Netzach are in equilibrium, as are Geburah and Chesed (Gedulah), and Binah and Chokmah.

The central Pillar, the Pillar of Mildness—Malkuth, Yesod, Tiphareth, (Daath), and Kether—is held in place by this balanced structure. When imbalance occurs, the excess energies give rise to what we commonly call "evil," or chaos. This is where the Qlipoth come in: they express all that is cosmically pernicious or antisocial to us.

The specific relations between Sephiroth may be explored in great detail; they give rise to the twenty-two paths of the primary Qabalah. While stationed in Binah, however, we are interested in the *synthesis* of the individual elements into an operative whole.

Take time to view the Tree from this vantage point, and a greater understanding should become yours. From here you may witness both the Gates of Life and Death (as you experienced before: not an entirely pleasant initiation, but then, they never are), and the truth beyond—the source of life, Kether, the symbol of godhead. It is said that the "roots of faith" begin here.

Binah at once creates and breaks down, allowing us a glimpse of the mechanics of the live metaphysics that constitute the cosmos. We did not create metaphysics: metaphysics created us. Binah never lets us forget this. Precocious mortals are snapped out of hubris in Binah. Here intellect, civilization, and academe, mankind's defense against the unpalatable void, mean nothing at all.

Just as Kali suspends her initiates' capacity to reason or act kinetically, so too does Binah reduce us to one primal impulse, one glyph of humanity. Her quality of understanding is instinctual, visceral. However, where as Kali reunites us with the sentient void, Binah carves us out and sends us in the opposite direction, down to Malkuth from which, in turn, Kali will eventually reap us. In Kali we go from ignorance through terror to initiation; in Binah we go from initiation through pain to temporary ignorance.

This may not sound very promising, but by scaling the Tree and revisiting Binah, we may acquire something of our prebirth understanding and develop absolute trust in the Divine Parent. This is the "Perfect Love and Perfect Trust" of Wicca. The more frequently and deeply we meditate on the Sephiroth, the greater this reclamation will be. Also, one of the messages of Binah is that of Grace; as Isis, Mary, the Mother, she is also the intercessor on behalf of her children. Like any mother, the Goddess will heed our prayers, when heartfelt.

The import is, in the final analysis, positive.

# Chokmah

## "The Illuminating Intelligence"
### SEPHIRAH 2

As we progress to the final Sephirah, topping the right-hand Pillar of Mercy, we are able to divorce feeling from thought and attain a more objective overview of reality as it is.

This is an informed perspective—informed, that is, both by experience as an individual in the present incarnation and by long-term patterns within the spiritual plan. In other words, one is attuned to the highest aspects of wisdom: an appropriate state, considering that Chokmah is essentially the portal to the House of God.

Chokmah, in such close proximity to Kether, benefits from the refined energies emanating from the Tree's resplendent crown. It is the first differentiated energy after the Divine Spark, and its qualities, though not personal, are male and dynamic. Because it is the first expression of "other than God," it is titled the "Crown of Creation." It might be argued that all things are God, of course, but clearly there are degrees of proximity to the ineffable source, Malkuth being furthest away and Kether closest. At the same time, "Kether is in Malkuth, and Malkuth is in Kether," or, as the adage attributed to Hermes Trismegistus puts it, "As Above, So Below." By now you will be acclimatized to these continual paradoxes, and hopefully able to meditate on Chokmah without inhibitive confusion.

The deities affiliated with Chokmah are those of wisdom and learning. Thoth, for example, rules over science, books, and the art

of the scribe. Likewise, Hermes is relevant here, being the bringer
of the word of the gods. Athena, as pure cerebral force, and Metis,
whose name means "measured wisdom," are also suitable attributes. Maat, against whose celestial featherweight all hearts are
weighed on death, also epitomizes inner truth. Ancient Egyptians
talked of "living by Maat," her name being analogous with principles of cosmic rectitude. To them, she represented the very essence
of spiritual wisdom, the core attribute of Chokmah.

However, in their lesser form these deities are better attributed
to Hod, where they provide immediate practical effects. This wisdom of Chokmah supersedes that which can be logically ascer-
tained, and transcends infinitely the learning of Hod. Chokmah is
pure wisdom, something we are unlikely to experience from our
flesh-encased individual standpoints in Malkuth. Just as Kether is
barely perceptible to human consciousness—by the sheer fact that
human consciousness is typically too limited to encompass that
which created it—so too is Chokmah a tall order for us to get our
human minds around. Indeed, the entire Supernal Triad is by its
very nature beyond our sphere. This is why mystics, yogis, and
shaman have for so long used drugs or soporific states to approach
godhead—liberation from the body is the only way to experience
it. None of the channels so far mentioned—not the practical
magic and intellect of Hod, nor the Dionysian revelry of Netzach,
nor even the strongest of intuitions gleaned from Yesod, or the
spiritual guidance of Chesed—none of these can bring us to the
realization of God, which is the entire point of the process. The
mystic must levitate his or her consciousness upward (in the case
of Qabalah) upon the Middle Pillar. In psycho-physical terms this
means drawing the consciousness and lifeforce up the spine until it
emerges through the crown chakra, above which lies the point of
communion with the divine. This is the state of Samadhi aspired
to by yogis, or the mystical experiences of true saints (not merely
encountering godforms, such as the Virgin Mary, who could man-

ifest from a lower Sephirah such as Chesed, Netzach, or even Malkuth). According to Jewish tradition, between the exodus from Egypt and the Babylonian exile in 586 B.C.E., there were over one million "prophets," men and women who could spontaneously commune with God simply because of the high spiritual state they existed in. Nowadays, this state is obtainable through meditation on the Tree and the vibration of various sounds along with a conscious raising of Kundalini energy. It can take many lifetimes to attain, and like most spiritual phenomena follows a time law of its own, arriving only at the moment of optimum relevance—so do not be dismayed when it proves a difficult feat. Practice is the key to success.

The informing influence may be seen in the caduceus adjoining the chalices of the two figures in the Tarot Two of Cups. This symbol of Mercury, or Hermes, indicates the high quality of communication between the characters. A winged lion's head hovers above them, its implication that brute forces have been mastered by the mind. The man and woman depicted are thus in a state of perfect companionship, unfettered by sexual concerns. There is empathy between them, and attraction; the man touches the woman's hand gently, and they look one another in the eye with honesty. Each holds a cup of friendship and emotional fulfillment. The wisdom indicated by Chokmah is here epitomized in the perfect understanding between male and female. A relationship based on the qualities of this card will be a long and happy one. To many beholding this card in days of yore, the idea of such equality between the sexes must have been "illuminating" indeed.

Balance is a relevant factor to two of the other cards assigned to Chokmah: the Two of Pentacles and the Two of Swords. In the former, a man wearing what resembles a clown's or dunce's cap, juggles two pentacles. Around them is woven the ∞, symbol of infinity. Thus he is a cosmic juggler, and though money is implied by the suit, he is dealing with more than the material. He represents an entire mindset.

Those who receive this card are usually unable to settle down to
any particular lifestyle, creed, or even personality. Just as the entire
zodiac is attributed to Chokmah, so does every persona seem to
suit some aspect of this character; each person feels as if he or she
is always acting, playing the clown, when under the influence of
this Sephirah. This masking, the loss of personality, can be an
advantage, and is deeply relevant to Chokmah's position on the
Tree, whose path to Kether is that of the air-brained Fool. But on
a mundane level it is leading to confusion and an inability to com-
mit to any one course of action. Even the Fool has to choose a
path: the nature of his quest is to travel, experience life, move on.

Added to this are the possibilities perceived by the querent at
this juncture; the ships visible behind the juggler represent potential schemes, adventures, and plans. In the meantime, unable to
focus on any one course of action, he ends up borrowing time and
money from sources he is unable to repay. Perhaps he is also mud-
dling his spiritual and material ambitions, as indicated by the proximity of the infinity symbol to the pentacles. Either way, the qualities of Chokmah—wisdom and insight—are required to remedy
this situation.

The other card concerned with balance is the Two of Swords. A
blindfolded, white-robed figure whom I have always imagined to
be female but who may well be either, sits on a stone seat before
the sea, a crescent moon behind her. Her arms crossed against her
breast, and she holds two swords in perfect balance. Her expression
is blank.

At first glance one might imagine such a pose to be uncomfortable, but the image is serene, meditative. She is as one with her
surroundings, just as in Chokmah the illusion of independence
from cosmic consciousness is dismissed.

The stone seat suggests the throne of Isis, and also the Aralim of
Binah, whose name means "thrones." Thus she is supported by
nature in its most disciplined, goddess-orientated sense. She is at

peace with the organic expression of her soul—that is, her body—and exhibits perfect control of her physical faculties. She is adept not just intellectually, but also physiologically; she is able to use the power centers of the human vehicle to further her spiritual advancement. The fact that the seat is hard stone suggests both the austerity of training undergone, and the wisdom of ages, an allusion to Binah's supernal counterpart, Chokmah.

The sea and moon imagery are also clearly Isian, again suggesting the qualities of Binah, which are created by Chokmah's projection into this feminine Sephirah. Yet despite the principles of flux and reflux which rule these bodies, the woman remains stable, seated in wisdom as she is. This is duality in its most positive sense: the figure of the Two of Swords understands the illusory nature of "reality," and beholds with her inner eye the force behind form, and the single cosmic consciousness behind force. Thus it is that she prepares to progress into Kether, where the illusion of separation from God is burned away entirely.

The Two of Wands is of a less-esoteric nature: a businessman stands between two budding staffs, a globe in his hand, green land and sea before him. Great potential is evident from the imagery, with the burgeoning wands promising future reward and the globe suggesting travel and adventure. Indeed, the recipient of this card might consider enterprise in any sphere of the Qabalah, or any area of the globe. All things are possible.

The image of holding the world in one's hands is appropriate to Chokmah, which proffers a total overview and total control of all aspects of being. Needless to say, these states are not reached merely through creative visualization (if only!), but are the hard-won rewards of years and even lifetimes of continuous effort. Just as the merchant in the Two of Wands has established his kingdom in the material planes, so has the initiate of Chokmah attained the spiritual kingdoms.

The key to Chokmah is in Binah, and vice versa.

The energy flowing between the two is at the very root of all creation; they are the Universal Parents, the two poles of opposite qualities rendering one another dynamic and procreative. In *The Lost Book of Paradise* we witness this dynamism as played out between Adam and Eve. Before Eve has even been created, Adam craves her, just as Chokmah craves the receptivity of Binah. In chapter 1, Adam desires: ". . . all words swallowed like seeds/by the earth/to rest there, pregnant," an analogy of the properties of Binah. Likewise the naming power is possessed by both Adam and Eve, a feature of Binah; the ability to encompass force in form, to classify, categorize, render a thing individual. It is this very feature that causes the trouble in Eden—the dichotomy of consciousness—the point at which the effusive power of Chokmah is contained and made finite by Binah.

Later in the text, in chapter 13, we find another perfect description of the Chokmah-Binah dynamic, when Samael declares: ". . . there is no loss/in Paradise that is not found/in the next moment—one moment is all/there is, or two moments: all is coupled/nothing or something, dark and light/inside and out—now/and then." This sounds, among other things, like an attempt to understand time, one of the qualifying factors of Binah. It also expresses the magnetism between the opposite Sephiroth, their ability to mutually compensate and draw out life-giving properties.

Finally, when Adam undergoes sexual congress with Lilith, whom he has mistaken for his rightful partner Eve, he exudes the energies of Chokmah reaching out towards Binah: ". . . my body/wants to find you and invent/itself in your image/to feel I was created and know/my limit in yours, the bottom/in which I can press no farther/rooted as the colossal palm . . ." (The colossal palm is the Tree of Knowledge.) He goes on to mention his teeth "locked/in solid milk/silent," expressing both the maternal and taciturn aspects of Binah. Here, the energy of Chokmah has met its equal and opposite, locking it into a silence of forms.

In exactly the same way is the lifeforce inherent in the male channeled into the female and locked into her, eventually to emerge encapsulated within "new" walls of flesh. This is the reason for such overtly phallic imagery seen in Chokmah.

# Getting from Binah to Chokmah
## "The Luminous Intelligence"
### PATH 14

This path is associated with the letter *Daleth* (ד), meaning "door." This is an appropriate analogy for the path that connects the primordial female with the primordial male Sephirah. It is the door between form and force, and of course the path is reciprocal, meaning that there is an equal flow in both directions. Like the currents between Hod and Netzach, Geburah and Chesed, there is a point of cosmic balance between the two, the Middle Pillar of Equilibrium.

The Tarot card ascribed to the Fourteenth Path is the Empress.

This path is sacred to Venus/Aphrodite/Laksmi/Hathor, and it is not difficult to see why. It is a most beautiful path, one that might be walked most appropriately barefoot.

It is a late spring morning, and the air is alive with the sound of larks and bluebirds. Dew sparkles on your toes, and the light breeze is invigorating. Youth and beauty are yours as you walk the path of Daleth.

This morning, the earth seems girdled by love. Nature reflects the sentiment, bringing forth bright roses that fill the air with a delightful aroma. Some are yellow, others a thousand shades of damask, pink, and red; savor them as you pass.

The air is luminous. As you walk, your whole body is revived by the redolent emerald earth. You cannot help but snigger as a flock of white doves swoops above you, making the sense of cliché rather acute. However, better this than the cliché of misery—you won't complain.

*Amour* is in the air, indubitably. As you continue to walk from Binah to Chokmah, the celestial sun shining overhead, you feel compelled, magnetized. It is similar to the sensation of moving between Geburah and Chesed, in that you feel highly motivated, but the feeling is much more pleasurable here. In this place, you are at peace. Here, all your hopes are germinal, you have the universe to look forward to—you are about to inherit the earth.

A little way along the path sits a throned pregnant woman, her hair the color of corn. Her complexion is pink and cream, her eyes clear blue. A slightly smug smile plays about her lips. She knows that she is further along the path than you are.

Despite this, you accept her as beneficent and divine. Certainly there is nothing malefic in her, or even challenging. The most she might accuse you of is being too restless. *Settle down*, she says, *and have a family. Be stable.*

If you have already "been there and done that," she will tempt you into stately solipsism. The Empress and her surroundings are delightful, and she wants you never to leave. Here, you can be happy, free of challenge, protected.

The danger, of course, is of becoming complacent, losing sight of the goal. *But if you did*, she whispers through the ears of corn, *if you did, it would be as one who has progressed well beyond the conscious bounds of most.*

It is tempting to accept the fruits of the unfinished search for godhead in lieu of the cosmic consciousness itself. Possibly, it is the final pitfall in the Tree. This path is like Eden, and it is full of sensual promise. Futurity shines from the branches of the Tree, and the serpent, *Teth* (ט), dominant on the tier below, connecting Geburah and Chesed, is still an influence.

Place an offering at the feet of the young Empress. She is at the beginning of her cycle—in the future, sorrow will be hers—so allow compassion to inform your perception. You know that she, as an archetype, is immortal. Her happiness is immortal as well, but she is pregnant, like Binah, and like Binah she will mourn in the future for her imprisoned child. It is like looking at the photograph of someone who lead a happy, prosperous life, but was eventually murdered.

There is, indeed, no point in feeling envy for another, however established and unshakeable they seem, as all of us suffer in equal measure, sooner or later. All incarnations are necessarily variegated by joy and sorrow, but there are also inherently happy incarnations and troublesome ones. Eventually, all of this evens out. Nobody ever gets away scot-free . . . and nobody goes unavenged!

If there is one thing the Qabalah should teach us, it is that there really is a "Scheme of Things." Look at Yesod and its lesson: a glimpse of the machinery of the cosmos, a knowledge that all is for a purpose, even the apparently superfluous or incongruous. Or at Tiphareth, sphere of redemption: things only seem mundane because we are used to them that way. We sully the symbols with disrespect and negative thoughts, and their essential purpose is even more difficult to perceive.

Such are your mediations as you take your leave of the young Empress and progress along the path to Chokmah.

As you travel, the atmosphere becomes less feminine. You seem to perceive male pheromones on the breeze, a not unpleasant scent. The doves are replaced by peacocks, the emerald green grass becomes thick with forget-me-nots and bluebells. Above you, every constellation you can imagine spans the sky, though it is only late afternoon.

You feel happy but awe-stricken. You arrive at the blue portal to Chokmah with a bounce in your step and holy terror in your heart.

You knock at it nervously, twice.

## Encountering the In-House Deities

The God-form in Chokmah is known as *Yah* or *Jehovah*.

The Archangel is Raziel. This is an exceptionally epicene Angel, yet proud and dominant in his bearing. He carries a sword of flashing metal and a set of scales of brilliant sky-blue.

Beneath him are the *Auphanim*, whose name translates as "wheels." This name suggests one of the most obvious quantum leaps in the consciousness and physical evolution of man. One of their Angelic duties is to dispatch visions of God to worthy seekers. A vision is necessary rather than a direct experience because the latter would be too much for the individual to bear. These whirling forces are themselves breathtakingly splendid, emitting a starry silver-gray refulgence, tall blue-green wings behind their backs (when static, anyway), and bodies of strong, fierce red-green momentum.

## The Temple of Chokmah

This is an exceptionally simple, geometric Temple. Two gray pillars hold up the roof. The floor is blue. The sky behind and between the pillars is blue streaked with white and gray cloud. Walking barefoot, robed in plain gray, we feel ascetic and Hermit-like in this sacred space. We are close to God, but still independent.

At the center of the Temple floor is a phallus-shaped font. No feminist nightmare this: it reflects the male in all of us, or rather, the male in all of us echoes this primal energy source. There is a door straight ahead, even though there are no walls; it leads to cornfields and maternal protection. The woman sacred to this portal wears the zodiac of Chokmah in her hair. Three other portals are evident: the Hierophant, the Emperor visible through glass, and the glimmering, foppish Fool. We choose not to activate any of these energies at this time.

The only paraphernalia to be found here is a pile of wands, almost tinder but not yet lit. As we pick one up, a particular stream of thought becomes emphasized and concentrated. Picking up another, we find that the same applies to it. There are as many wands as you have themes in your life at present. You may use each to clarify a particular chain of thoughts and events, and to determine their outcome.

# Entering the Sephirah

Chokmah, as you know, is the polar opposite of Binah.

Place yourself mentally in the gray sphere at the top of the Pil-lar of Mercy, and look around you. Try to absorb the archetypal atmosphere, as you do in every Sephirah.

The traditional symbol yet again is a bearded male: perhaps is comes as a surprise considering his lofty status, but this character is, metaphysically speaking, a bit of an old goat. Crowley expresses this aspect of godhead admirably in his poetry, particularly "White Stains" (though with a strong Christian theme!). Chokmah's sym-bol is the Tor or Tower, and the erect phallus. Initially, the bearded male of Chokmah appears to belong more to Netzach, home of the satyrs and children of Pan, and he certainly seems incongruous in terms of orthodox religion with its strong sexual taboos.

However, it's going to take a great deal of male energy to fill the void that is Binah, so a forceful, passionate male principle is well in order. Indeed, as each Sephirah emanates its predecessor—and the "aim" is always balance—Binah must be as concave as Chokmah is convex. There is some controversy over which came first, Binah or Chokmah, and, though Binah befits the third place numerologically, my instinctive feeling is that Binah may have preceded and thus engendered Chokmah. In many ways, the line-age is irrelevant, but the qualities of Binah are so primal and so like the universe itself—starry Nuit awaiting the fertilizing seed, so intrinsically void—that it seems natural for her to have come first. Others might argue that the first expression of Being or Becoming would be Positive, the Negative state of Binah coming later. Binah is not merely the opposite of Chokmah; it is a third of intelligent, light-bright Kether.

Either way, Chokmah and Binah created one another, and form the prototype of the dynamic that rules over the whole of our little slice of creation: the male-female principle of magnetism, fertiliza-tion, and procreation. Of course, these raw energies do not really go about contained in archetypal expressions such as Isis or Pan, but it is helpful for us to envisage them as such. Their qualities are expressed on a microcosmic scale as this divine masquerade.

So, on one level, we may consider Chokmah as the lusty ruby-lipped male, hypnotized by the desire to plunge into Binah. It is no mere physical urge that drives him; his motives are metaphysical. The phallus of Chokmah is symbolic of the channel required to keep these compelling energies in balance by tipping them over into Binah, the female and receptive Sephirah. The best simile we have is that of sexual activity, and certainly our workings on the Malkuth plane seem to be miniature, grosser versions of the Chokmah-Binah dynamic.

So, our representative of Chokmah emerges from a cave carved in the gray rock of the Sephirah's surface, full of excess energy. His "lust" makes him appear half-animal; his aura is erratic, sparkly, crackling with electricity.

Binah in turn glamours him like Lilith, dark and powerful, flaunting, and concealed, pungent with the musk and mystery he longs to plunder.

Soon, you will begin to feel the mental will to ascend, but the instinctual urge to return to Binah. Binah, though less elevated than Kether, calls to you to return, and Kether may begin to seem impersonal, abstract. Sitting in Chokmah you witness the shocking radiance of the Ketheric "sun" above, and, further down, the compelling void of Binah into which you long to thrust yourself nihilistically.

If you do not feel this to be so, that is also fine: the Supernal Triad takes us all in different ways. However, you may feel inclined to project sideways rather than up. Kether overflows into Chokmah, and Chokmah into Binah.

Either way, contemplate the following as you sit on the lush grass beneath the cave entrance, the sky superblue with Ketheric energy, a waft of male pheromones occasionally assailing your nostrils, the pulse of impatience perceptible in the fertile earth. . . .

Chokmah's desire for Binah is that longing we all must incorporate with our opposite in order to create the whole: like Plato's image of humans once having been superpowerful hermaphrodites, rent asunder by jealous demigods and condemned to spend the rest of their days seeking their "other half." This has nothing to do with monogamy or other civilized concepts; it can operate on a plethora of levels. All occultists know that this energy-dynamic is the fundament of magick, and at its most potent is not physical, but rather a fertilization on the Inner Planes.

Without the force of desire for difference that creates the "Rainbow Bridge" between Binah and Chokmah, there would be no Tree of Life.

What motivates you in your own life? Try to look at the root causes, the energies behind your actions. Who are the prime movers of your psyche? Consider in depth the reason for their effect on you. Try to be as honest as possible, and then interpret these relationships in the light of what you have learned and experienced in Chokmah.

Bathe in the Ketheric refulgence and reassess your life plan in the light of these considerations. You do not, of course, have to act on them, but try to imagine what it would be like if you followed an alternative route or psychological/mental policy, particularly if you feel that your current mode of being is overly influenced by others or another, and is not entirely self-chosen. Chokmah is a good place to make new plans for achieving what we most want out of this present incarnation, and even, if you are particularly advanced, out of the sum total of all incarnations.

For those aspiring to Kether, or Samadhi, this will be a natural progression. Quite simply, visiting Chokmah can make it obvious to us what we are doing planted in Malkuth.

The magickal tool relevant to this Sephirah is, of course, the wand. Here, however, it is the impetus behind the wand that is of relevance, rather than the tool itself. Chokmah represents the creative urge in its most primal manifestation, the raw energy of procreation.

Remember how the wand you invested with energy in the Malkuth exercise sprouted leaves and blossoms as you consecrated it? Pull it out now and wield it a little—feel how quickly and accurately it conducts your thoughts and will. Test it: you're in the right place for this now. It is particularly good for initiating creative projects, and bringing propitious circumstances for creativity. In Chokmah, it becomes a will-controlled phallus, capable of fertilizing what the Magician intends, with long-term oversight, to produce a specific result. Unlike the human equivalent, it is not slave to the caprices of hormones and psychology, but is more like the astral sword in its precision. However, the sword is primarily a tool of the intellect; the wand proffers a creative, organic alternative.

Still sitting by the satyr's cave, enjoying the dynamic colors and vibrations of Chokmah, breathe deeply in, deeply out, until you feel relaxed and freed of immediate concerns. Raise your wand either in your mind's eye, or actually, if you possess one. (Alternately, raise your arm on the physical plane and maintain the image of the wand and Chokmah "landscape" mentally.) Use your wand to conduct and contain some of the potent energies of this sphere.

Elevate your consciousness to the upper, right part of your brain, take one deep breath, and, as you exhale, ask yourself which you feel most drawn to, transcendental Kether or organic Binah.

If your urge was to elevate (and try to be honest about it— what was your *instinctual* response?), you have reached a point in your life-death cycles at which you are capable of finding a path to ascension. You should concentrate your energies on spiritual matters, and be capable of abnegation without damaging your life path.

If, however, you found yourself attracted to Binah, it is clear that you still have work to do on the material planes, and thus will be returned to Malkuth until you have completed that work. (Of course, your response may also be down to transient moods—this test is by no means definitive!)

Whatever your predicament, it is possible to bathe in the refreshing rays of Kether/the Creative Source at any time through meditation, and the more you meditate, the more like the subject of your meditations will you become.

You can be anything you want to be. All that is required is will, visualization, and divine grace.

# Kether

## "The Admirable or Hidden Intelligence"
### SEPHIRAH I

*B*efore you attempt to imagine the ascent to Kether, take stock of your astral journey so far. This does not mean the mere process of having conducted the visualizations/meditations, but the points at which you felt you "had contact." These will be either the visualizations with which you had the most natural rapport, or those of particular relevance to you at the moment. You will know when your mind touched the Inner Planes and affected them; this is live magick.

The processes that were mental/academic are no less valuable for it, however; you are finding your way around the Tree, testing out and learning its properties. Just as one cannot be all things to all men at all times, it is unrealistic to anticipate an in-depth rapport with each Sephirah at any given time. There will be dreamy days when Yesod is the mind's natural abode, or days of intellectual stimulation when Hod is the station that appeals most. During times of pronounced spirituality, Kether, Chokmah, and Binah will proffer the elements required, each very differently, as we have seen.

Whatever your experiences on this internal trip, you are establishing a route for yourself, which, visited frequently, will soon lead you in new directions. The ramifications are countless.

Every symbol already mentioned might be said to apply to Kether, as it is the sum total of all, the perfection of all modes of creation. Perhaps the diamond is the best attribution for this reason; its

strength and purity are made from compressed carbon, the compressed life of a million different sources over the course of the
evolution of the planet.

The Aces of the Tarot apply to Kether, the *primum mobile* of the
Tree. These are the fundamental impulses behind the energy of
each suit, and epitomise the qualities of each element.

The Ace of Cups, depicting the fountain of life overflowing the
rim of a giant chalice, represents the source of emotion, creativity,
and imagination. Its element of course is Water, and thus it relates
to the twenty-third path, that of the Hanged Man, whose elemental attribution is Water, and to Hod, also known as the Water
Temple. The emotional, effusive Ace of Cups might seem inappropriate to intellectual, dogmatic Hod, until we recall that Hod is
the Sephirah in which knowledge is received from on high, making it both receptive and reflective, two of the most obvious qualities of water.

Meditation is another key to the qualities of this card, as indicated by the lilies floating on the water at the bottom of the picture. Lilies and lotuses have long been symbolic of the spirit rising
above the dross of the subjective and subconscious, their flowers
blooming like the crown chakra in unfettered lucidity, the chaos
beneath the water transformed into beauty. So too might the sciences of mantra, yantra, and inner vision transform the souls of
men. The Ace of Cups here symbolizes the introspective capacity,
a necessary preliminary to the exuberance it also represents.

When the Ace of Cups appears in a reading, great joy is indicated. The Venusian dove flying in at the top shows incoming
love, the disinterested nature of which is emphasised by its whiteness and the equilateral cross of Tiphareth it holds in its beak.
Tiphareth of course represents the prophets or divine messengers,
the intercessors on behalf of man. Thus love both on a personal
and a celestial level are indicated, the potential for a mystic experience. Likewise, as the dove is sacred to Netzachian Venus, is the

power behind creation available to be tapped. Spiritual elevation and great creativity are possible when the Ace of Cups is chosen.

The aspect of love is echoed by the Ace of Swords, whose appearance in a spread often indicates the initiation of a powerful new love affair. The seventeenth path (between Tiphareth and Binah) is that of the Lovers, and its Hebrew name translates as "sword." However, in this case the love, though spiritual in essence, appears as subjective, and is not of the calm, happy nature of the water trump, but rather of a passionate, fiery nature.

There are two schools of thought on the elemental attributions of Swords and Wands; Alex Sanders, for example, and no doubt many of his Wiccan initiates, had Swords as Fire and Wands as Air. The Golden Dawn however, from which the bulk of contemporary occult work originates, attribute Swords to Air, the sharp, intellectual suit, and Wands to Fire, the element of creativity. Both have arguments for and against, the most common being that as fire burns wood, Wands seem inappropriate to this element. Also, as in the case of the present discussion about the Ace of Swords and its spiritual implications, Fire seems appropriate. This card is transformative, with the power of purification and transformation. The hand of the Magician that brandishes the sword will direct it with surety to whatever psycho-spiritual cankers need removing. On the side of Air, however, the card and the entire suit indicate the power of the intellect, new ideas, new thought processes. Ultimately, it is for the individual to decide on their attributions (with the exception of this reference, I have maintained Swords as Air and Wands as Fire throughout this book).

An austere, gray landscape spans the bottom of this card, for its implications are never easy. Great conquests, both psychological and physical, are possible, but with its jagged peaks and despond-inspiring vales, it is reminiscent of the landscape of A *Pilgrim's Progress*.

The Ace of Wands, with its burgeoning leaves and slightly phallic tip, is the essence of procreative power. Ideas and projects flourish under its influence, and the positive effect of nature and natural surrounds is palpably felt. It also indicates communication with those of the same spiritual "tribe"; it is like a flag held at a convention to usher its clan forth.

The Ace of Pentacles represents, in effect, the gift of life in Malkuth. The pentagram, as discussed in the Malkuth section, represents the powers of the five elements; Earth, Air, Fire, Water and Spirit, unified by the circle of the Magician. From this combination springs all life on earth; thus, anything is possible. This is echoed by the archway at the bottom of the card, always a symbol of potential. In this case the arch is natural rather than manmade, representing the gifts of the gods. Thus on a purely material level it suggests a gift or lump sum of money that will have transformative qualities for the recipient—for example, a legacy that enables one to travel, or to study—but on a more abstract level it represents the gift of opportunity.

Everything that makes life good is indicated in this card, which contains the elements of all the others. Being the Earth suit, it represents Malkuth, and one again we are party to the residence of Kether in Malkuth.

All of the Aces might be said to relate to the twentieth path (between Tiphareth and Chesed) because its Hebrew letter, *Yod* (ʼ), translates as "hand," and all four magickal symbols are being brandished by the hand of God, or the Magician as God's representative. Yod is also ascribed to the fifteenth path, that of the Emperor, and it may also be in this "hand" that the Aces are deemed to be held. As with any such divinations, it depends on the interpreter and situation to define the correspondences.

This is the path of the Hermit, and indicates the necessity of withdrawal from the world in order to achieve inner peace. The combination of the sagacity and innate wisdom of the Hermit with use of the four most powerful celestial tools would be total mastery over the obstacles that stand between us and the light (represented by the Hermit's lamp). In other words, it would lead us straight to Kether.

# Getting from Chokmah to Kether
## "The Scintillating Intelligence"
### PATH 11

Reaching the crown of the Pillar of Equilibrium from the top of the Pillar of Mildness involves taking the eleventh path, that of the Fool.

The Hebrew letter assigned to this route is *Aleph*, meaning "ox" or "bull." As well as being sacred to Jupiter, ruler of civilizing Chesed, the bull denotes the beginnings of agriculture, and the spiritual force of Kether. It is also a mighty beast, at times worshiped as a god for its ferocity and strength, over which mankind has assumed eventual control. The bull also represents the element of Earth, and this attribution underlines Kether's intimate relationship with Malkuth, the earth sphere.

The path is represented by the Fool, a subject worthy of a book of its own. The guise of Foolishness has long been employed by satirists and social critics, the definition being very far from the "idiot" with which it is habitually connected. Shakespeare's Touchstone in *As You Like It* is a perfect example of the wise Fool, employed as his name suggests as a reality check in an Arcadian idyll. In British folk plays and morris and sword dances, the Fool, often wearing a dress and appearing as a cross-gendered bearded lady, undergoes a symbolic death and resurrection reminiscent of the death of the Celtic God of the Old Year (see Tiphareth) and crowning of the God of the New Year; also of the abduction and reemergence of Persephone (the mourning of Demeter); the death of Osiris and his resurrection in the Underworld; the crucifixion and burial of Jesus and his consequent re-emergence; the death of John Barleycorn; in other words, an epitome of all the lateral seasonal myths. The theme of sacrifice and a visit to the Underworld is prevalent in the folklore surrounding the Fool. He is often cut down by his own; sometimes by his very offspring, but he emerges victorious at the end. That many morris dancers wear soot upon their faces is reminiscent both of the mining communities from which they originate and of the purifying fire and debris thereof which cleanses and from which new life emerges phoenixlike.

Just as the Book of Job tells us that "The just and upright man is laughed to scorn," so is the visionary often perceived as mad. This brings us to the fact of genius frequently being perceived as Fool-ishness; any harbinger of the new will find it a struggle to shake the Binah statis of the social norm. We cling to the old form for dear life, preferring "the Devil we know" to a new dispensation. In the old days we would have burned the prophet for heresy; now we simply accuse them of being mad or having taken too many drugs, so that like Cassandra they are doomed to prophesy unheeded. Of course, some of them really are unbalanced. It is in situations like this that the virtue of Malkuth, discrimination, comes in handy.

Envisaging yourself in Chokmah, surrounded by its soft gray-blue hues, begin to move upwards along the path. It is coastal, the black sea of Binah distantly visible to the left, the sea beneath the cliffs to your right a deep ultramarine.

There is something different about this path to all the others you have travelled. Each, of course, is unique, but the atmosphere here is sharp as salt, more exciting. It is windy on the path, and each time the breeze touches you it seems like the very breath of God. It sanctifies you on contact.

As you progress on the upward slope you notice a multicolored shape flickering against the blue sky in the distance. Its path is per-pendicular to yours, and it is heading towards you. Growing closer, you recognise it to be the flamboyant figure of the Fool, and he waves. He dances towards you in a blur of color, zigzagging here, stopping to chase a butterfly there. He brandishes a white flower about his person. Clearly he is not normal.

You feel nervous. What kind of thrift-shop-pilfering lunatic is he, with his great bat-wing sleeves, his green tights and Dick Wittington-style boots?

Also, his dog seems disturbed. It leaps up and yaps continually, sometimes getting its teeth round his foot and being shaken off, other times jumping up and nipping him on the legs. It is a wonder his tights aren't ruined by now.

Still, something compels you to wait. He is fascinating, the path he weaves mesmeric. Over his shoulder he carries a stick, a bag on the end of it. You are just wondering what might be in it, daydreaming a little perhaps, when all of a sudden he is upon you. He grins, reading your mind.

"Air!" he cries, opening the bag and flourishing it wildly to reveal that it is empty. "Air is all that is necessary!"

Chat to him a while. As you do so, consider why this wise and childlike person, so full of beans, so close to the godhead, is given the title he is.

You realize that his magickal prowess is externalized and infinitely surpasses your own; you realize how much more you have to learn. His flashing teeth and the flower he holds are so white that they are difficult to look on, indicating his fundamental purity. This Fool is a vision of self-expression and all that may be attained with joy in conjunction with Divine Law.

The colors on his tunic are ever-shifting, you notice. Beautiful astral scenes appear when you keep your eyes fixed on it, and they seem to perfectly symbolize whatever you are thinking. When he talks, the colors change. If he alludes to wisdom, the tunic becomes gray-blue. If he talks of tears, it becomes black. Habitually, as he witters, the scenes flash by quick as a blink. As you think this, a chameleon appears in the folds of the tunic.

Grasping at nothing with a smile and a wink, the Fool produces a fan made of red feathers like the one in his cap. He hands it to you. This strikes you as peculiar at first, the air being perfectly temperate and not in the least stagnant—indeed, it sounds as if there's about to be a storm, judging from the thunder you can hear rumbling in the background—but you take it with good grace, remembering that you still have your descent to consider.

The fan makes you travel faster. Your feet seem to lift off the ground and you are drawn to wherever your will takes you, which is, if all is going well, to the brilliant white sphere of Kether.

Gradually, all colors begin to fade except for the dazzling white that seems to have made an imprint on your retina from the Fool's flower, and this expands. Tiny flecks of gold scud across its surface, then vanish. Soon, there is nothing left but glowing, pulsating, living light of ineffable whiteness.

## Encountering the In-House Divinities

The godname in Kether is *Eheieh*, meaning "I am that I am," or "I will be." The state of *becoming* is of course most relevant to the primary Sephirah.

Its Archangel is Metatron, from whom the philosophy of Qabalah was originally received. He is incredibly tall and bright, with a voice like thunder. Sometimes he appears to be wearing an auric robe of purple; at other times it is white. He is the most intelligent and thus powerful of all the angelic entities. In Malkuth he manifests as Sandalphon; the two Archangels are often said to be one and the same. When he has his feet on Malkuth, it creates "the sound of sandals" denoted by the name "Sandalphon."

The order of Angels beneath him is the *Chayoth ha-Qadesh*, the Holy Living Creatures. These fiery, blue-green divinities are responsible for bringing light, literal and metaphorical, to the world, as well as heat and the quality of love. Without any of these, civilization would never have existed, or, without the latter, would have destroyed itself long ago. As their title indicates, the Holy Living Creatures are also akin to the Bull, Lion, Man, and Eagle of the four quarters, the Kerubim William G. Gray ascribes to Malkuth.

Again we witness the reflection of Malkuth in Kether, and Kether in Malkuth. These forces are building blocks of the cosmos, and of course the physical world contains all the effects of these forces and processes.

## The Temple of Kether

This is the Holiest of Holies, the loftiest sanctum, the highest Tree house and most difficult to attain. It is reminiscent of the Temple of Binah in that all that one seems to do in it is exist, and even that not consciously. It is intimately connected with breath.

At first you are aware of the air entering and exiting your body; then of the life-force existent in you. The body becomes akin to a Temple, and then the Temple is the white light of Kether, and you one of its many epicenters.

The breath of God blows on this place, vivifying beyond anything imaginable in Malkuth. Light of living purity emanates from every angle and facet of this diamondlike Temple. Mind-shattering music moves us through aeons of evolution in milliseconds. Through all this we are suspended in sentient amnesia; we merge with greatness, forgetful of all that we have ever been and all that we will become. Individuality dissolves like an iceberg in a warm current. We return to the Ocean.

Describing Kether is impossible—it really has to be experienced by you, the individual. If it truly is, you will not return! The best we can hope for is to perceive the concept of Kether. In the light of your journey up the Tree, you may be able to imagine what this might be, and that is all we can hope for at this stage.

If not, the following visualization should help put you in a suitable frame of mind.

## Visualization in Kether

Sitting cross-legged on the floor of your favourite room, or any place that is saturated with your presence, take several deep breaths of the familiar ambience, and think of your life to date, very factually, as if you were reading a report of it.

Name? Date of Birth? Achievements to date?

Take stock. No need to go into great detail, and definitely don't become emotional; simply be honest and swift in your assessment. Try to encapsulate the essence of yourself as you are, now, and have been in the past.

After a couple more deep, relaxing breaths, imagine yourself rising a little out of your body. Feel the sensation of lightness and ascent, enjoy the beginnings of your release.

Now, imagine your friends, partners, and ex-partners, all of the people who have influenced your life, both positively and negatively. Think of how you came to Malkuth at the same time, in the same environment, to influence and help one another. Your souls are linked inexorably. Just as their dynamism has propelled you in certain directions and alchemically altered your constitution, so too has your energy sent them out of the orbits they would have inhabited had you not been around. Even if the primary sensation is repulsion, the dynamic is been present. Think of those in your life with whom you have forged such a spiritual bond, those who have helped define your personality and life path.

Now feel your bodies beginning to separate as you gradually exit through the top of your head or your solar plexus, depending on how you are constituted, until you find yourself on the roof of your abode.

Envisage the tiles beneath your feet, the aerial of your TV if you have one; construct the scenario as accurately as possible. Most importantly, take a good look at the view.

This is the environment in which you currently exist. Think about the community in which you are operating, your local vicinity, the features of your village/town/city.

Who do you interact with on a regular basis? If you are employed, move further up until you can see your place of work. This is where you, the individual, are assimilated into the community. If you are a full-time parent, the schools of your children are an obvious alternative, or any other place in which you interact with the "public"; the library, gym, local shops, etc.

Rising higher still, almost at cloud-level now, you observe with increasing detachment your known environment in its wider context. Now you are able to see unfamiliar territory, and the streets, houses, and buildings familiar to you look very small indeed.

Moving up through the chilly clouds, you find yourself still rising, rising, like a helium balloon with the string tied to the solar plexus of your distant, invisible body.

Between gaps in the clouds you glimpse the great expanse of the country you are in, and feel an objective affinity with the place that harbors you and your personal effects.

Higher, higher, into the blackness of Nuit you drift, until the white edges of the land appear, and the big blue of the ocean. Still ascending, you see the side of the globe on which your country is carved. Enjoy your vertiginous vantage point as you ascend still higher, still further into the endless, unfathomable depths of outer space.

When you feel inclined, look up.

There above you hangs the dazzling orb of Kether, white-hot and rainbow-aureoled, high-pitched and infinitely refined.

Will it let you in?

You hold your breath with anticipation as you attempt to merge with the light; and in you slip, into the sentient brilliance that holds no coherent form, and offers no point of reference, but simply is.

Experience the spiritual light for as long as you feel able.

You have finally made it, in thought at least, to the top of the Pillar of Mildness or Equilibrium, the Sephirah of brilliant, intelligent white light in which the individual personality is dissolved. Beyond this lie the three veils of "negative existence," the unknowable creative void. Enjoy its unsullied atmosphere and allow it to work its own magic on you. There are times when it is good to abnegate personal will and hand oneself over to the Powers-that-Be, and a meditation on Kether is an ideal scenario for quieting the ego and engendering divine grace.

This is also the place to crystallize your highest aims into potential manifestation. The diamond-light of Kether can help clarify and magnify your intent; it is composed of celestial inspiration. Like carbon compressed until it transforms into diamond, the organic matter, the "raw material" of Malkuth may be infinitely pressured and refined in Kether. You do not need to will it specifically whilst meditating here; simply be aware of your aims as you enter the visualization. Kether is zen *satori*, and in this luminous, meaningful void, full waking consciousness is not appropriate. Allow the impetus to be innate and spiritual.

When you wish to, gradually lower yourself back into the starry night sky, and follow that string. You may be surprised to find a body bearing a particular name and set of statistics waiting to receive your soul.

When I was younger, this experience of re-encapsulation (even after sleeping) used to cause great confusion. If you find it disturbing or disorientating, the best antidote is to eat something, watch TV, stroke an animal, or play some really loud, meaningless music.

This may sound the antithesis of a spiritual experience, but do not forget everything on every plane is equally valid when in balance with its equal and opposite. Kether is in Malkuth, in that we carry a microcosmic version of Kether in the soul, and Malkuth is in Kether, albeit differently.

Let the light of Kether inform your actions in Malkuth by always taking an objective overview and looking for the highest good in any situation. Kether is, of course, the ultimate goal of the aspiring soul, and this exercise has merely given you (and me) some idea of what it might be like to abide there. From Malkuth it can never be truly experienced, though highly adept yogi(ni)s experience a fraction of it in their Samadhi ecstasy. We have a long way to go to reach the exulted state that is Kether, but the important thing is to strive.

With the discrimination of Malkuth, the imaginative intelligence of Yesod, the integrity of Hod, the compassion of Netzach, the beauty and devotion of Tiphareth, the determined energy of Geburah, the obedience to divine will of Chesed, the understanding of Binah, and the wisdom of Chokmah, we have everything we need to get there.

# Daath and the Abyss

## Daath, the Invisible Sephirah

*T*he Sephirah Daath did not exist as such in the original Judaic Qabalah. It was used by members of the late Golden Dawn to embody a concept; that of an "invisible sun" and "son" which concentrated and then dispersed some of the energies of the Supernal Triad. It means "knowledge," and is said to be an amalgam of the properties of Binah, Chokmah, and Kether, but in a greatly diminished sense, more like a shadow reflecting their form than a container of their properties.

Strategically placed above the Abyss, directly beneath the path of the high priestess, *Gimel*, Daath is intimately connected with the processes of the thirteenth path and the occult tightrope walk across the Abyss. As the exhausted Priestess teeters above Daath, she hears its siren call, the lure into its bottomless depths. Superficially it promises knowledge, but the priestess intuitively perceives that such an attainment is premature, and that the real "gift" of Daath, of the Abyss, is annihilation. This too may prove a temptation, for by this stage she is desperate for anything that might alleviate the aridity of her spiritual thirst; burdened with the weight of her own being, she staggers on.

Many nasty tales are told of those who fail on this path, and tumble into Daath and the chasm beneath. This will not happen during a visualization by any means, but when one wholeheartedly asks for initiation into each Sephirah and path between them, the effects become entangled with daily life, and the myth reenacts itself time and time again until the lesson is learned. The Gimel path definitely gets the prize for dearest-won liberty, but liberty is exactly what it offers; of mind, body and soul, as it would, its finishing point being Kether. Though Daath is a relatively recent addition to a centuries-old structure, it is I feel an appropriate one, echoing the experiences of many who went before.

Daath exists not so much in a place as between places. Neither is it a Sephirah as such, but rather the idea of one. It represents the relationship between the Supernal Triad and the seven Sephiroth of the lower Tree as well as that between the ordered perfection of the Supernals and the chaos of the Abyss. It epitomizes a state between the mortal world and the realm of the gods, a place of the enactment of many a significant descent and ascent. Persephone's fall into the Underworld could be said to belong to Daath as well as to the thirty-second path, especially as it is closely connected with the experience of the High Priestess path. Other myths in which a character is snatched from grace by a trick may also be attributed to Daath, the fall from Eden being an obvious example. The end, ultimately, may be an empowered participant (once victim), like Persephone as Queen of the Dead, but the motives lie in a shadowy place and are difficult to perceive, giving rise to thoughts of futility and abandonment by the gods to those traversing this portion of the Tree.

The affiliations of Daath are not merely subterranean. As Daath is suspended between places; it follows then that it must have an "upper" end. Another part of Daath could be construed as symbolically mountainous, a place of communication with the gods. Like Hermes and Iris there are beings here who mediate between planes, but how trustworthy the information may be when processed is another matter. It is highly likely that false prophets abide in this conceptual sphere. It may seem possible to receive true Divine communion at some point during this process, as Daath lies so close to Kether, Chokmah, and Binah, but the interaction is likely to be contaminated. Daath processes universal psychic waste; it may be like trying to tune in with the Light from the base of a sewer. Likewise, powers encountered in this Sephirah might be deviant. It is a question of using the old Malkuthic discrimination to chose between oracles, or portents, or perhaps to abandon them altogether. It cannot be denied that crossing Daath and the Abyss is profoundly confusing, on all levels.

The God-name of Daath is, apparently, somewhere between IHVH and IHVH *Elohim*. Its Archangels are all those of the cardinal points; Raphael, Michael, Gabriel, and Uriel. Probably, they are keeping its influence in check. The first three have been described in relation to the their respective Sephirah earlier in the book; Uriel is mentioned in conjunction with Malkuth, though the Qabalistic correspondence to the earth sphere is Sandalphon.

The name of the Order of Angels translates as "shining serpents," echoing the element of temptation to self-destruct on this route. They hiss and lisp of easier ways, greater wisdom, better immortality. They provoke many a fall, of course, for that is why they are placed there.

The symbol for Daath is the prism, because of its energy-condensing and dispersing action. It may also, with retrospect, cast a clearer light on the mental and spiritual muddle of the Priestess path, defining and illuminating individual influences.

# The Abyss

During the talk given on his last birthday (titled "Awake in the Cosmic Dream"), the great mystic Paramahansa Yogananda confesses, almost gigglingly, that perhaps God thinks he made a bit of a mistake in creating us and giving us free will. "But it is done now, and He cannot take it back."

In Qabalistic cosmology "subtle beings" such as Samael and Lilith existed alongside Adam and Eve, with whom they copulated and created duality; for Adam and Eve could no longer trust their own instincts, and "fell" from pride and security. They were not specifically evil, for, as the tenth-century B.C.E. matriarch Devorah Bat-David points out in the *Sefer Gan Eden*, "there is no will to disobey but rather a capriciousness to creation itself, so that catastrophe is comparable to natural disaster."

The remorse of the Great One, this notwithstanding, must be mighty. Along with the problems caused by other deviant creations; Lucifer for example, and a multitude of trials and errors we cannot even conceive of, there must be some undesirable repercussions in the consciousness of God. And as God thinks, so are entire universes created; we may conclude that Daath and the Abyss are the Qabalistic equivalent of the "places" created when all was not well. These are, needless to say, horrific.

I imagine the Abyss as the cosmic sewer and Daath as its plug. Whenever I have a ritual bath I seal the plugs with salt, refusing access to the Malkuthic and Yesodic demons which are the friendlier face of such forces. Perhaps this takes on board the medieval horror of human waste products perceptible in Christianity and Islam, the latter even producing rules as to which foot to place before the other when entering a WC, but of course the medieval mind has worked upon the Qabalah, and such correspondences are not surprising. Excreta is also the microcosmic equivalent of unwanted material, and anyone who's ever been to India will know that there are animals which will feed off it, just as there are demons and bizarre entities willing to feed off God's and humanity's waste. Not a pretty image, but one worth being aware of. Perhaps it is this realm of annihilation that is perceived briefly on the thirty-second path courtesy of the *assafoetida*—stench.

According to William G. Gray, the Abyss is ruled by Shaitan and presumably his Djinns, which seems a suitable attribution considering the pious Islamic aversion to physical waste, its presiding Angel (now semi-Demonic?) being *Ridya* or *Musukiel*, meaning "the Veiler of God."

Thus we see why "crossing the Abyss" is such a feat. Not only is the path long and hard, but the thought of that which must not be thought on emanates like a miasma from the chasm below. On the Gimel path, psycho-physical circumstances may become so hard that thoughts of the Abyss are knocked out of one; in some ways, it is too much time to think which leads the mind astray in the Daath/Abyss direction. The eyes must be fixed on the cleansing spiritual sun with absolute faith; this keeps the mind busy. It is true that "the Devil makes work for idle hands to do." If the mind begins to unravel, it sends out astral streamers which may get caught on an aberration, jerking the consciousness into a darker realm. This certainly is not helpful. Intense yogic concentration is required over a period of time to maintain a positive reality. If this is maintained, then the Chasm may be crossed, and a higher degree of immortality achieved. Spiritual grace is regained, despite the Fall. We prove the will to strive towards God, whatever the consequences. It is for this reason that adepts run the risk of annihilation by treading the thin wire above the Abyss.

# The Remaining Paths

*T*he paths we have not travelled in this exploration are, of course, of equal importance to those we have. All are necessary as psychological processes; in real life, none may be omitted.

## Getting from Malkuth to Hod
### "The Perpetual Intelligence"
#### PATH 31

The Hebrew letter ascribed to this path is *Shin* (ש), meaning "tooth." The glyph of this letter looks like a three-pronged fork of fire, and indeed Fire is its elemental attribution. Its Tarot image is that of Judgement, in which the souls of the dead are called forth by the mighty Archangel Gabriel, who sounds the trumpet of redemption, quite literally blowing new life into them.

The ground surrounding the open tombs looks more like water than earth, being blue and undulant, thus suggesting the astral sleep of Yesod. Death, it tells us, is just an illusion, a spiritual trance-state. So, of course, is life in Malkuth; here, the fire of the divine pierces the consciousness of the living zombies of Malkuth. *Wake up!* it cries. *Time to open up the consciousness of your bodies, which have become as tombs, and start ascending the Tree.*

Thus we witness on the thirty-first path the beginnings of spiritual awakening, or the calling from on high, a condition well suited to its position at the base of the Tree.

Because of its connection with Hod, the powers of communication are also implied. This is both the communication of the divine with the individual, and the interaction of humans on spiritual subjects. Groups in which religious ideas are explored and the sense of "other" extrapolated are thus part of the experience of this path. Church meetings, pagan moots, coven gatherings, and meaningful cult activities originate here. Just as the grinding of teeth (appropriate to this image out of the Book of Revelation) begins the process of rendering food digestible to the stomach, so does this path help us ruminate on the concept of the divine and make it digestible to us.

Asbestos is attributed to this path, for it resists destruction by fire and represents immortality, the part that is left when the fire of God has burned away the dross, clearly an appropriate correspondence for the Judgement card. Other symbols include the fiery-red poppy, recognized as relevant to the subject of eternal youth and eternal life to all who have stood at a Memorial or Veterans Day service on November 11. A modern connection, of course, but relevant to the implications of the card—Gabriel's trumpet blast recalls these and similar services honoring the transcendence of personal will in favor of a greater good.

With Hod's informing mentality at one end and the physical state at the other, this path is fixed in "Perpetual Intelligence." It rules the transition from androgynous thought into physical categorization, thus regulating solar and lunar properties. It is much more civilized than its counterpart, the Moon path (see "Getting from Malkuth to Netzach"), and is concerned with obeying the higher dictate rather than following the individual intuition.

# Getting from Malkuth to Netzach
## "The Corporeal Intelligence"
### PATH 29

The Hebrew letter of this path is *Qoph* (ק), which means the back of the head. This connects it immediately with the medulla oblongata, through which cosmic sustenance is said to enter the system. This celestial prana is absorbed for as long as it is willed that one should live, and is received whether one is aware of it or not, thus illuminating the connection between this path and instinctual, almost dumb survival. Certainly the intellect has no influence here.

The path's Tarot card is the Moon, bringing to mind a plethora of relevant deities, particularly goddesses: Artemis, Levanah, Hecate, Selene, Isis, to name but a few. With regard to the Moon, all of these divinities represent instinct, intuition, and nature. It follows that another attribution is sorcery, magick. However, as the process is "corporeal," concerned with the body, the type of magick possible here is not the elevated, but rather the visceral revelry of the medieval coven (that is, those which were solely responding to the Christian creed), the psychokinetic activity of the menstruating girl. The shenanigans of Stephen King's *Carrie* could be attributed to this path, in which the will power of Netzach filters through the subconscious and arrives within the sphere of operation in Malkuth unfettered by comprehension.

Due to the aquatic implications of the Moon, the astrological sign attributed to the twenty-ninth path is Pisces. This connects it with the twenty-eighth path, from which it is "hooked" from above (the Hebrew letter for the twenty-eighth path is *Tzaddi* (צ), which you will recall means "fish-hook"). Both paths, and indeed this whole section of the Tree, are concerned with the subconscious, its contents, and their influence on various levels of individual existence.

The Tarot image depicts this perfectly, with the cray fish of subconscious impulse exiting the deep, uncharted waters of the psyche and journeying between two canines who howl at the moon. This represents a time when nothing is certain—*"entre chien et loup"* as the French call twilight—a time when dog may appear as wolf, or vice versa. Illusion is the key element, and the trump is so-called in the Tarot of the Old Path.

Because the path is concerned with corporeal issues, the special implication of this card in conjunction with it is mental illusion, or lunacy. The path represents madness, particularly hormonal, which cannot be held in abeyance: the sacred delirium of the oracle, the intuitive menstrual insanity of the Black Isis. It follows that Lilith is native to the Twenty-Ninth path, her physicality and special magick reviled by Adam, who represents the light of conscious reason. Significantly, he also represents shame. The casting out of Lilith indicates the inability of "civilized" mankind to face up to instinctive impulses—particularly those of desire—which are subsequently cast into the ocean of the subconscious where they redouble and triple their power. The result is a terrifying, seductive demon who visits the "virtuous" in their sleep!

Thus we see the influence of the subconscious on the physical vehicle. Likewise is the path specific to neuroses, phobias, and all reflexive and instinctual reactions. We are still very much "in the body" as we ascend to Netzach from Malkuth.

## Getting from Yesod to Netzach
### "The Natural Intelligence"
#### PATH 28

The Twenty-Eighth path connects the Moon sphere with the Sephirah of Venus, and is thus highly feminine in nature. The nine Muses spring to mind as suitable attributes, particularly as Netzach is the sphere of creative power. This path, connecting the will with the subconscious, is replete with imagery significant to the "green ray," working of nature magick.

As already mentioned, the relevant Hebrew letter is *Tzaddi*, the fish-hook.

The Tarot image itself is the Star, representing a naked woman pouring water from two flasks, one into a pool, the other onto the earth. On one hand this reflects Aquarius, the Water Bearer and astrological correspondence to this path. On the other, the pool represents Yesod, the earth Netzach. The woman's actions symbolize the dividing of the energies of the path between the two Sephiroth.

The traditional magickal image of Netzach is a beautiful naked woman, and such is the character in the card of the twenty-eighth path. Free of all inhibitions and perfectly at one with her natural surroundings, she represents not so much nature worship as Nature herself. However, the eight eight-pointed stars shining above her indicate an additional element; that of humanising intellect (eight being the number of Hod) and reflection. I do not mean to imply that the path is cerebral—it is not. Rather, the potential indicated by the celestial bodies is what differentiates the human condition from its animal nature. The star is the star of hope, of aspiration: *ad astra per aspiramina.*

A bird perches in a tree at the back of the image, about to take off. The eagle is sacred to this path, but the long-beaked bird depicted here looks more like a pelican or an ibis, the latter a moon bird sacred to Isis and Thoth. This connects it both with the twenty-ninth path and the sphere of Hod. It indicates the new ventures and inspirations which are likely to present themselves as one travels the twenty-eighth path. Some of these may well be deeply unusual, the products of the astral sphere of Yesod and the elfin Tír Na-n Óg, which is Netzach.

# Getting from Hod to Tiphareth
## "The Renovating Intelligence"
### PATH 26

The Hebrew letter ascribed to this path is *Ayin* (ע), meaning "eye." Thus we perceive instantly that the quest it represents involves the tenuous properties of vision and perception. Of all the senses, sight holds the strongest sway. We judge all sorts of things by appearance, whether we mean to or not, from people to situations to physical scenarios. Yet as we know, the ensuing assessment is often faulty.

The spiritual eye on the other hand cuts through the material delusions to the heart of any matter, and it is this spiritual insight which is one of the gifts of the twenty-sixth path. By the light of the sun of Tiphareth, we learn to assess on the grounds of inner wisdom rather than by the form and appearance of Hod.

The Tarot card ascribed is that of the Devil. In the *Rider-Waite* deck, the Devil, in the form of a winged satyr, sits with a torch in his left hand above two loosely chained figures, a man and a woman. They are horned and have mock tails—the man's of flame, the woman's a vine bearing grapes. An inverted pentacle shines from the "third *Ayin*-eye" of the lofty horned deity.

Much has been be said on the subject of the Devil by pagans and Wiccans defending their sacred imagery against the encroachments of Christian symbolism. Some have redesigned this trump in objection; or, possibly, restored it to its original state. Juliet Sharman-Burke in *The Mythic Tarot* presents the Devil as Pan; and Ellen Cannon Reed in *The Witches Tarot* substitutes the old Christian misconception of the witches' god for the real thing—Cernunnos, the Horned One. In Howard Rodway's *Tarot of the Old Path* the central figure is missing altogether, and the card title changed to "Temptation."

All of these are excellent updates on an image prone to be the bane of the Craft. Waite's image, however, is not outdated, as there is nothing "evil" about it when we shed that immediacy of judgment invoked at first sight: nobody is being tortured and nobody held against their will. Despite the iron chains about the necks of the two figures, they seem perfectly happy, and are quite capable of removing them should they so chose—but they do not. What is popularly construed as vice is doing them no disservice at the moment. The Bacchanalia suggested by the grapes and fire is to some extent necessary for the shedding of the protocol of Hod. In order to ascend from this most cerebral of spheres, a bit of free-thinking is required, and flying in the face of convention as the Devil clearly does, can be an elevating experience.

There is also a great deal of raw, chaotic energy indicated by the animal nature of the satyr, and by his inverse pentagram. Here, the elements have precedence over spirit, which is now at the lowest point of the pentacle-star. What better antidote to the confines of the lower personality and its proclivity to toe the line than this?

There is nothing deliberately cruel on this path; it is on the line between Chesed and Hod, and is thus informed by mercy—but there is a danger of harm through ignorance. As Rodway's title emphasizes, its traveller is continually tempted by excess. Here again we have the theme of illusion, for as the junkie deludes himself that he can give up after just one more hit, so might the traveller of the twenty-sixth path believe in his or her ability to keep total control. Relinquishing it is the aim, though not necessarily through the use of intoxicants. The temptation might be for illicit sex, the energy of which can be extremely elevating, or for drugs, or just the old falling-over water. In regular readings the Devil can indicate greed and materialism, though unless the esotericist craves the material stability of the lower Tree, these factors are not likely to be relevant. More typical is the problem of ignorance presented by the symbol of the Devil.

The quest of the path, or one of them, is working out to what we are enslaved, and breaking those bonds, to be as free and uninhibited as the mountain goat which, as Capricorn, is ascribed to it. As the "renovating" intelligence its energies may be used to reassess the concepts by which we have been trained to live, replacing them with a more suitable personal alternative, or just recognizing that there is more than one way of looking at a thing.

# Getting from Yesod to Tiphareth
## "The Tentative Intelligence"
### PATH 25

This is the path of Temperance, a suitable attribute as it runs straight up the Middle Pillar of Equilibrium, and Temperance is an example of perfect equipoise. The ultimate goal, Kether, is resident at the top of this Pillar, and it follows that a key characteristic of the twenty-fifth path is aspiration. This also equates it with the spinal column; the top, or Kether, being the crown chakra.

Temperance represents the cleansing activities that improve the intake of celestial light, such as chakra and aura purification. Physiologically, Tiphareth relates to the central chakra, the solar plexus, usually envisaged as golden. This skeletal attribute seems appropriate to the Hebrew letter of the path, *Samekh* (ס), meaning "prop."

One of the symbols of the twenty-fifth path is the rainbow, again recalling the auric spectrum of the chakras. Iris, the goddess of the rainbow, is a temperate deity who abides in the spiritual and material worlds with equal fluency, and the irises depicted in the Tarot card recall her function as intermediary between spheres. She is one of the messengers of the gods, and is thus linked with Tiphareth, Sephirah of intercessors.

The figure in the card is a white-robed angel, winged, but standing with one foot in the water, the other on dry ground. She pours water from one chalice to another, allowing neither to be full or empty at any point. She maintains the flow of life forces. In a chakric sense, she preserves the balance between energy centers. The sign of the sun sits above her forehead. Light radiates from her, and from a distant source at the back of the picture. Whether it is a golden citadel or the sun itself we cannot tell, but it suggests a supportive spiritual force. The recipient of this card in a reading often has access to an energy bank in an unseen quarter, and is already tapping into it unconsciously.

The special qualities to strive toward on this path are fluency in diverse spheres of life, and of course the art of temperance itself. The angel has one foot in the Styx, giving the perspective of awareness of physical mortality. Or is this the water of life, or the subconscious pool of watery Yesod? It is all of these, and all contrast with the green terra firma on which her other foot rests, suggestive of the power of Netzach and the properties of Malkuth.

Balance is particularly important when we recall that the path which crosses this one is the twenty-seventh, that of the lightning-struck Tower. It is at the conjunction of these two paths that the Tower stands, or rather, that the experience of the Tower is felt. An angel of mercy is certainly required to help the initiate overcome the repercussions of this mind-shattering process. The faith which Temperance represents is the required remedy for the dark night of the soul here indicated. Healing flows down from Tiphareth as a response to the injuries received as the striving soul struggles towards the light; the angelic spirit of Temperance is reminiscent of Raphael and Michael, Archangels of healing.

The astrological correspondence of this path is Sagittarius, wryly hailed by Jim Morrison "the most philosophical of all the signs." Certainly the serene overview proffered from the standpoint of Temperance offers the salve of stoicism to the wounded, and the promise of better times to come. Sagittarius is the archer, and from this path we shoot arrows of aspiration at the sun; not, hopefully, to witness them burning up, but rather to return to us fired by flames of celestial inspiration and purification.

# Getting from Hod to Geburah
## "The Stable Intelligence"
### PATH 23

The Hebrew letter describing this path is Mem (מ), meaning "water." At first glance, the attribution of "stability" to this most pliant of elements seems inapt, especially as the image representing it is that of a hanging man, hardly the most "stable" of positions. Yet a little enquiry in to the nature of the image—the man's tranquil expression, and the fact that he hangs by the ankle, not the neck—reveals it to be a deliberate posture, not an affliction; rather yogic in fact.

Part of the confusion inspired by this card is due to its title: "Hanged Man" rather than "Hanging Man." Those unfamiliar with its import react instantly to the images inspired by the implication of the character having been hanged, both an irreversible fact and a punishment. Were the verb in the present tense, the act would sound more deliberate, and also unfinished, a factor of great importance to its meaning. This card is about processes: as the posture suggests, the querent is "between places," earth and the heavens, Malkuth and Kether, Hod and Geburah. The halo emitting from the head of the hanging man should disperse any further doubts as to his culpability; few criminals are equipped with glowing crown chakras. Turn the card upside down, and he seems almost to be pirouetting in the tree, as light and lithe as a trained ballet dancer. No, he is happy to be so positioned, and there is a higher purpose to this uncomfortable-looking act. The tau cross of the branch confirms that the hanging man is in the process of gaining wisdom through suffering.

Everything been gained by deliberate abnegation and discomfort is relevant to this path; it represents the potential fruits of hardship. As the unusual nature of the card suggests, this especially includes unconventional processes that may even seem horrific to other people, but which are adhered to in the hope of reaching a spiritual goal. At the time of receipt of this card, however, the goal has not yet been attained, and further "sacrifice" is necessary.

Water cleanses, and so this path is one of purification. The water of Hod washes away mundane concerns, and the spirit is committed to the definitive fire of Geburah. Unwanted traits are destroyed by sheer determination, and, if the sacrifice is properly performed, immortality is gained.

The equilateral cross formed by the legs of the hanging man sug-gest Tiphareth, especially as they are transposed upon the trunk of the tree, which could be equated with the Middle Pillar. The spine of the hanging man runs parallel with it, suggesting a prop that is both natural and fed by the elements. "Primitive" nature supports the act; a certain wild-child streak is necessary to carry this feat off. Bowing to convention—represented in part by the tidal pull of Hod—will get one nowhere on this path.

The sacrificed gods of Tiphareth all knew this process. Christ was eventually "hanged from a tree," and Odin spent nine days dangling on Ygddrasil in order to attain the Runes, the Norse equivalent of Tarot. In order to attain his spiritual vision, Odin gouged out one of his eyes, providing us with an extreme example of loss of one thing—liberty, comfort, physical sight—leading to the attainment of a less-transient state.

Transience is what is recognized by those familiar with this path; they have attained an overview from which vantage point no process seems interminable. In other words, they have transcended the immediacy of the body's concerns and the fluctuating nature of the mind's. The closer the goal becomes, the stronger the force of Geburic determination to succeed. Thus, through the process rep-resented by the twenty-third path, stability is indeed attained.

## Getting from Netzach to Chesed
### "The Conciliatory Intelligence"
#### PATH 21

Between the undisciplined power of Netzach and the compassion-ate law and order of Chesed lies the path of the spinning Wheel of Fortune. As though we were riding a Ferris wheel at a fairground, we are shown the blue sky of Chesed and then plunged back into group mind of the crowds, then taken up again. Drunk on the ambrosia of life which bubbles out of Netzach's springs, giddy with following every impulse to its ultimate conclusion, with surfing the ley lines of nature-cosmic Netzach, our stomachs drop as the wheel sweeps once again up into the cerulean. For a moment, quiet and fresh air calm our senses as we rock there, suspended on the Ferris wheel of the Fates. The sisters pause, look at one another, and nod. A spindly hand pulls the lever, the blue blurs away in a rush of air, and again we are plunged into the chaos of the excited populace.

Jupiter rules this path, as befits his personal combination of sociability and underlying discipline. It represents both a stage and an overriding aspect of our spiritual development, its primary concern being spiritual destiny. The Hebrew letter ascribed to it is *Kaph* (כ), meaning "palm of the hand." A visit to one of the fair's Gypsy caravans will complete the implications of this imagery.

This is one of the most exciting paths on the Tree. Contemplating it, the same thrill of anticipation can be compared with the feeling as a Gypsy is about to make an utterance over your fortune, or as the Tarot reader concludes the reading. If they are good oracles, they will not omit to tell you that fate is not entirely fixed, and that personal choice—free will—can make all the difference at any point. As the saying goes, "The stars indicate, they do not compel." This path gives the clues we need to help us on our way.

Methods of divination are developing rapidly in conjunction with increased awareness of different genres of spirituality and the enthusiasm now being felt for them. No longer the province of trained priests and priestesses or hereditary witches alone, many people are involving themselves in do-it-yourself prediction. The methods are almost as varied as the practitioners, ranging from using any of the vast array of Tarot cards now available, to Runes, pendulums, crystals, and aura-chakra skrying. More maverick techniques include the New Age tendency to see life as a metaphor of inner reality, and thus all events as symbolic. A pain in the right knee thus becomes relevant to how one relates to one's mother, tripping on a flagstone indicative of a hitch in one's life path, and so on. There is a great deal in all of this, but the participant runs the risk of being semiotically roused to the point where every little thing assumes gigantic proportions and requires analysis. Giving such work a time limit helps (either by asking that important clues be perceived today, specifically, or by confining them to a ritual divination).

Then there are the types of methods employed by the Temple Ov Psychick Youth, for example, such as flicking between television stations and formulating sentences of apparent import from the random words encountered. This may sound silly, but it is merely the ultramodern equivalent of Aztec and Druidic divining by the spilling of guts, and, like all forms of skrying, relies on the imagination of the individual to make it work. The words are taken symbolically, not just in their flat sense; an advertisement for washing powder thus accessed, for example, might mention cleaning power, whiter than white, dissolves all grease and stains. A young magician who has issues of guilt relevant to him at that time might conclude that a purification ritual is necessary; someone considering a meditation on Kether might conclude that the time is right, while another might simply deduce that the piles of washing in their room need to be dealt with. Combined with the aural emissions of other stations, the results could be as mind-boggling as any more traditional techniques, if not quite so pleasingly organic. (Personally, I find the very high wail emitted by the television utterly destructive to psychism, but others may not. It's a question of using what you feel the most fluent in and what is appropriate to you at that time.)

Whatever the method, the point is the ability to gain clues about our spiritual destiny. This is the path of quests, missions, individual grails. Where are we going, and what are we doing to help ourselves along the way?

The card itself must be one of the oldest designs, and it certainly represents the oldest of questions. For millennia man has sought to know the future, usually hoping to avoid mortality. Kings have knelt at the feet of withered hags thanks to this urge, obscure oracles have dictated the rise and fall of empires. When no heed is taken of them, disaster ensues. Look at Cassandra, doomed to be disbelieved as Troy fell in her mind's eye, an image soon to be brought to realization because of her "blind" compatriots.

Because of the capacity of the individual to divine their own future when the mood is right, and also to cut the overworked oracle some slack, riddles are the traditional answer to a query. The sphinx sitting on the Wheel of Fortune is obviously the ultimate riddle-setter, and the sword she holds in her left paw indicates her ability to cut to the heart of a matter using unconventional methods.

A Muse, or the entire set of Muses—particularly Urania—the inspirer of astrologers, and Calliope, of epic poetry, might also be a suitable attribution, as the Delphic Oracle traditionally delivered her answers in hexameters, the meter being proof of Apollo's presence behind the mouthpiece. Homer, the most Muse-inspired of poets as far as the ancient Greeks were concerned, sang in hexameters, a rhythm widely perceived as conducive to prophetic accuracy.

The corners of this card, like those of the World image, are guarded by the four Divine Watchers: man, eagle, bull, and lion. Each reads a book here, no doubt perusing the script, or possible script, intended for the querent. The sphinx smiles smugly from the top of the wheel, controlling without effort the demonic-looking creature at the bottom of the wheel described by Waite as "Hermanubis." The sphinx is a symbol of Malkuth, and thus represents the stability of the earth plane carried through into the celestial spheres. All is not airy-fairy in the ether, but solidly conceived. She thus represents the reconciliation of earth and heaven, body and spirit, represented by the *Sepher Yetzirah*'s title for the twenty-first path, the "Conciliatory Intelligence."

The serpent seen slithering down the descending side represents the infamous Typhon, Set of Egyptian lore. Though traditionally labelled "evil," his inclusion in the image shows that even seemingly negative energies are essential to the dynamic of the universe. The polarity theme is deeply relevant to the Qabalah, which has as its extremes severity and mercy—and thus Equilibrium—as its Central Pillar. Also, without Kether "overbalancing" into Chokmah, and Chokmah tipping over into Binah (i.e., repeated states of Qlipothic imbalance), there would be no living Qabalah and hence no universe. Typhon might be said to represent the essential "darkness" of Qlipoth, without which the light would be unrecognizable.

A syncretized form of Anubis and Hermes, a psychopomp, this jackal-headed chimera stands for descent into the Underworld. Death is as inevitable a part of the wheel's rotation as birth; the spirit is guided by the sheer inevitability of rebirth. The card is not mystical, but rather factual. It stands for the processes of existence, yet seems mystical to us, since we rarely attain the philosophical understanding it represents. Even if this is understood intellectually as the cycle of Samsara, the concept will not take root until assimilated by soul-understanding. The card tells us that all is changing, that we must go with the flow, and that ultimately we are evolving upwards. Even the processes that seem like a backward step are challenges to be welcomed, not shied away from. Written on the wheel is the word "rota," an anagram of Taro, referring to changes that are allotted the querent.

The creatures in the Tarot image are representatives of different aspects of the Cosmic Intelligence, as are Archangels and Choirs of Angels, and like them they have specific tasks to perform. The Wheel of Fortune may seem like a fairground ride to us, controlled by those whose integrity is uncertain—a mere flight of sensation—but the illustration is intended to show that it is not. Instead our "rota" is a carefully planned and protected part of the universal calendar, every day of significance, even those which seem bad or void. Nothing goes to waste in this view of the World.

Though both Regardie and Waite mention seven spokes on the wheel, in my Waite deck there are definitely eight shown! Personally I prefer this number, reflective as it is of the eight sabbats and esbats of the year, but it is certainly a mystery that the man who helped design the pack quotes "seven radii" as the proper number and then produces a deck depicting eight of them. Did he review his decision? I doubt it, as seven is a number more suited to his time and personality than the womanly eight.

Either way, we witness in the image the creatures of Ezekiel, the Guardians of the Watchtowers, Lords of the Elemental Quarters, four guardian Archangels, etc., abiding foursquare over the circular spinning wheel, thus giving us a framework of reference. Events may seem to be flukes, the whimwhams of fickle circumstance—the sort of apparently mindless energies we encounter in Netzach—but they fall under the jurisdiction of Chesed, seat of law and order. Recognizing this is the most important of the many lessons of this path.

## Getting from Tiphareth to Chesed
### "The Wilful Intelligence"
#### PATH 20

The *Kaph* or "palm that has just been read" is that of the next Tarot character we are to meet, the Hermit. In his *Yod* ("hand") he holds the illuminating lamp, one of the symbols of Netzach on which the Wheel of Fortune is based; in the other he holds a staff, the wand of Chokmah and "prop" of twenty-fifth path of Temperance. He is setting off to follow the advice of his inner dictate, rejecting earthly concerns and goals for a while, aiming for a more permanent, inner truth. This is a path of wisdom, thus the connections with Chokmah. In *A Garden of Pomegranates*, Regardie describes the letter *Yod* (ʼ) as "the index finger on the hand, with all the other fingers closed," thus phallic and "representing sper-matozoa." The latter is a secretion sacred to Chokmah, Sephirah of primal fecundity.

This bearded Mage represents perhaps the most popular mental image of the initiate. The Hermit has set himself aside from the norm; in the Victorian era he was regarded as the epitome of spir-ituality, of man's most earnest strivings towards God. In an age in which science, particularly evolution theory, was rocking the the-ological boat and inspiring much depressed and wretched athe-ism, the Hermit was held in very high esteem. Those of the upper classes in Britain who wished to gain grace by being patrons to such spiritual seekers (so much more convenient than doing it oneself, dear) kept hermits in their gardens—quite seriously! The vogue did not last much longer than a decade, but a craze for "ornamental hermits" certainly took hold in the upper echelons of British society. This may well have been the cause for the ubiquity, in proper libraries, of Tennyson, whose poem "The Mystic" per-fectly exemplifies this Victorian regard for hirsute men of sack-cloth. Of course, it was in this environment that the Golden Dawn first flourished, many of its members being both wealthy and well educated. The class division and backdrop of the Industrial Revo-lution and pending godlessness explains a great deal about the pompous, moribund style of much European esoteric writing at this time.

Just as the wilfulness mentioned in the path's Sepher Yetziratic title was (and often still is) required to break away from orthodox dogma, so is it necessary in order to separate oneself from society, whose group mind engenders illusion, in order to see clearly with inner vision. This is another of the benefits of the Hermit's lamp.

The planetary ruler of the path is Virgo, thus showing that the path is virgin, not trodden before. In the card there is snow at the Hermit's feet, indicating both physical hardship and this "untouched" quality. Its experience involves going where the body and/or mind have not yet had the conviction or opportunity to venture, and its key trait is solitude.

With the twenty-third, sixteenth, and twelfth paths (those of the Hanged Man, Hierophant, and Magician respectively), we find here the most Hermetic of processes. This path involves will, intellect, meditation, discipline. It represents a time of purification, of contact with the godhead. At the end of it, the initiate emerges with his or her energies redoubled and with a crystal insight into the personal spiritual quest. Magickal abilities are augmented under its influence; no longer is the Wheel of Fortune dictating one's moves, but the individual will. The hand that holds the Wand describes its own universe (within the confines set by the Lords of the Inner Planes, at least).

## Getting from Tiphareth to Binah
### "The Disposing Intelligence"
#### PATH 17

The Hebrew letter corresponding with this path is *Zayin* (ז), meaning "sword." Its Tarot card is the Lovers, and its zodiac sign the Gemini twins. The line of force runs between Tiphareth, where the personality and individuality are fused, and Binah, where spirit and force are given form.

Like love itself, Tiphareth is healing and radiant; Binah, conversely, is restrictive and sorrowful. What more obvious analogy could there be for the results of unwise love, or even of giving way to love at all? Since time began, or Binah first bore us, women everywhere have known its effects, through the joyful pangs of childbirth, the pain of fruitless labor, or the sorrow of being loved and cast aside, or "ruined." No wonder the Mater Dolorosa waits at the end of the path to tend to her pitiful child. In cultures where girls are taken from their families, friends, or tribe to be married, a similar atmosphere prevails. The union of lovers can be painful on a multitude of levels.

However, there is much that is joyful and positive about this path, particularly at its onset. The card itself depicts Adam and Eve in Eden before the Fall. Raphael hangs behind them, both of his hands raised in protective blessing. Tiphareth in Assiah fills the garden with warmth and growth. They are naked and relaxed. Eve looks upwards, indicative of her spirituality, while Adam looks at Eve, presumably thinking how appealing she looks. Between them in the background lies a dark phallic mound, above which hang billowing clouds which touch both Adam and Eve on the head. They are conjoined by the mist of their lack of knowledge, entirely innocent at this stage. The serpent also watches Eve from the apple tree. His head is within striking distance of her neck.

The card is full of rainbow color, just like the world when we are in love. Everything is beautified by this perspective; for a moment we glimpse God in another person, and through that feeling we perceive God in everything. Of all intoxicants, the drug of love must be the most potent. It gives spiritual and physical inspiration, aspiration, strength, and confidence. As Robert Graves knew, the relationship with the human Muse is a relationship with the Goddess. The human lover might change, but the element essential to inspire love—the channel to the God(dess)—remains. In being in love, we are attempting to sublimate Malkuth into Kether, or at least into Tiphareth. It can never be sustained; the personalities of the participants inevitably interfere eventually. But just occasionally, in the eyes of another, we behold the divine, and this is one of the purposes of being here in Malkuth. (Witches regularly reaffirm this divinity by calling down the God or Goddess quite consciously into the priest and priestess. To the best of my knowledge, Wiccan marriages or handfastings rarely end in disillusionment; if they come to a natural end, it is with loving respect that partners decide to let one another go forward.)

Twin souls—such as lovers are, at least initially (and on some levels, permanently)—are represented by the symbol of Gemini.

The Roman god of the Old and New Years, Janus, is also relevant, with his two faces on one head, each looking in a different direction. Both are reminiscent of Plato's idea of man and woman originally forming one superunit, possessed of formidable powers.

When this card appears in a reading, it often means that a love affair is either taking place or pending, but it is not always a straightforward matter. Depending on the positions of the other cards and the intuition of the interpreter, it can imply that an important decision needs to be made, often regarding a severing of attachments—*Zayin*, the sword, may be required. In *The Mythic Tarot* the scenario is that of Paris being forced to chose between the lovely but shallow Aphrodite, intellectual Athena, and powerful, vengeful (but charming) Hera. Poor boy! He cannot put a foot right for doing wrong—a proclivity towards any goddess in particular will mortally offend the others. This is an example of the sort of dilemma that might be faced on this path; the choice between people or situations of equally appealing value, all very different. In the end Paris was goaded into making a choice, and the Trojan War was the result! Hopefully not all decisions made on this path will have such dire consequences.

Traditionally, the card often represented the choice between family and lover, the sword thus effecting the healthy cutting of childhood ties and initiation into adulthood. It cuts the umbilical cord that binds child to mother, both physically at birth and emotionally throughout childhood.

Adam and Eve lost their childlike innocence and associated themselves with matter rather than spirit. Their independence was thus asserted, and though the implications were doubtless bad, the increase in their knowledge cannot be denied. So this is very much a process of personality development, of growing up and "getting real," as well as of love and its psychological effects. It is the safety of childhood we are "disposing" of when we tread the seventeenth path, with its pretty illusions and belief in being the center of the universe. The sting of reality was felt in Eden, and unfortunately it is felt here too. It is, perhaps, meant to jab us into seeking the only permanent love: that of God, the Cosmic Intelligence.

## Getting from Chesed to Chokmah
### "The Triumphal Intelligence"
#### PATH 15

This is a Taurean path, thus also connecting it with Netzach, the sphere of natural power. Bulls are sacred to Jove/Jupiter, confirming that its lifeblood flows from Chesed. Its Hebrew symbol is *Vau* (ו), meaning "nail," another ferrous item. Iron is sacred to the twenty-seventh path—between Hod and Netzach, intellect and energy—both of which are relevant to the experience of the fifteenth path. Here, the higher self vies for power with the animal instinct, though one can be sure so high up the Tree that this is in a fairly elevated sense.

The card ascribed is the Hierophant, or Pope—but I infinitely prefer its allocation to Chiron, King of the Centaurs, which may be found in *The Mythic Tarot*. He is the archetypal wounded healer, his horse's body allying him with the natural world and instinctual (re)action, while his man's head and upper body lend transcendent understanding and aspiration. He is also half-mortal, half-celestial, reminiscent of the Hermit as a cave dweller of solitary nature. Like a typical Taurean he is hard working, and both Hierophants are erudite. The scroll held in the Centaur's hand reflects this, while in the *Rider-Waite* deck two crossed keys sit at the pontiff's feet. The doors he will help us to open are both intellectual and spiritual.

Nails, as the implements used to pin Christ to the cross, have obvious significance to the theme of self-sacrifice. Chiron, though mortally wounded, is a healer; and (theoretically) clergy and popes should put others before themselves. The blood-red robes of the Papal Hierophant refer to the Passion of Christ, a passion different to that of Netzach in that it is not corporeal, but similar in that it reflects a lust for life, in this case the lives of others. The white of the Hierophant's sleeves, hems, and feet is intended to represent this fundamental purity, this complete lack of ego. It is in this sense—of high aims presiding over physical pain and other concerns—that the path is "triumphal."

The wisdom represented by the traditional allocation is that of the established body of learning. In a reading, the card may indicate the Christian Church and institutions such as marriage, or some other long-established organization that carries with it an aura of fear and sanctity. This can take the form of a school with a reputation for excellence, a university, or even a successful business (usually a very big company). Such places have figures of authority who are often austere and lofty, and a strict sense of hierarchy pervades the atmosphere. It is for the newcomer to work their way from the bottom of the heap to the top, proving their worth as they rise. The sort of plodding effort for which earth signs are so famed is exactly what is needed on this path. Its ultimate goal, after all, is Chokmah, wisdom, and that never comes cheap.

One of the main fruits of this path (as any, in its own way) is the improvement of magickal ability—in this case, of the power behind it. The color of the path is indigo, recalling Yesod, the dreamy Sephirah whose creative capacity is so essential to effective magick. The image is the vessel that carries the will, and it is the power of the Netzachian bull that sustains it.

The essential feature of the sixteenth path is that of external esotericism: doctrine, ritual, and hierarchy. A spiritual pecking order may be established on the Outer Planes, but on the Inner, the superiority complex will drag one to a downfall. It is, after all, the humble Fool who finds his way to Kether, in the end.

# Getting from Tiphareth to Chokmah
## "The Constituting Intelligence"
### PATH 15

The fifteenth path is also concerned with established order, in this case the deeply "constitutional" aspects represented by the Emperor. The Hebrew letter is *Heh* (ה), meaning "window," and the astrological sign that of Aries, the Ram. Two ram's heads on the Emperor's throne face the onlooker, while two are seen in profile on its back. Four is significant both as the number of the trump and as the numerological equivalent of the traits represented by its figure; those solid qualities of the well-established, benevolent patriarch.

Behind the enthroned Emperor are mountains such where a goat or ram might feel at home. The rocky terrain suggests that the Emperor has conquered much in order to establish his kingdom. His white beard indicates experience, and recalls the Hermit, upon whose snowy locks is now placed the crown of worldly achievement. It may seem topsy-turvy to have the Emperor and Empress, both of whom are so obviously established in Malkuth, near to the top of the Tree, but it is significant that the world of the spirit must be mastered before true success in the material world may be established. Besides which, both are of godly proportions, the Emperor representing Jupiter, Thor, Zeus, and any number of father gods, and the Empress Demeter, Laksmi, and all the stately females of the pantheons.

The image of the Emperor in *The Tarot of the Old Path* is particularly pleasing, depicting a very dapper-looking chap, more like a crowned musketeer than a middle-aged emperor, his legs in a position suggestive of recent or intended action. I like the dynamism of this image, for the Emperor is not at the end of his reign but still implementing change. With children playing in the background and lots of green and growth indicated, it suggests the futurity which is so essential to this path. "Constituting" it is indeed, but the whole point of constitutions is that they last, generation after generation. This is the Ten of Pentacles (relevant to Malkuth) carried into the spiritual realms; the attainment of material desire, the ability to use it to the betterment of others. Like Chesed it is ruled by benevolent masculine force (by masculine I refer to the traditional sense of Apollonian learning: the founding of citadels, the establishment of a logical order that provides the framework for other, perhaps more ethereal or imaginative, lives). Yesod offers a glimpse of the machinery of the universe, and the fifteenth path offers a glimpse at the machinery of the constitutions upon which spiritual growth is founded.

The regal aspects of the Emperor reflect Tiphareth, the most royal of Sephiroth. As the sun casts light on the obscurest nooks and crannies of our globe, so does the Emperor's beady eye, courtesy of the falcon sitting on his shoulder, assimilate every small detail of his kingdom. In order to provide effective rule, it must. Of course, the falcon is both an object of fancy to the ruler, who employs it as sport, and a merciless bird of prey. Any socialist would point out that a royal personage is also a predator, or at least springs from a line of them; the Emperor would fight to preserve his position, though he is hopefully beyond trying to unfairly increase it. Despite the fact that Aries is ruled by Geburan Mars, there is little aggression in the card as allocated here on the Tree, though the Emperor is bound to be somewhat jingoistic at times. After all, he needs to buoy his people up, make them feel proud that they are living in his domain. Though pride in one's origin and native country is perfectly natural, it is only healthy when accompanied by an appreciation of other peoples' as well—so any jingoism felt while working the path is to be transcended, not nurtured!

The letter *Heh*, symbolized by a window, again shows this quality of sight, of perspective. From the window of the fifteenth path we view the territory in which we live and breathe, and our small but significant place in this microcosmic scheme of things.

The ruby red of the Emperor's clothes recalls that of the Hiero-phant, but here the implications are different. One might go so far as to say that they are the color of spilt blood, as wars were fought in the establishment of this empire. Its stability, however, suggests that further bloodshed may be avoided through obedience to benevolent rule. Situations such as the French Revolution arise when the ruler is detached from the ruled. In *The Tarot of the Old Path* it is particularly evident that the Emperor is both involved with his people and active in their welfare. So are happy kingdoms established on all levels, that we may progress happily ever after!

# Getting from Tiphareth to Kether
## "The Uniting Intelligence"
### PATH 13

On this path, the Abyss of Daath is crossed. The High Priestess, the card corresponding to this journey, must prove herself worthy of the title. If she is to be successful, she must cling to her integrity despite the effects of Tiphareth's Qlipoth, who are likely to plague her in the form of false spiritual hopes, false dawns, and masculine bullying—often using a human vehicle to express themselves.

In the *Rider-Waite* deck she wears the equal-armed cross of Tiphareth on her breast, but here it is white, lunar, purified. Outer Plane energies go very much into remission on this path, and though outer circumstances may go crazy when it is being worked, the High Priestess responds mainly on the inner. She is the most tacit, tentative of Tarot characters, her only interest (at least, at this point) the development of her occult prowess and higher understanding of the universe.

Crowned with a full moon or globe between silver horns—recalling the Egyptian Hathor and Isis—she sits in sky-blue robes between the left-hand Pillar of Severity, which is black and marked with a *B*, and the right-hand Pillar of Mercy, white with a *J*. The letters refer to *Boaz* and *Joachim*, which are the names given ie twin columns in the Temple of Solomon. Why these columns were named at all is mysterious, but their presence here obviously reflects the balanced rule of the divinely appointed leader.

Behind her hangs a cloth depicting pomegranates, a reference to Persephone as *Kore*, Queen of the Underworld, and behind that may be glimpsed the sea. At the feet of the High Priestess lies a crescent moon, recalling Selene, Artemis, and other new moon goddesses. A scroll sits in her hands, partially concealed by her cloak. It bears the word "TORA," and refers to the Jewish Torah, or perhaps the system of learning found in the Tarot, both of which representing esoteric knowledge. It is not entirely visible, like the subject itself. Some is deliberately concealed, other aspects inferred. Even though we cannot see the rest of the scroll (or life), we know it is there.

This route bears a strong connection to the Moon card, as all of its prime deities are moon goddesses, and the aspect of instinct remains. However, where those on the moon path barely know whether their next step is onto a shadow or into a crater, the High Priestess is well aware of her every move. She is more like the moon herself than the effects caused by the moon; she has an overview, she is reflective, she contemplates while the world is dark and others sleep.

The relevant Hebrew letter is *Gimel* (ג), meaning "camel." The main feature of the camel is that it carries its sustenance on its back, just as the High Priestess must be self-sustaining. She will require refreshment from hidden sources on this difficult journey, and the strength to carry the weight of what she encounters, as help will be nowhere to be found. At times this may even feel like the weight of sin, a hunchbacked deadweight, for the process of the thireenth path is very exacting. Issues from the past haunt her like phantasms; unresolved dilemmas run their tingle-fingers up and down her spine at night. Unknown spirits tip-tap at her chakras.

THE REMAINING PATHS 251

This path can certainly be classed as one of the Qabalah's "dark nights of the soul." However, as its ultimate goal is Kether, it is not surprising that the route is a testing one. Nothing but purity finds admittance to Kether, and the resulting freedom after the painful confines of the thirteenth path is a bliss in itself. Though the Magician attains Kether through brilliant true magick, and the Fool through childlike confidence, it is the Priestess path that is perhaps the most natural to us in Western society. We are not nurtured in a manner conducive to the Magician within, though many a Renaissance incarnation worked this path; and as to the Fool's carefree innocence, few could lay claim to that when sober. The way of the Priestess, however, is a path of therapy, intense introspection, and correction, and thus befits our psychological training. It may not be right, but the fact is we have been taught that the path of spirituality is a stony one, and with all the imposed psychological warps of society, it will take some effort for its members to look for the divinity within, revere the God/Goddess in everyone, and accept responsibility for their own actions. The latter is the true meaning of karma: cause and effect.

One of the animals sacred to this process is the dog; a creature obviously affected by the moon, and one that used to be sacrificed to Hecate in order to gain her favor. The triple aspects of the Moon Goddess as maiden, mother, are crone are amply demonstrated: Selene, Kore (as "mother" to the dead), and Hecate, to name but one combination. This is very much a process of growing up, of taking on a spiritual burden and then being relieved of it; even a very young Priestess will feel like an old woman, at times, on this path. Hecate is one of its protectors, and it is she who initiates the participant into each new stage of the journey.

The thirteenth path is "uniting" because it joins Tiphareth, sphere of individuality, with Kether, sphere of spirit. The quest is to maintain individuality without ego. It unites all of the aspects of our being, and results in a fit channel for the Goddess.

The psychism encountered on this journey will be selfless; questions regarding one's own destiny will misfire and cause grief. However, mediumship relevant to others will transpire, healing should flow freely, and a great deal of good may be done for others, while the practitioner suffers within. A very purifying process, and very Binah! Of course there is a strong relationship between the Superior Mother and the Isian Mother Superior in this process of receptivity, understanding, and compassion. The path of the Empress crosses that of the High Priestess, offering a little help along the way—even if it be the mere thought of happier times, the outside world, and unconditional love. Persephone in the Underworld must have felt just this breeze of sun-scented air when she thought of her mother Demeter and the sure fact that they would see one another again, someday. Those working this path may comfort themselves with the knowledge that the ineffable sunlight of Kether grows ever closer.

## Getting from Binah to Kether

### "The Transparent Intelligence"

PATH 12

The Hebrew letter of relevance is *Beth* (ב), meaning "house." The house usually contains all of our worldly effects, from the personal and fanciful to the essential, and more often than not represents the sum total of ones time on earth. Importantly, it is also the sanctuary, the place of inner life. Within the privacy of our own four walls, we can be ourselves. Chances are, the Magician would not go out of doors looking and feeling the way he appears in the card: robed in red, with a white tunic and headband—certainly his modern representative would save the ritual robes and melodrama for home and temple! So, this path epitomizes what is personal and free from the critical eye of society; it is a path in which trust is possible, confidence felt. Here, we are "at home" with our inner nature.

Quite right too, so close to Kether: like his counterpart on the eleventh path, the Fool, the Magician is cavalier in his attitude to conventional concerns. As Hermes and Mercury he shows the feisty streak of the trickster; he cares not one jot what others think of him. He knows what he wants, and he is sure to get it. The brilliant white of his robes show that he has passed the spiritual tests that give him the right to be so certain. The red of his robes show sacrifice in the past; his achievements are the fruit of a great deal of labor. The red also indicates an animal instinct, now reduced to a wrap for convenience, decoration. His will controls every part of his nature.

We have already looked at the imagery of this card in depth in the Malkuth section, but let us revisit the Magician's symbols briefly. On the table before him are the tools representative of all the elements: wand, sword, pentacle, and chalice, and he holds aloft another wand, his left hand pointing towards earth. Clearly he is channelling energies, directing them through his body. About his waist is an ouroboros serpent, a symbol of infinity. The sideways eight that also represents the eternal hovers above his head.

Flowers grow in the foreground of the card, lilies and roses alike, representing Netzachian energy, Ketheric purity, and the cultivation of spiritual arts.

His intelligence is "transparent" because the Magician can see "through" everything now, through the layers of illusion that veil the godhead. Nothing is real to him but the spirit and forces of spirit.

As Mercury is both a godform attributed and the astrological sign of this path, we may conclude that Hod, Sephirah of Mercury, is strongly affiliated with it. The Magician is an intermediary between gods and mortals; he walks shamanically between worlds, mixing the energies of each with craft and ease. He travels like quicksilver, fluent in all the tricks of the trade. He communicates, translating the language of the celestial into terrestrial form, a typical feature of Hod. Likewise is he conversant in the protocol and established order of the Mercurial sphere.

Recalling that the name of this path is *Beth,* "house," it is interesting to note the domestic aspect of Hermes. As servant to the Olympian gods, kindler of fires, chef, and cupbearer, he represents domestic order. His competence at apparently menial tasks is significant to the Magician, who unless (s)he has toiled as a neophyte will never attain to the grade of *Ipsissimus* ("utter master") represented by Kether.

As a thief he also steals into the houses of others; indeed, in one Homeric hymn his half-brother Apollo accuses Hermes, not unreasonably, of "stripping more than one poor wretch bare this night." Apollo has already lost his herd to Hermes in the famous comic scenario, and though he attained the lyre from the event, his wariness is wise. Though a good shepherd and handy man-about-Olympia, Hermes is a law unto himself.

Hermes is also known in his capacity as psychopomp to lead the spirits of the dead to their rightful abode—another "house" connection. He is connected both with the Persephone myth and that of Orpheus and Eurydice, in which instance he guides Eurydice "home" to the Underworld once Orpheus has blown it by turning to look at her. He likewise leads those who have difficulty in parting from their living loved ones into the chthonic regions of Hades—hopefully with a kind word or two. He is, after all, a diplomat par excellence.

The Magician's affiliations with Binah are harder to trace. His nature is very different to that of Binah: where she is internal, he externalizes; where she is dark and restrictive, he shines like Apollo and moves about with expansive ease. However, as a high-grade initiate, he knows Binah, and has moved through her processes. He may not be like her, but he has swum her psychic seas and knows her currents. He is the action that links Binah with the Primal Source; he recognizes her as the origin of many of the elements that constitute him. She is the base, and Kether, of course, is the goal.

# The Remaining Tarot Cards

Kings, Queens, Knights, and Pages are ascribed to the four worlds of
Atziluth, Briar, Yetzirah, and Assiah, respectively. As mentioned
previously, the Emperor and Empress are often closely associated
with Atziluth and Briar, which is understandable owing to their
greater regal status. But this convention messes up the Tarot pattern somewhat. It seems to me quite fitting that the court cards
should represent the realms of existence, the Pages obviously learning and active in the material plane, the Knights dynamic and protective in the mental, the Queens presiding over the formative
world, and the Kings representing the archetypal or conceptual.

# A Qabalistic Tale

## Malkuth

*T*he bride was sitting in such a position that the blues and greens of the stained glass window melted across her face and the sacred rose shone on her forehead like a *bindi*, but she was not aware of the precise aesthetics of the imposed pattern. She was drinking in the color like an elixir, praying for strength, praying that her feet would not be noticed. Beneath the antique lace of her wedding dress were the appendages that were her disgrace, always tightly clad in lace-up Victorian boots, never before revealed. Today, however, she must go discalced, a symbol of surrender. Nobody would deny that the bride looked stunning.

Incense wafted from the drapes, trapped there for perhaps a hundred years or more, the sylphs and zephyrs of this day the ones to release it. She could see the candles responding to their handiwork, the salamanders flickering with glee, making the wax course faster, faster, like unstoppable tears. Though a newcomer might say it was empty, she could see that the chapel was busy, performing elaborate tricks of the light, the black pillar shadowed one minute, the next minute white, crowded with blithe spirits who were here for the show, entertained by the spectacle of a sacrosanct space preparing itself for this union. She turned her grandmother's ring on her middle finger, as she always did when nervous.

The physical guests would be arriving soon. She worried about Malach. He detested churches so, a spot of melodrama he had developed from conversing with her familiars from an early age. They had egged him on, amused by his pliancy, quite unlike his mother. She was an exacting mistress, always in control. Until now.

Surreptitiously she removed her boots, fingers fumbling with laces long-tied.

She shuffled her bare feet under the pew, causing a scratching sound which reminded her of rats beneath the floor boards. *Not a particularly pleasant wedding day allusion,* shrieked the Scottish witches across the aisle, who never missed a trick. *Hubby will be here soon, and you should be thinking on love, not rodents, dearie!*

Yes, indeed.

Rise through matter. Rise.

She wriggled the monstrosities back into their rind of convention, hoping that the hem of her dress would not let her down. She would walk in mincing steps like a little lady, a living doll, and her feet need never show. She would rely on the organist's cacophony to conceal her audible disgrace, the feral scrape of claw on stone.

The organ sounded out with a blast which made her gasp for breath. The peacock-colors slid off her face and she was pale, petite, quite an ordinary girl, albeit one in shock. A man in black, definitely human, was bent over the keyboard, utterly immune to her presence, having a quick practice. The bell tolled ten.

Time to go, to clear the way.

She stood up, feeling the cold through the soles of her shoes, her small white hands, mostly hidden by creamy lace, preparing to grab the nearest pew should she slip. In her mind's hypersensitive eye her claws scraped down the aisle, while in fact she clip-clopped quite nicely into the tiny vestry and out onto the angelica-green grass of the graveyard.

She waited round the back, plonked in all her finery on the gentle slope of the cemetery, close to the stream. She thought of the inhabitants of the tombs, of how they bide their time. She thought of them rising, rising, pale and intent on the merest hint of a trumpet, a chink of salvation. Rising from the cold tomb to be born again, this time to be supported.

Barely a traditional bridal antechamber, true, but it befitted her needs. The undines delighted her ear with Enochian babble, like Eden before the Fall. The sun and moon made themselves known, casting her at the center of their sacred circle. *You have evoked me,* she thought. Then, *All creation has been invoked. What is the Magician's will? Show us the way, we wish only to please.* The tiniest flicker of an ironic smile hovered at the edge of her mouth, and vanished. *Let us be what we are best at being.*

Down the black-and-white tiles of the Temple of Malkuth strode the groom, his best man bringing light in the shape of a lamp, both of them very righteous and erect in their spotless morning suits and top hats. The groom, smelling of wood and spices, was dressed in black but for his green shirt, red shoes, and yellow carnation. The glamourous crowd sighed in appreciation, the hearts of the women beating with butterfly's wings, heads tilted sideways. From obscure nooks elfin eyes peeked excitedly. What a lovely altar, with its thick smoke, elegant golden cross, silver chalice, ritual sword, and pentacle altar cloth! The priest flicked his wand towards the choir stalls.

The organ intoned the beginning of the bridal march, and a frisson of excitement passed through the assembly. Necks hitherto smooth developed tendons like twisted trunks of trees as eyes green, blue, and brown turned to rest on the vestry.

*Here comes the bride.*

*Here comes the bride, see how she slides.*

Scritch-scratch on her owl's feet she approaches the altar, a bouquet of graveyard weeds in her hands, eyes veiled, yet vulnerable.

*Will imperfection be accepted?*

Beneath the freshly plucked ground, the local dead echo her question. When Gabriel calls them to pass through Judgment, will he be exacting, cruel as Yahweh, or merciful of their faults? Despotic overlord or gentle teacher?

She watches her handsome man, awaiting his reaction, fear veiled.

The smooth solid groom turns Netzachian eyes on her, and smiles. Malach groans from his grandfather's side, but really he is glad. He has seen his mother humiliated before, and though a paternal authority figure is anathema to him, he does not wish to witness the demise of blushing bride into public laughing-stock. Despite the imposed frills of his vestments, he is glad he is here to witness something going right for his mother for once.

The priest wears both dog collar and antlers—this is a progressive church. Or, to tell it truly, he wears astral antlers, visible to most of the assembly, but not to those sundry persons one always feels obliged to invite to such occasions; the land-ladies and hair-dressers and old school friends with whom one shares nothing but memories of companionable tedium. To these, all seems quite ordinary, except, that is, for the strange bouquet of bindweed and— is it groundsel?—surely not. The graveyard weeds. But then she always was a queer bird.

She stands at the altar, relieved beyond description. *Redeemed,* she thinks. Her pseudo-feminist friends would shriek if they heard that: *redeemed by marriage, by a man?* But of course the male body was merely symbolic. This husband-to-be was knitting her to the material world while allowing her freedom in the spiritual realms. Allowing? It's a fact. He is flesh of my flesh, and I need that to operate down here. Meantime, spirit flies up through aethyrs towards celestial light. Abridged version, of course.

" . . . to be my lawful wedded wife . . . "

*He smiles into my eyes. He doesn't mind about my feet.*

" . . . till death do us part."

Sniggers from the discarnate wedding guests, inevitably. *Concentrate. My turn now. No obeying, of course, but lots of sincerity.*

"I, Kallah von Binah, do take this . . . to be my Holy Guardian Angel . . ."

The belfry chimes out twelve of its best, and the miscellaneous jangle of wedding bells fills the air.

They step out into the purple-gray path, rice and confetti getting caught in their hair. The crowds cheer, and Malach smiles sulkily at his mother. She smiles back, radiant in her ascension. Proudly she bears the mark of scorn long-passed. The elementals and the light-bearing best man sparkle with merriment.

And now the crescent moon is risen in the purple sky, and it is time to move on.

## Yesod

She lies on her back, spellbound. A silver chalice of moon juice, a third of it spilled, sits nearby, pomegranate pips floating in its liquid pearlescence.

Her husband strokes her hand, doting, somewhat smug. *My love,* he whispers.

Delicate lace and softest velvet, visible drifts of musk like layered clouds, bed scattered with rose petals and endlessly falling, and a smile of love which would make a paradise of the Abyss. The bridal chamber is enchanted by scent and sound, color, and texture, all forms of silver and violet and sensual pleasure. Bells in the dark window liven the air, silhouetted by the moon, the indigo sky. Candles burn in silver chandeliers, nine to each cluster, their flames wild and lithe. A censer hisses as it devours another lump of gum. Eastern aromas flood the room.

Melodic chanting provides a backdrop to the words of promise which issue from her dark lover's mouth—poetry mostly, his or someone else's—it matters not what he is saying, but merely how he says it. Their naked bodies are beginning to dissolve, not into one another, but quite literally, limbs now lines of illumination, mostly white, some auric interference, shades of blue and green and purple and so on, but mostly brilliance uninhibited by such specifics. Their flesh is getting very thin, and lighter and lighter while also falling into the bed or whatever lies beyond it, their arms now entwined, the moon turning purple, eyes shutting in soporific surrender. . . .

She kicks off the silver sandals she has employed to prevent scratching the ebony floorboards, kicks them off in her sleep, and they fall like molten moonlight, like shooting comets in some other person's universe. Drifting higher on the perfumed air, held fast by Malkuth but no longer inhibited by him, she rises, following the call of Gabriel. He blows a golden trumpet, and some of those whose flowers she stole earlier rise up with her, raising grateful arms towards the graceful Archangel, stretching them for the first time in what feels like aeons, rising up and up and up through the planes.

An eagle swoops above the airy plateaux at which spirits collect, an astral layer of the living dead being ushered back from Limbo. She knows this destiny can never be hers: it belongs to those who do not live to learn, but live to die, who know no whisper of immortality. "Once-borns" she calls them, at least before they reach this stage. *Chances are, the Ashim will give them a second chance now, set them on the Wheel.* At least they have made the effort to rise out of their graves, and the Angels never ignore human endeavor, it being what they wish and work for.

Over and beyond, and now she is alone with just the purple seas and pink clouds streaked with menstrual red. She travels, searching. A moon, a silver huntress, a mother, a triple-faced hag. She rides a dog-star through the empyrean and reaches a Planet of Women.

These figures are tidal and infinitely perceptive, they are held in the sway of the deities. Others dance, beckoning wheat and shy shoot from the darkness with rhythms of promise and pleasure. Some sit in shafts of golden sunlight teasing answers from complex dilemmas, exchanging thought and concept with a minimum of fuss, sure-thrusters like the Queen of Swords, precise in every detail. Others wander in gardens of silver and yew, holding hands in labyrinths, exchanging Sapphic whispers, fluttering with love tokens and billets-doux, giggling, coy, playful as kittens. But what of these?

She grows impatient. Yesod is replete with sidetracks, distractions. *Get to the point!*

What is the point? It is one in three, or three in one: pick a dream, any dream. A fantasy will carry you, but to employ the power, first find the root. What is the root of this mandrake dream? Solid Hod will rebuff illusion . . . so go find Hod.

Get behind, behind. You will drift forever on the illusory waves of Yesod, lulled by the steady breathing of yourself, your partner's breathing, lying on your backs enwrapped, floating on a thousand million possibilities of every thought. To get to the root, go beyond.

# Hod

She breathes. It is like going to work the day after a sabbat. The power has shifted, now she cannot be drifty, prophetic, but must be logical, sane, disenchanted. Cynicism is the best antidote to Yesod, a real party-killer, with the smell of the incense still in her hair and the silver power of Hecate glinting in her eye she concentrates on the external. Not quite the external of Malkuth, which is very general, but the precise academic channels of dogmatic Hod. Communication, debate, lecture, and tutorial, these are necessary to train the brain, the soul. Discipline.

Forget the perfume and silver sandals that fell through space, forget the happy couple who fell from grace. *Let's analyze them.*

Her husband sits before her, very earnest. She looks him straight in the eyes, ignoring their sparkling mahogany irises in favor of the cool blank stare that is like parchment waiting to be written on. Upon the virgin page she draws a black caduceus, concentrating on every detail, every scale, every twist and twine of serpentine intellect. He smiles, respecting her skill. Quick as a flash he responds with his own sigil of explanation, a condensation of some celestial truth, some proof of mind over matter, the mercurial swiftness of a demigod, no less. She laughs. Take that, she says, producing an antidote to his intellectual serum in milliseconds. It is a trick, but he may not notice. She waits to see. It has worked.

The game of cerebral chess continues well into the evening, but then it is time for bed. Glad of the respite he chases her up the winding staircase, clapping his hands as he goes. She shrieks and streaks ahead. He grins. *Time to get her back,* he thinks peskily. *In Netzach I can spook and double-dare her.* Radiant Michael laughs, holding hands with Haniel across the power-stricken way. *Travel carefully,* he bids them, *And with faith.* Haniel awaits.

A nightmare of incongruous circumstance follows.

Their bower is struck by lightning. (*A terrible omen for our wedding night,* she thinks.) Fire cracks the mirror and blackens the chamber, eating up the beautiful drapes and turning her lace to rags. The lovely musky spirits flee to some more pleasant place, and melodramatic demons flock by for a laugh. All becomes jagged and strange, and the young bride develops a cold sore right in the middle of her ruby-red lips.

"It's the stress," she explains. "My blood is boiling up!"

She thinks he is looking at her with disdain, revolted by her weakness, her physical appearance or some such. *He will leave me now,* she moans internally. *How can he rejoice in being wed to someone like stupid me?*

As she thinks this, her hair turns from rich red-brown to gray, and her face ages by a hundred years or more. She can see it in the shattered mirror of their room. Her groom, still clutching a chess piece from their earlier tryst, seems not to notice. Is he stupid? She asks herself—and if so, what horror! For she is pledged to him now. She turns teary eyes to him, and hot salt drips to her crow's feet.

"Do you love me?" she whinges neurotically. "Even now that I am old and gray?"

"Are you?"

"Yes, you idiot, look. What shall I do?"

He turns eyes of love on her, but she determines to make him see. *Take me in all my imperfections* is her silent plea. She stares at him with such determination, such self-disgust, and such manic snake's eyes that he does indeed see, and he is shocked. She is revolting, casting herself in such a moldering mold, feathers of fungus where once were lustrous lashes, a gaping blackness where once were violet-sweet teeth and fresh breath as of a virgin!

Still, a knight he is, a champion to the Goddess. He knows the many guises of womanhood, her power, her faults, her everlasting magick. Smiling, he kisses the hag that had been his young bride, kisses her on the wrinkled, bitter lips in the parched room that had been a silver and violet bower, he sups the breath of the bearded hag in scorched rags in a stricken tower no longer a bower. And he smiles. His Lady is once again a lithe and *fèrique* child.

# Netzach

They run hand-in-hand through a strange elfin land. She wears a dress that leaves nothing to the imagination, secure now in his love, her perfection enhanced by the certainty of his commitment. She breathes the scent of his skin, warm spice, and woods, incense to her senses, a foundation from which to project the fantasies of her individual will. Here, though they are one, she is beginning to perceive that they are also very different, each with their own race to be and run. While she is sun and moon, he seems to be being absorbed into the element of Earth, attuned to Venus, first noticing the bright planet as they walked, now breathing love breath on her neck and talking of procreation. She thinks it is too soon. She already has Malach, and must return to him soon enough. She does not yearn to create others like her, as he does. She hopes it will not re-invoke the Tower, her defiance of his urges. He smiles, emollient, serene. *I'm in no hurry, Lady*, he says. *I was born under the sign of the Ox. I can wait.*

The Leo in her insists on stoking the fire. All must be processed, all cleansed. So, despite the fragrant emerald-green grass, the soft Netzachian sunlight shed by compassionate Tiphareth, the lure of brown eyes filled with love, the roses shining from tangle thicket, she presses on.

*I am becoming a nag*, she thinks, but she cannot help herself. *He is mine now, this little slice of perfection, this passport to Eternity. He is mine and I must know him.*

So as they cruise hand-in-hand the mounded gateways of faery land, talking of Puckish sprites and Naiads and Nature Muses, of spooks and witches and spirits of the forest, she tries to break him. Silly girl, but she cannot help herself. She is still held fast in the naked arms of Malkuth, remember.

His pentagram revolves from day to night. What had been spirit upright becomes spirit in plight. Below the elements it rests, victim of forces external. He grows thin and pained, even here in Netzach, where love is famed. Sometimes they glide together, featherlight in Venusian night, Sir Gawain and radiant Lady Ragnell, the world put to rights. At other times they follow lampen light to faery bower where Christian concept is not yet conceived, and time stands still. A single tear might then be glimpsed between his long dark lashes and his sensual lips. She catches it, a pearl, and treasures it. No faery jape or goblin deal will part her from this talisman so dear, replete with green ray energy, so sweet and filled with faery fiddle music, a fertility rite condensed and sublimated in his eyes.

They dance together in circular motion, their moves marked out with standing stone and arcane statue guarded by hoary elementals, ancients even to their kind. The Quarters make themselves known, as do the gods and goddesses, those of Olympia, Avalon, Kam, and the like. Pantheons are united here, together as if never parted. What can they do?

*Sweet Lilith, never let me go.*

But Lilith is a demon by any other name, and her fate is sealed.

*We require a greater light,* she says. *Something less glamoured, less transient. The sun there: that's the way.*

And so the couple resolve to follow the sun.

## Tiphareth

The prophet stood in the street in rags, speaking but rarely listened to. He was heard by random passers-by, who picked at his wisdom and crafted it to their needs, but his meanings were seldom hearkened.

He was a true prophet, more's the pity: a humble-looking man, his beggar's body disguising a soul of genius. He had "been there and done that," Qabalistically speaking and on all other levels; in the right environment he could have guided many souls into the light. However, aside from throwing the odd pentacle into his upturned hat, most of the populace centred their attention on another speaker, an impressive-looking Buddha-bellied chap, golden skinned with an aura as bright as the sun itself. This man never begged. He did not need to. People willingly gave up an entire year's wages, all the corn in their store houses, all of their pigs and cattle for a few words of advice from this Lord of Beneficence. With his stentorian voice, commanding eyes and indubitable ability to perform magic and miracles, they felt sure the investment was a sensible one.

The warped prophet, his gnarled hands always supplicating passers by to listen, even when they had rejected him a hundred times before, caught the eye of our young bride, and instantly a rapport sparkled between them. Her husband, still in love, placed five bright pentacles in his cap, and went to move on.

"Stop!" whispered the honeymooning woman. "We ought to listen to this man. I feel he may have something for us."

"For you, and all the rest of this creation," creaked the rusty oracle.

The handsome husband was rendered momentarily unattractive by ennui, a danger to all Taureans.

"All right, my love," he sighed, only slightly exasperated. He would listen to the golden Buddha while his other half wasted her ear on the mendicant: neither would notice. He turned a humoring face on the couple and bent his ear to the flow of genius coming from his left.

". . . Osiris risen," he heard. ". . . And I have returned to teach you the pitfalls of the Underworld, so that you need not suffer when you are called into the Halls of the Assessors. Yes I, and only I, can show you how to nullify your karma, how to gain powers beyond human imagination, how to become immortal and empowered. . . ."

Even without looking, the husband could see the speaker's aura pulsating with light and life, sending out signals in etheric Morse code, black-white-black-white-white-white-black. Spiralling mandalas on the surface of his bodies, tiny vortexes of darkness leading to . . . where did they lead? He traced the source, gradually, gradually growing closer to the innermost essence of the guru-master-prophet. His eyes, meanwhile, remained fixed on the bearded mage before him.

The lusty young bride was listening to this man as she had never listened before. Her feet were turning from hideous claws into shapely flesh as she stood beautified by the grubby luminary, and she thought of young Malach, and how he and his generation could benefit from the simplicity of this creed.

"Love and be loved," squeaked the aged mystic. "Be always bathed in your own beauty, because believe me, all here are truly beautiful. I have been to Hades and seen the lost souls lodged there, and I have visited Christian Hell, where obscenity reigns in a manner unimaginable on earth. I have seen the ugly and the sad, the half-made and the unbegotten, the thoughts of darkness when the Abyss was gaping wide, and each here, even the most wretched of fake prophets contains more light than all of these fragments of creation put together. Never doubt that you are beautiful and cupped in the loving hands of the Creative Source. I come from Kether and Binah to tell you that you are treasured in the trove of creation, each of you a priceless immortal gem. The diamond is often covered by debris when it is unearthed, but that does not stop it from being perfect on the inside. You, too, are perfect, crystalline, durable."

The bride stood rapt, devotion flowing from every pore of her being, while the husband tranced out on the mesmerising fractals emanating from this Christ-Come-Again. She felt herself falling into the well of his wisdom in willing surrender, and wishing to reward him with means more than physical.

"Allow me to kiss you," begged the youthful beauty, "though my lips be not worthy."

"If you have listened well you will know that we are both worthy of such an exchange," reprimanded the crippled reject, his understated halo faintly visible to her inner vision. The aura of his direct neighbor, the expansive golden god, threatened to swamp them any moment, but she refused the champagne fizzles of his sidelong glances in favor of the stout ale of the lowly beggar-prophet.

She turned ruby lips to his unsavory cheek, brushing it with the bee-stung lovelies which so delighted her beau.

Awoken from his stupor, the latter leaped forward and attempted to rend the two asunder.

"How can you kiss THAT?" he shrieked. "Even the feet of the true Messiah would shrink from contact with you now, thou filthy courtesan of Shaitan!"

Tears welling instantly and clogging her capacity for speech, the wronged woman stood mute and shamed before the throng. Images of pyres clustered in her mind.

"Have you forgotten everything I just told you?" hissed the true prophet through a bubble of spittle. "Be not wretched, for in so doing you cast us all down."

The bride looked around, and indeed all present seemed to have come down a psychic peg or two since her indulgence in inferiority. The previously enchanted appeared slovenly, those rapt seemed gullible, and each and every one of the motley crew seemed in some way debased.

The husband, strong and steady as an ox, picked his bride up bodily and began to remove her from the scene of hostility. The disgruntled crowd murmured, their muse broken, the golden hour lost.

"These are examples of the male-female dynamic at its worst," boasted the expansive golden man. A wave of feminist approval washed him clean of doubt.

"He certainly knows which buttons to press," nodded the true Mage to his only believer. Across the prominent muscles of her solid husband's arms the young bride nodded and smiled in agreement. She knew that it did not matter whether he received her confirmation or not, he was bathed in celestial self-belief and cosmic approval, however hidden that might be. *Funny that the other man called himself "Occult," when all of his powers were open for all to see.* And as she thought this, a bolt of light shattered their consciousness for a moment.

Raphael, his resplendent wings outstretched, was upon them, radiating healing, broadcasting love as if his whole future depended on the promo. Michael was not so very far behind him, his cloak engulfing the world it seemed for a second, maybe more on reflection, and the young couple were united in a way that they never had been before. They were small clinging sparks in a fire of consciousness. Around them the blackness longed to engulf them, but for as long as there was spiritual matter for their flames to subsist off, the darkness was held at bay.

# Geburah

They were carried to a chariot drawn by two shiny-coated sphinxes, one black, one white. The tethered animals were restless, pawing the earth and rolling their heads and eyes back, bristling with irate energy. No mysterious riddle-setters these, serene and aloof, but brute forces ready to devour those who had not the intelligence to avoid their path. Luckily for the potential victims their range was limited by their apparent inability to pull together in any particular direction.

Bride and groom were deposited inside the comfy carriage, and a set of reins placed in each of their laps. She had the white sphinx, and he had to try to control the black.

"Where are we going?" she asked reasonably. "We'd better decide that first."

"Home, of course," said the Angels. "Drive thee home."

The husband nodded his assent, and the animals instantly began to buck and rear in opposite directions. Grabbing the reins before they were flung out of reach, husband and wife felt their limbs nearly pulled from their sockets as they struggled to control the powerful pair.

"It would be much easier if they were in love!" screamed the woman.

"Very practical!" berated the man. "No, we need to control them, let them know who's boss."

She, however, was attempting to establish a psychic link with her sphinx in order to see what was upsetting it so. She summoned her familiars to help, and they were just about to make a breakthrough with the consciousness of the sphinx when the husband, who had found a whip, began to beat the animals. The enraged

steeds reared and roared, and the noise turned the hair of the ter-
rified passengers white. The momentarily exposed rows of blunt
teeth set in powerful jaws put mortal fear into their bones. A
whoosh of air, and the mighty animals were charging headlong
down an arid path dotted with lions and crawling with gigantic
serpents, dragging the rickety carriage and its helpless passengers
in their wake.

"See," said the man, rather more shakily than he would have
wished. "They're acting in unison now."

"Only in order to dispose of us!" cried the woman. "We'll crash
any minute if we don't slow them down."

Once the sphinxes had established a rhythm, however, they became again psychically accessible. This time she was taking no
risks. Catching her husband off-guard the young bride grabbed the
whip and flung it from the juddering carriage.

"What did you do that for?" he screamed, but she had already
slipped into a trance.

In the vision she approached the two creatures, who stood with
their backs to one another, noses in the air.

"Why will you not pull together except through necessity?" she
asked, but neither responded. She concentrated on the white
sphinx, and drew close to him, asking the same question. The animal, sure that only she could hear his reply, looked at her with
eyes clouded with tears. "She scares me," he said.

She approached the other sphinx and asked her the same question. Again, assured that her peer could not hear the answer, the
black sphinx replied, "He terrifies me. I see my own reflection in
him, yet strangely distorted, and my impulse is to flee."

The bride was surprised to find herself back in the teeth-chat-
tering vehicle, hurtling out of control towards annihilation. The
steeds were once again beginning to pull in opposite directions,
and disaster was pending. Husband and wife still held the reins,
but neither was effective.

"We need to steer together," she said. "Here, you take mine and I'll take yours for a while."

Holding the reins between her knees she pulled two mirrors from her wedding gown and held them high, so that each sphinx might see its own head reflected in the body of the other.

"Hmmm, he's quite a handsome beast really," mused the female of the species, and the male sphinx became filled with admiration for the fluent power of his partner. They began to move in unison again.

The Angels, who unbeknownst to our travellers, had been hovering above the carriage the entire time, guided the chariot out of the desert towards what looked like a walled medieval garden. The sign of Jupiter was painted on the portal in which they parked the enamoured sphinxes, and across the door in huge blue letters, "WELCOME."

## Chesed

The couple, still shaken from the ride, move gratefully into the open auric arms of the gardens of Chesed, which fill them with happiness and peace like a long-lost loved one's embrace. The aromatic lawns, healing herb gardens, and decorative shrubberies are as green as Netzach, the buttery light of Tiphareth blessing the plants with perpetual growth. Blue lakes of meditation soothe the grounds, while the sound of mantras provides the unshakeable spiritual energy by which the place is sustained.

Like a medieval tapestry, fair maidens and unicorns are woven into the scenery, each captured in perpetual perfection. *Incorruptible*, thinks our young bride wistfully. *How lovely to look always in the mirror and view unsullied beauty.* As she thinks this, her feet begin to twitch.

The couple walk down a path that is like an aisle, towards the castle of Jupiter. As they process they think of progeny, of having children of their own. She sends loving thoughts to Malach, and hopes he will appreciate some small additions to the family. *He is a good boy*, she reflects warmly. *Everything will be all right.* They find that they are holding hands.

The cheerfully festooned gates of the inner sanctum swing open as they approach, and the couple are surprised to find their wedding guests, with very few exceptions, gathered within.

"Malach!" cries the young bride, gathering her son into her arms. Looking over his small shoulder she beholds the smiling faces of all their families and loved ones past and present, and feels so intrinsically linked with the cosmic tribe that she wonders that she ever felt isolated. Unlike at earthly festivities she feels fluent with all. None are in competition, all are happy to be who they are, insecurity is a forgotten nightmare. The physical body stripped away and the astral and causal bodies exposed, all interactions are necessarily genuine.

The negative aspects of the past seem an illusion now, every ancient pain dissolving in the community cauldron, the physical version of which is awash with a vivifying fruit punch. Chalices are held in every hand, silver and gold ones studded with gems, each of them brimful of pleasure. The fermented fruits of past labor, supped in loving company, are a potent pro-life philosophy, she decides. Perhaps pain is worthwhile after all. Without it, this would not seem so good. She wouldn't swap these moments for anything.

She lolls happily against the chest of her universally approved partner, proud of him yet independent, glad to have such a handsome touchstone, glad to have her feet at last publicly dismissed as irrelevant. Ever since school she has lived in the shadow of her unsightly claws, but now all agree that they are of no issue. Love cures everything.

Big music fills the spaces between verbal exchange; the benevolent atmosphere expands wherever it is able, filling up every gap until the sense of community seems indubitable and loneliness a mad impossibility. Incense redolent of arcane tradition permeates the air, stabilizing rather than ethereal, like pipe smoke and coffee in an ancient library, or the scent of pine mingling with that of sherry on Christmas Eve. She recalls her parents leaving Father Christmas icing-powdered mince pies and a glass of sherry the night before Christmas, the fat stocking weighing on her feet in the morning, the little kindnesses buried beneath the landslide of a wrecked home. It delights rather than depresses her, and she sees the good behind the cloak of unhappiness in those whose fear and ignorance made a mess of her childhood, and she forgives them. The music, so grand and all-encompassing, eradicates the meanness in her soul. All narrow channels become wide in Chesed.

She talks with friends she had though gone forever; childhood companions, the close confidantes of adolescence, the flashing friendships of early adulthood. Passing empathies are represented en masse—she is surprised by how many she had touched and forgotten. Her handsome husband greets all without envy and she in turn meets the lovers of his past who had so intrigued her, and they share their pleasure at his being.

*All very New Age*, she begins to think with a hint of cynicism, but it is all too beautiful to abnegate. *Besides, a little love and peace is the perfect antidote to the warped world of mundane energy* . . . but even as she thinks it, nestling close into her proud husband's shoulder, Malach before her, friends and music and noise all around her, it begins to fade. . . .

# Binah

. . . and, inexplicably, she is alone. Strictly speaking, this statement is not true: she can still see and hear those around her, but she cannot touch them. Something has just plunged her into a state beyond their reach, a state of painful and solitary wisdom. Her aura, previously open to all, has become an impermeable bubble, and she feels sure that they resent her for it. Yet it was involuntary.

Grappling for her previous sense of belonging, she stares at her loved ones, her friends from the past.

"Medusa!" she hears them whisper one to the other. Or she thinks she does. "She'll turn this celebratory sabbat to stone."

She seeks out her messiah, the husband who should deliver her from the evil of isolation. He is leaning over his lover past, the one who left him for another, now long gone. Three swords pierce her heart, and her feet grow obscene. *Contaminated thou art*, she seems to hear. *Three queens rule thee, Priestesses of Trouble and Sorrow.*

Salt wells up in her eyes, oceanic in import. Black grief wraps itself about her like swaddling bands or tresses of Nephthys. *No difference between the two*, she thinks. *Birth, death, existence, it's all the same: one long tunnel of pain with the occasional stop at a station, possibly pleasant, possibly not.* Bitter tears course down her face, but no one notices. None, that is, but Malach, and she turns a cheerful countenance on him. "Mummy's fine, darling," she says, her heart breaking. "She's only crying because she's happy. Silly Mummy!" Malach, reassured, smiles and runs off to play with marbles under the tables.

The punch she imbibed earlier feels toxic in her stomach; it is turning to acid in her soul. The scene blurs and slurs to the left, dragging her consciousness with it. She fears she will faint.

Now she is falling down a well of bottomless grief, and now, with a thump, she is sitting on a stone throne near it. She remains beside her partner, but their minds are in different dimensions. She feels unworthy, fears for her past and her future, but above all, she rages at the necessity of the process in the first place. *God, you bastard*, she screams within. *Why so much suffering? Why the fall from grace, from Eden, why divorce from the cosmic source, why the pain of birth and death. . . .*

She tries to explain a little to her husband, conscious that her feet grow ever more warped as she speaks.

He rebukes her, whispers harshly that she is ruining his day. She curls in on herself, scabs bleeding, utterly repulsive. The well commits an upsurge of black energy, the type that used to carry a sacrificed soul away on it. The greater good, the greater good. The mantra of pain-riddled, rheumatic Binah.

Where have all the lovely friends from Chesed gone? Though she knows they are still here for her, she feels burdened by the knowledge of this grief, and by expressing it she would ruin everybody's day and year and life. Such burdens are not lightly broken. And so she holds her tongue, wrapping the agony around herself like a cloak, her insight turned ever inwards in the mandala of the Mater Dolorosa.

## Chokmah

"What's the matter, my love?"

His voice comes to her from outer space. She is shocked. Does he really care?

"Where's your faith?" he mutters into her hair, placing his arm around her black-clad shoulders. "Remember how we tamed the wild sphinxes? Yours are running away with you now."

She knows he is right. Again, reality shifts. Her grief, though real, appears pathological, an unnecessary addition to the grief of the Mother. Demeter wants Persephone released, not mourning in the Underworld.

"Hades had me," she says, then, embarrassed at her psychodrama. "How's the party going? I think I must've drunk too much punch."

"I'll say!" The husband is fond. "You went out like a light. I carried you outside. You came round every so often but were talking nonsense. Everyone's worried about you. How do you feel now?"

"Bizarre."

"Fancy some air? We could climb the hill to the Tor."

She looks up at the looming tower, its crown indubitably in clear ether. Grays and silvers streak the skies around it. "Can we take the spiral path?"

They circumnavigate the Tower for many hours, growing ever closer, a procession of two. She goes barefoot, salving her bleeding claws on the wet earth. The mud is cool and soothing, and the increasing altitude clears her mind. The moon and sun become apparent, both vast harvest orbs, equidistant from the Tower's ancient crenellations.

"It's beautiful," she gasps. The sounds of the party below are festoons on the breeze; and soon, the breeze becomes wind. Pinning the sky to the heavens are the silver tacks of the zodiac, each sign clearly visible, the Lion and the Bull balanced by the Scales, Mars and Venus in equilibrium, Sothis blessing the union.

The black bands unravel as they ascend, revealing the fresh young bride once more. Malach's voice floats to his mother's ear, an angel's coded whisper. Below them stretch the green hills and vales of Netzach, the carefully tended gardens of Chesed, and on the other side, the distant walls of the city of Hod, the raised arena of Geburah, smoke-swathed, and the Well of Binah, directly below. The water in the well, an unlidded eye, is as red as the sun and the moon. Spirits crafted of purest ether press in around them, Ketheric impulses personified. Some have messages of hope and trust and divine providence; others are simply wisdom incarnate, and their wordless presence is effortlessly elevating.

They reach the smooth mound from which the tower thrusts, and roll their hot bodies in the cold green grass of the crest. She rolls until she is on top of him, and sees the sun and moon reflected in his irises, flecks of fire in deep mahogany. Thick black lashes, girlie, flutter beneath manly eyebrows, the thin mouth opens for air. He breathes the musky perfume of her, her dark hair redolent of Yesod streams around his face. Now all he can see is the moon-in-water of her countenance, green eyes, mischievous, feline, reflecting his, red smiling lips, mouth full and succulent, incisors gleaming, longer than most. She had told him when they were first courting of an earlier boyfriend terrorized by these sharp teeth, but he would give her every drop of his blood at this moment, every iota of his life fluid. Nothing matters now but he and she, this moment on the mount of Chokmah.

The wind descends on Chesed, heaves a sigh, and blankets them with sounds of music and revelry from below. Their union is celebrated as it is consummated.

# Kether

She is seeing light so bright it dissolves all solids. Diamond-bright, at first perceived in spectra, aureoles of tears of sorrow or joy, she knows not the difference—or perhaps it is sweat. It matters not where the good salt that creates the substance of spectrums and spiritual structures like ice-bright towers of purity shining light, not reflecting but actually creating, issues from. The origin is nearing, the brightness behind Assiah and Briar and Yetzirah and Atziluth, the spark which set the fires of all creation ablaze.

*In the beginning,* sighs the wind, drawn by Angels of resplendence unimaginable, ten Angels on ten winds, each of a different tincture, each from a different angle, each carrying a very different yet equally important aspect and scent of knowledge:

*In the beginning there was Consciousness, a consciousness beyond the collective projections of man into the universe . . . suprahuman, suprademigod, supragodform; All-Being, yet not all-Knowing, because if it had been, it would have stopped right there. Sages say that it was lonely, however, and so began Creation. Yet, not as we know it—that took many aeons of cosmic space-time, but a gradual spilling of this consciousness into untouched places. And as it grew it also unbalanced, and as it unbalanced it caused states of being which were not intended, and whose import became the opposite of that intended. And the opposites enhanced the intended, and before long Light and Darkness had sprung up, and in their wake, good and evil, pleasure and pain, and all the other dichotomies and contradictions and paradoxes of creation.*

And so the Angels whispered continually, and quite unnecessarily, because they had heard it all before, a thousand times. *We're just reminding you, lest you forget . . .*

*Lest you forget. . . .*

# The Wedding

The organ music was coarse and dissonant. The organist was inept, totally inappropriate for a wedding. *He would ruin the day, surely?* He played on, oblivious to her glowers.

She sat in the tiny chapel, her wedding dress of green, her chestnut hair reddened by the stained glass roses, her creamy skin an accolade to the Creator—but her lips were moving in supplication.

For what does she pray, this maiden so fay, so belle, so beyond all need? *She need not,* sigh the Scottish witches, watching her with pride. *The girlie's feet are healed,* they cackle.

Not long now until the guests arrive: she must flee. Rather than sit alone she will sit in the graveyard. The dead won't mind if her feet are warped, their own being so much worse.

She alights a family burial mound, a relic from the pagan days, and swiftly unlaces her tight Victorian boots. He has never seen her feet, of course—he would not be marrying her now if he had.

They peel off like two rinds, long-bound by string. But rather than the taloned claws expected, the boots removed reveal two perfect, creamy limbs of unparalleled symmetry.

# Appendix

## 555
## Playful Correspondences
## to Get You in the Mood

| SEPHIRAH | READS | ARTWORKS | MUSIC | VISUAL IMAGE | SCENT |
|---|---|---|---|---|---|
| Malkuth | James Joyce, *Dubliners*, *Ulysses*<br><br>T. S. Eliot, *The Wasteland* | Photographs | Kate Bush, *The Sensual World*<br><br>The Jam<br><br>Hip Hop | Beautiful Dark Woman with Peacock's Tail | Dark Musk, Dittany of Crete |
| Yesod | Lenora Carrington, *The Seventh Horse*<br><br>Salvador Dali, *Hidden Faces*<br><br>Romantic / French Symbolist Poetry | Réné Magritte, *Le Chateau des Pyrénées* (*1961*)<br><br>Max Ernst Surrealist | The Orb<br><br>Edith Sitwell & Peter Pears, *Façades*<br><br>Massive Attack & Liz Fraser, *Group Four* | Lunar Arch above Purple Astral Seas, Levitation, Dreams | Jasmine, Cinnamon |
| Hod | Fyodor Dostoevsky, *Crime and Punishment* (Also relevant to Geburah)<br><br>Voltaire, *Candide*<br><br>Classics & Classical Studies | M. C. Escher | Johann Sebastian Bach<br><br>Wolfgang Amadeus Mozart | Androgynous Intellectual<br><br>Sharp, Effete Young Man, or Female Androgyne<br><br>Setting The British Library / Old University Town | Storax, Cannabis, Sandalwood |
| Netzach | C.S. Lewis, *The Lion, the Witch and the Wardrobe*<br><br>Fairy Tales | Richard Dadd<br><br>Arthur Rackham<br><br>Edmund Dulac | British Folk: Shirley Collins, Steeleye Span, etc.<br><br>Current 93 *Tam Lin* | Beautiful Young Woman Bathing in Liffey at Beltane | Grass, Cannabis, Damiana Smoke, Musk, Rose |
| Tiphareth | The New Testament<br><br>*Bhagavad-Gita*<br><br>Myth of Isis and Osiris | Gustav Klimt, *The Kiss*<br><br>Botticelli<br><br>Medieval Devotional | Georg Friedrich Handel, *Messiah*<br><br>Faith and the Muse, *Cantus*<br><br>Maurice Ravel, *Bolero* | Solar Deity: Christ, Osiris, God of<br><br>Waning Year Sacrificed and Risen<br><br>Love/Lovers | Acacia Frankincense |
| Geburah | Anthony Burgess, *A Clockwork Orange*<br><br>Norse Myths | Russian Propaganda Poster-Art<br><br>Mark Rothko | Beethoven, *Symphony Number 9*<br><br>Richard Wagner<br><br>Thrash/ Death Metal<br><br>Anything "tribal" Punk, etc. | Fierce Warriors Going into Battle | Tobacco, Ale, Sweat, Pine, Cypress |

| SEPHIRAH | READS | ARTWORKS | MUSIC | VISUAL IMAGE | SCENT |
|---|---|---|---|---|---|
| Chesed | Dr. Frederick Lenz, *Surfing the Himalayas, Snowboarding to Nirvana*<br><br>Anthony Storr, *Feet of Clay*<br><br>Tal Brooke, *Lords of Air* | *La Dame et L'Unicorn*<br><br>Tapestries in Musée du Moyen Age, Paris | Nick Cave and the Bad Seeds, *Mercy Seat*<br><br>The Police, *Invisible Sun*<br><br>Sisters of Mercy, *Temple of Love*<br><br>Mantras | A Unicorn (the true guru is as elusive as . . .)<br><br>Maat, Weighing the Heart Against the Feather of Truth | Pine |
| Binah | Dion Fortune, *The Sea Priestess, Moon Magic*<br><br>Angela Carter, *The Passion of New Eve*<br><br>Tanith Lee, *Vivia* | Charles-Auguste Mengin, *Sappho*<br><br>Images of Pieta | Lisa Gerrard, *The Mirror Pool*<br><br>Current 93, *Our Lady of Horsies*<br><br>Kate Bush, *The Ninth Wave*<br><br>Dead Can Dance, *Into the Labyrinth* | Lilith in Positive Aspects, Empowered and Vast as Star-Spangled Nuit | Civet, Myrrh, Dark Musk |
| Chokmah | Paramahansa Yogananda, *The Divine Romance* | Traditional Images of Bearded Father-God | Music of the Spheres | Unpersonified Creative Impetus, Raw Force | Musk [Civet, Ambergris] |
| Kether | — | — | Music of the Spheres Om | Boundless Intelligent Light | — |

| SEPHIRAH | TO PREPARE | EXPRESSION OF VIRTUE | VICES TO CONSIDER | SIGNS OF ZODIAC | DAY OF WEEK |
|---|---|---|---|---|---|
| Malkuth | You're there already | Intelligent Discrimination | Materialism<br><br>Mental & Physical Laziness<br><br>Alcoholism | Taurus; Virgo; Capricorn .<br><br>[Aquarius] | Monday/any |
| Yesod | Consider<br><br>Astral Projection | Creative Imagination<br><br>Faith in own Convictions | Impracticality; Escapism<br><br>Sexual obsession | Cancer | Days when moon visible<br><br>Friday night for dreaming |
| Hod | Do some Mental Arithmetic | Truthfulness, Logic, Self-Control | Dissimulation, Dishonesty, Coldness, Fickleness | Gemini Virgo | Wednesday |
| Geburah | Think of someone or something that makes you angry<br><br>What are the principles behind your aversion? | Courage, Tenacity, Strength, Justice | Mindless Destruction, Lack of Respect, Intolerance | Aries<br><br>Scorpio | Tuesday<br><br>Thursday |
| Chesed | Decide on the moves you will make to further your spiritual path<br><br>Join a magickal group<br><br>Go to a Pagan Moot (employ discrimination!) | Obedience to Higher Intelligence/ Purpose/ Inner Dictates | Authoritarianism. Bullying | Sagittarius, Leo | Thursday,<br><br>Sunday |
| Binah | Walk by the sea at twilight | Understanding of place in scheme of things, Acceptance, Discretion | Clinginess, Reluctance to accept change | All, especially Capricorn, Aquarius | Saturday |
| Chokmah | Meditate on your prime spiritual motives and impulses | Wisdom, Motivation | | Pisces | Thursday |
| Kether | Meditate on the light | All | None | All | All |

# Bibliography

Bonner, John, *Qabalah, A Primer*, Skoob Esoterica, London (1995).

Baudelaire, Charles, *Les Fleurs Du Mal*, Classiques Français (1993).

Crowley, Aleister, *777 and Other Qabalistic Writings*, Samuel Weiser (1998).

Drury, Neville, *Echoes from the Void*, Prism Press (1994).

Fielding, Charles and Carr Collins, *The Story of Dion Fortune*, Star and Cross Publications, Texas (1985).

Fortune, Dion, *The Mystical Qabalah*, Aquarian Press (1987).

———, *Applied Magic and Aspects of Occultism*, Aquarian Press (1987).

Gray, William G., *Ladder of Lights*, Samuel Weiser, Inc. (1981).

Halevi, Z'ev ben Shimon, *Psychology and Kabbalah*, Gateway Books (1986).

Hoffman, Edward, *Opening the Inner Gates; New Paths in Kabbalah and Psychology*, Shambhala (1995).

Homer, *The Iliad*; translated by Robert Fitzgerald, Oxford University Press (1984).

———, *The Odyssey*, Oxford University Press (1984).

Hurwitz, Sigmund, *Lilith, the First Eve*, Daimon Verlag (1992).

Kaplan, Aryeh (ed.), *Sepher Yetzirah*, Samuel Weiser (1997).

Knight, Gareth, *A Practical Guide to Qabalistic Symbolism, Volume One*, Kahn & Averil (1997).

———, *A Practical Guide to Qabalistic Symbolism, Volume Two*, Kahn & Averil (1998).

———, *The Practice of Ritual Magic*, Sun Chalice Books (1996).

———, *Larousse Encyclopaedia of Mythology*, Paul Hamlyn Limited (1959).

Levi, Eliphas, *Transcendental Magic, Its Doctrine and Ritual*, William Rider & Son, London (1923).

Matt, Daniel Channon (ed., trans.), *Zohar*, Paulist Press (1983).

Otto, Walter F., *The Homeric Gods*, Thames and Hudson (1979).

Parfitt, Will, *The Elements of the Qabalah*, Element Books Limited (1997).

Reed, Ellen Cannon, *The Witches Tarot*, Llewellyn (1997).

———, *The Witches Qabala*, Samuel Weiser (1997).

Regardie, Israel, *A Garden of Pomegranates*, Rider & Co., London (1932).

Rosenberg, David, *Sefer Gan Eden, The Lost Book of Paradise*, Hyperion (1993).

Scholem, G. G., *Major Trends in Jewish Mysticism*, Thames and Hudson (1955).

Sitwell, Edith, *English Eccentrics*, Penguin (1962).

Waite, A. E., *The Key to the Tarot*, Rider (1991).

Wynn Westcott, Dr. William, *Sepher Yetzirah* (facsimile), Cambridge (1887).

Yogananda, Paramahansa, *Autobiography of a Yogi*, Self-Realization Fellowship (1990).

————, *Awake in the Cosmic Dream*, Self-Realization Fellowship (1998).

Zwi Werblowsky, R. J., *Cabala*, Purnell, Man, Myth and Magic series. Undated.

# Index

Adam, 32, 174, 194, 221–222, 228, 243–244
Akasha, 51, 59, 186
Ain Soph Aur, 6, 9, 27, 54
Aleph, 25, 88–89, 209
Angels, 8, 10, 17, 24–25, 65, 76, 96, 111, 128, 130, 146–147, 164–165, 180–181, 212, 221, 239, 262, 271, 273, 279–280
Anubis, 74, 239
Aphrodite, 106, 117, 195, 244
Apollo, 33, 59, 77, 85, 88–90, 94, 107, 122, 238, 254
Aquarius, 229, 284
Archangels, 10, 96, 124, 127, 145–146, 164, 212, 221, 233, 239–240
Archetypes, 2, 43, 74, 173, 180
Ares, 142, 179
Aries, 247–248, 284
Artemis, 56, 64, 66–67, 77, 106, 227, 250
Asbestos, 226
Ashim, 25, 46, 262
Assiah, 10–11, 24, 56, 77, 119, 129, 166, 243, 255, 279
Astral Plane, 58, 69, 99, 105
Astral projection, 89, 284
Athena, 85, 89, 91, 93, 190, 244
Aura, 47, 61, 65, 69, 111, 132, 154, 181–182, 200, 232, 246, 267–269, 275

Ayin, 229
Azrael, fire of, 57

Bacchanalia, 118, 231
Baldur, 122, 135
Baudelaire, Charles, 38, 158, 285
Bear, 37, 39, 49, 69, 110, 137, 139, 162, 164, 198
Beth, 252, 254
Binah, 2, 11–12, 20–22, 27–28, 39, 42, 46, 88, 91–92, 112, 124, 127, 147, 150, 158, 173–187, 192–196, 199–203, 205, 207, 210, 213, 217, 219, 221, 239, 242, 252, 254, 261, 269, 275, 277–278, 283–284
Blake, William, 35, 69
Briah, 10, 24, 55–56, 119
Buddha, 8, 22, 75, 268

Cancer, 180, 284
Capricorn, 231, 284
Chakras, 94, 171, 232, 234, 250
Chalice, 50–52, 108, 110, 113, 124, 185, 206, 232, 253, 259, 261, 286
Chariot, 178–179, 271, 273
Ches, 178–179
Chesed, 10, 12, 19–20, 22, 25, 27–28, 64–65, 83–84, 86, 106, 121–122, 127, 150, 157–172, 178, 185–186, 190–191, 195–196, 208–209, 217,

289

231, 235, 240, 245, 248, 273, 275, 277–279, 283–284

Chokmah, 11–12, 21–23, 25, 27–28, 88, 127, 158, 173, 176, 178, 180–181, 185–186, 189–203, 205, 209–210, 217, 219, 221, 239–241, 245–247, 277, 279, 283–284

Christ, Jesus, 2, 8, 39, 63, 94, 119, 121–122, 125, 132, 135, 176, 209, 235, 245, 282

Christianity, 117, 121, 125, 222

Coleridge, Samuel Taylor, 70–72

Cronos, 175–176

Crowley, Aleister, 1, 4, 26, 199, 285

Cybele, 91–92, 113

Daath, 127, 180, 186, 219–223, 249

Daimos, 77, 178

Daleth, 178, 195

Demons, 123, 155, 222, 264

Diana, 56, 77

Dionysus, 91, 100, 129, 190

Djinn, 113

Dove, 206

Eagle, 11, 59, 61, 212, 229, 238, 262

Earth, Plane of, 40, 79, 120, 166, 238

Eden, 32, 39, 57, 163, 174, 194, 196, 220, 222, 243, 245, 259, 276, 286

El, 62–63, 65, 111, 164, 166

Elements, 13, 16, 40–41, 43, 45–46, 51–53, 63, 67, 88, 95, 107, 143, 182, 206, 208, 235, 253, 264
  Air, 12–13, 24, 43, 50–53, 67, 88–89, 95–96, 113, 127, 182, 205–208
  Earth, 24, 43, 45, 50–51, 88, 182, 208–209, 265
  Fire, 24, 43, 50–51, 62, 95–96, 182, 207–208, 225
  Water, 24, 43, 50–52, 62, 88, 96, 182, 206–208

Elements, King of, 113

Elohim, 95–96, 111–112, 146, 180, 221

Equilateral cross, 121, 134–135, 206, 235

Equilibrium, Pillar of, 31, 195, 209, 232

Ezekiel, Creatures of, 240

Fish, 34, 125, 227

Fortune, Dion, 283, 285

Gabriel, 8, 63–65, 68, 221, 225–226, 260, 262

Gawain, 266

Geburah, 4, 10, 12, 18–19, 21–22, 27–28, 64, 106, 121, 127, 141–157, 159, 162–164, 178–179, 185–186, 195–196, 217, 233–234, 271, 278, 282, 284

Gedulah, 19, 157, 186

Gematria, 6

Ghob, 113

Gimel, 219–220, 223, 250

Goblins, 113

Golden Dawn, 207, 219, 241

Graves, Robert, 243, 262

Guardian Angel, 39, 87, 261

Guardians of Watchtowers, 240

Gurus, 19, 22, 167

Hades, 58, 89, 254, 269, 277

Haniel, 111, 264

Hathor, 91, 117, 195, 249

Heh, 247–248

Hera, 244

Hermaphrodite, 90

Hermes, 88–90, 189–191, 220, 239, 253–254

Hod, 10, 12, 15–16, 18, 22, 27–28, 43, 55, 63, 83–103, 106–112, 115–116, 127, 165, 185–186, 190, 195, 205–206, 217, 225–226, 229–231, 233–235, 245, 253, 263, 278, 282, 284

Incarnations, 47, 197, 201
Infinity, Symbol of, 191, 253
Iris, 56, 220, 232
Isis, 2, 22, 39, 56, 74, 112, 122–123, 173, 175, 181, 184, 187, 192, 200, 227–229, 249, 282

Judaism/Judaica, 1, 3–4, 22, 31, 173–175, 181, 191, 250, 286
Jupiter, 164, 209, 236, 245, 247, 273
Jove, 157, 245
Justice, 19–20, 39, 64, 96, 124, 127, 145–146, 166, 181, 284

Kabbalah, 3–4, 6, 285
Kali, 2, 91–92, 155, 175–176, 186–187
Kaph, 236, 240
Karma, 29, 35, 38–39, 138, 146, 150, 179, 251, 268
Kerubs, 59
Kerubim, 46, 65, 96, 212
Kether, 3, 11–12, 20–23, 27–28, 32, 35–36, 39, 46, 62–63, 88, 94, 119–122, 157–158, 164, 173, 185–186, 189–190, 192–193, 199–203, 205–217, 219–221, 232, 234, 237, 239, 243, 246, 249, 251–254, 269, 279, 283–284
Khayyam, Omar, 17
Kore, 250–251
Krishna, 8, 122–123, 133, 135, 151

Lamed, 145
Laurel, 59, 123
Leo, 77, 122, 266, 284
Levanah, 227
Lilith, 174, 194, 200, 221, 228, 267, 283, 286
Lion, 11, 42, 59, 61, 162–163, 191, 212, 238, 278, 282

Magick, 1, 4, 6–7, 36–37, 53, 89, 98–99, 106, 123, 133, 152, 163, 183, 201, 205, 227–228, 246, 251, 265
Malkuth, 7, 10–14, 16–17, 19, 22–25, 28, 31–60, 62–66, 69, 71, 74–77, 83, 87, 90–91, 97, 102, 105, 107, 110, 112, 114, 118–120, 122, 128, 132, 141, 157, 161, 172–175, 178, 180, 185–187, 189–191, 200–203, 208–210, 212–214, 216–217, 221, 225–228, 233–234, 238, 243, 247–248, 253, 257, 259, 262–263, 266, 282, 284
Mantras, 170, 273, 283
Mary, Virgin, 175
Mathers, S. L. MacGregor, 2
Meditation, 4, 6, 11, 29, 32, 38, 44, 92, 101, 105, 121–122, 155, 160, 162, 167, 191, 203, 206, 216, 237, 242, 273
Medulla Oblongata, 126, 227
Mem, 88, 233
Metatron, 3, 212
Moon, 14, 17, 56–57, 63–64, 68–69, 76, 80, 85, 113, 115, 169, 174, 183, 192–193, 226–229, 249–251, 259, 261–262, 265, 278, 283–284
Morrison, Jim, 233
Mother, 2, 38–39, 45, 64, 68, 71, 75, 85, 91–92, 107, 174–175, 178, 180, 183–185, 187, 236, 244, 251–252, 258, 260–262, 277–278
Mozart, 282
Muse, Muses, 51, 72, 228, 238, 243, 266, 270, 282

Naiads, 266
Nature, 9, 11, 14–16, 18–19, 21, 23, 27, 34, 38, 42, 49, 63–65, 70, 77, 89, 91, 96–97, 105, 112, 114, 125, 137, 141, 144, 153, 155, 157, 160–162, 168, 173, 175–176, 180,

182, 190, 192–193, 195, 206–208,
227–229, 231, 234–235, 245,
252–254, 266
Netzach, 10, 12, 16–17, 22, 25, 27–28,
43, 55, 83–84, 87, 90–91, 93,
105–119, 121, 124–125, 136, 171,
179–180, 185–186, 190–191, 195,
199, 217, 226–229, 233, 235–236,
240, 245, 264–266, 273, 278, 282
Nixsa, 113
Nymphs, 52, 113

Odin, 74, 235
Oils, 57
Oracle, 90, 228, 238, 268
Osiris, 94, 122, 135, 173, 209, 268, 282

Pachad, 142
Paralda, 67, 113
Paris, 244, 283
Path, 1–2, 6, 16, 18–21, 26, 32–33,
45–46, 56, 58, 71, 75, 86–98, 106,
109, 111–112, 121, 124–126, 145,
160, 162–163, 174, 176, 178–179,
186, 192, 195–197, 206–209,
219–220, 222–223, 225–254
Peacock, 47–48, 97, 282
Peh, 109
Pentacle, 50–51, 54, 143, 159, 177,
230, 253, 259, 267
Pentagram, 208, 231, 266
Perfumes, 57
Persephone, 41, 58, 74, 86, 178, 209,
220, 250, 252, 254, 277
Phallus, 199–200, 202
Pillars, 27, 88, 100, 175, 198
Equilibrium, 18, 25, 28, 31, 145,
175, 178, 186, 195, 209, 215,
232, 239, 278
Mercy, 19, 21, 25, 27–28, 65, 86,
88, 122, 127, 134–135, 157–159,
163–164, 166, 186, 189, 199,
231, 233, 239, 249, 283

Severity, 27–28, 33, 88, 155, 162,
175, 181, 186, 239, 249
Pisces, 227, 284
Plath, Sylvia, 20
Plato, 174, 201, 244
Pluto, 58
Poe, Edgar Allan, 70, 72–73
Poetry, 70, 199, 238, 261, 282
Poppy, 226
Prana, 9, 92, 133, 227
Protection, psychic, 7, 9, 13, 18

Qlipoth, 2, 13, 80, 122–123, 163, 166,
186, 239, 249
Qoph, 227

Reed, Ellen Cannon, 29, 230, 286
Regardie, Israel, 2, 5, 26–27, 240,
286
Resh, 93
Runes, 74, 235–236

Sacrificed Gods, 2, 235
Samekh, 232
Samsara, 239
Sepher Gan Eden, 177, 222
Sepher Yetzirah, 238, 286
Sephirah/ Sephiroth, 2, 4, 6–7, 10–11,
13, 16, 20–21, 23–24, 26–29, 31,
34–35, 39, 41, 43–44, 46, 55–57,
62–65, 68–70, 76, 83–84, 86–87,
89–92, 95–96, 98, 105–108, 110,
114, 119–120, 122, 124, 127, 130,
133, 141, 144, 146, 148, 157–158,
161–162, 166–167, 170, 173, 175,
178, 180, 185–187, 189, 191–195,
199–201, 205–206, 212, 215,
219–221, 228–229, 232, 241, 246,
248, 253, 282–284
Seraphim, 146, 165
Serpent, 126, 163, 196, 239, 243, 253
Set(h), 34, 42, 49, 63–64, 74, 111,
127–128, 131, 142, 145–146,

159–160, 162, 166–167, 197, 216, 238–239, 241–242, 262, 271–272, 279

Shaddai El Chai, 62–63, 65

Sharman-Burke, Juliet, 230

Shekhinah, 31, 39, 62, 173–175, 180

Shin, 88, 225

Sphinx, 42–43, 238, 271–273

Swastika, 164

Sword, 41, 50–53, 64, 93, 96, 111, 127, 145–146, 149, 164, 181, 197, 202, 207, 209, 238, 242, 244, 253, 259


Tarot, 3–4, 6, 10–11, 28–30, 40, 46, 49, 58–59, 61, 68, 73, 76, 84–87, 97, 107–109, 123, 125, 141, 143, 157, 159, 162, 168, 176, 178, 191, 195, 206, 225, 227–230, 232, 235–236, 239–240, 242, 244–245, 247, 249–250, 255, 286
    Mythic, 30, 85, 107, 230, 244–245
    Of Old Path, 29, 87, 228, 230, 247, 249
    Of the Witches, 29, 230, 286
    Rider-Waite, 29, 40, 85, 162, 230, 245, 249
    Morgan-Greer, 29–30

Tarot, Major Arcana, 3, 30
    The Fool, 88, 192, 209–212, 251, 253
    The Magician, 16, 34, 46–47, 50–51, 53, 55, 59, 90, 106, 108, 157, 177, 202, 207–208, 251–254, 259
    The High Priestess, 219–220, 249–250, 252
    The Empress, 108, 178, 195–196, 247, 252
    The Emperor, 157, 168, 198, 208, 247–249, 255
    The Hierophant, 198, 245–246, 249
    The Lovers, 176, 207, 242, 275
    The Chariot, 178–179, 273

Strength, 15, 18, 29, 33, 53, 65, 96, 100, 111, 141–142, 148–149, 152–154, 156, 162–163, 166, 206, 209, 243, 250, 257, 284
The Hermit, 160, 208–209, 240–241, 245, 247
The Wheel of Fortune, 40, 238–240, 242
Justice, 19–20, 39, 64, 96, 124, 127, 145–146, 166, 181, 284
The Hanged Man, 97, 206, 242
Death, 39, 43, 56–58, 78, 106, 120–121, 125–126, 141–142, 150, 155, 164, 176, 186, 190, 209, 225, 239, 260, 276, 282
Temperance, 124, 164, 232–233, 240
The Devil, 29, 97, 210, 223, 230–231
The Tower, 97, 106, 109, 233, 266, 278
The Star, 112, 229
The Moon, 56–57, 63, 68, 76, 85, 115, 169, 183, 226–228, 250–251, 261–262, 278
The Sun, 10, 17, 67, 69, 93–94, 97, 113, 127–129, 163, 169, 174, 230, 232–233, 248, 259, 267, 278
Judgement, 29, 97, 225–226
The World, 10–11, 24, 35, 43, 58–61, 74–75, 93, 109, 125–126, 129, 131, 136, 156, 158–159, 173, 175, 182, 193, 208, 212, 238, 240, 243, 247, 250, 266, 270

Tarot, Minor Arcana, 30, 159, 176
Cups 11, 40–41, 68, 84, 108, 124, 144, 159, 178, 191, 206–207
    Ace, 206–207
    Two, 191
    Three, 178
    Four, 159

Five, 144
Six, 124
Seven, 108
Eight, 84
Nine, 68
Ten, 40–41
Pentacles, 10, 40, 86, 108, 124, 144,
    159, 177, 191–192, 208, 248,
    268
    Ace, 208
    Two, 191
    Three, 177
    Four, 159, 177
    Five, 144
    Six, 124
    Seven, 108
    Eight, 86
    Nine, 68
    Ten, 40, 248
Swords, 10, 40–41, 73, 85–86, 107,
    124, 143, 160, 176–177,
    191–193, 207, 263, 276
    Ace, 207
    Two, 191–193
    Three, 176–177
    Four, 160
    Five, 143
    Six, 124
    Seven, 107, 143
    Eight, 85
    Nine, 68
    Ten, 40
Wands, 11, 40, 73, 86, 107,
    123–124, 128, 143–144,
    159, 177, 193, 198,
    207
    Ace, 207
    Two, 193
    Three, 177
    Four, 159
    Five, 143–144
    Six, 123–124
    Seven, 107

Eight, 86
Nine, 68
Ten, 40
Taurus, 284
Temple Ov Psychick Youth, 237
Temura, 6
Tennyson, Alfred Lord, 241
Teth, 163, 196
Thor, 112, 142, 149, 247
Throne, 76, 167, 179, 181, 192, 247,
    276
Tiphareth, 2, 10, 12, 17–18, 22, 28,
    33–34, 62–63, 69, 87, 94, 97, 106,
    119–139, 141, 145, 158, 160, 176,
    180, 185–186, 197, 206–209, 217,
    229–230, 232–233, 235, 240,
    242–243, 247–249, 251, 266–267,
    273, 282
Time, 1, 4, 8, 15–16, 18, 20, 22, 37, 40,
    42, 44–45, 61, 66, 68, 70, 72,
    76–78, 83, 85–86, 94, 101–102,
    109, 115–116, 118, 122, 127–128,
    131, 133, 136, 142, 144, 147, 150,
    152, 155, 160–161, 164–165, 167,
    169–170, 175–176, 182, 184, 186,
    189, 191–192, 194, 198, 203, 205,
    210, 214, 220, 223, 225, 228, 234,
    237, 240–242, 252, 258–259,
    261–262, 264, 266, 272–273
Tor, 199, 277
Tree of Life, 1–3, 27, 32, 103, 117, 123,
    141, 157, 201
Trinities, 175
Typhon, 239
Tzaddi, 125, 227–228
Tzadqiel, 164–165
Tzaphkiel, 180–182

Vau, 245
Veils of Existence, 23, 26, 215
Venus, 28, 105, 108, 111, 113,
    179, 195, 206, 228, 265,
    278

Waite, A. E., 286
Weapons, magickal, 7
Well, 2, 4–5, 7, 19, 23, 29–30, 39,
    41–45, 49, 57–58, 61–62, 68,
    75–76, 80, 89, 92, 97, 99, 117, 119,
    126, 131–132, 137, 143–144, 149,
    152, 159, 163, 171, 177, 183–184,
    192, 196, 199, 209, 212, 220, 222,
    225, 229, 241, 244, 248, 250, 264,
    269, 276–278
Wicca, 187

Yesod, 4, 10, 12, 14–17, 21–22, 28,
    33–35, 39–44, 46–47, 55–81,

83–85, 87, 90, 92–93, 96–99,
    106–107, 120–121, 128, 147, 178,
    180–181, 185–186, 190, 197, 205,
    217, 225, 228–229, 232–233, 246,
    248, 261, 263, 278, 282, 284
Yetzirah, 10, 24, 55, 119, 130, 238, 255,
    279, 286
Yod, 208, 240
Yoga, 6, 167
Yogananda, Paramahansa, 33, 89, 121,
    221, 283, 287

Zayin, 242, 244
Zodiac, 183, 192, 198, 242, 278, 284

# ☾ REACH FOR THE MOON

*Llewellyn publishes hundreds of books on your favorite subjects! To get these exciting books, including the ones on the following pages, check your local bookstore or order them directly from Llewellyn.*

## Order by Phone
- Call toll-free within the U.S. and Canada, 1-800-THE MOON
- In Minnesota, call (651) 291-1970
- We accept VISA, MasterCard, and American Express

## Order by Mail
- Send the full price of your order (MN residents add 7% sales tax) in U.S. funds, plus postage & handling to:

**Llewellyn Worldwide**

**P.O. Box 64383, Dept. 0-7387-0002-9**

**St. Paul, MN 55164–0383, U.S.A.**

## Postage & Handling
- **Standard** (U.S., Mexico, & Canada)

If your order is:

$20.00 or under, add $5.00

$20.01–$100.00, add $6.00

Over $100, shipping is free

(Continental U.S. orders ship UPS. AK, HI, PR, & P.O. Boxes ship USPS 1st class. Mex. & Can. ship PMB.)

- **Second Day Air** (Continental U.S. only): $10.00 for one book + $1.00 per each additional book
- **Express** (AK, HI, & PR only) [Not available for P.O. Box delivery. For street address delivery only.]: $15.00 for one book + $1.00 per each additional book
- **International Surface Mail:** Add $1.00 per item
- **International Airmail:** Books—Add the retail price of each item; Non-book items—Add $5.00 per item

**Please allow 4–6 weeks for delivery on all orders.**
**Postage and handling rates subject to change.**

## Discounts
We offer a 20% discount to group leaders or agents. You must order a minimum of 5 copies of the same book to get our special quantity price.

## FREE CATALOG

Get a free copy of our color catalog, *New Worlds of Mind and Spirit*. Subscribe for just $10.00 in the United States and Canada ($30.00 overseas, airmail). Many bookstores carry *New Worlds*—ask for it!

**Visit our website at www.llewellyn.com for more information.**

## THE TREE OF LIFE

### An Illustrated Study in Magic

### ISRAEL REGARDIE
edited and annotated by Chic Cicero
and Sandra Tabatha Cicero

In 1932, when magic was a "forbidden subject," Israel Regardie wrote *The Tree of Life* at the age of 24. He believed that magic was a precise scientific discipline as well as a highly spiritual way of life, and he took on the enormous task of making it accessible to a wide audience of eager spiritual seekers. The result was *The Tree of Life*, which adroitly presents a massive amount of diverse material in a remarkably unified whole.

From the day it was first published, this book has remained in high demand by ceremonial magicians for its skillful combination of ancient wisdom and modern magical experience. It was Regardie's primary desire to point out the principles of magic that cut across all boundaries of time, religion, and culture—those fundamental principles common to *all* magic, regardless of any specific tradition or spiritual path.

1-56718-132-5, 552 pp., 6 x 9, 177 illus.,
full-color, 4-pp. insert                                    $19.95

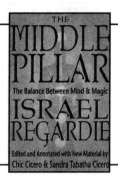

# THE MIDDLE PILLAR

## *The Balance Between Mind & Magic*

### ISRAEL REGARDIE

edited and annotated with new material by
Chic Cicero and Sandra Tabatha Cicero

Break the barrier between the conscious and unconscious mind through the Middle Pillar exercise, a technique that serves as a bridge into magic, chakra work, and psychology. This classic work introduces a psychological perspective on magic and occultism while giving clear directions on how to perform the Qabalistic Cross, The Lesser Banishing Ritual of the Pentagram, the Middle Pillar exercise, along with its accompanying methods of circulating the light, the Vibratory Formula, and the building up of the Tree of Life in the aura.

The Ciceros, who knew Regardie personally, have made his book much more accessible by adding an extensive and useful set of notes, along with chapters that explain Regardie's work in depth. They expand upon it by carrying it into a realm of new techniques that are directly related to Regardie's core material. Especially valuable is the chapter on psychology, which provides a solid frame of reference for Regardie's' numerous remarks on this subject.

1-56718-140-6, 312 pp., 6 x 9, illus.                    $14.95

**To order, call 1-800-THE MOON**

Prices subject to change without notice

PATHS OF WISDOM

*The Magical Cabala in the Western Tradition*

JOHN MICHAEL GREER

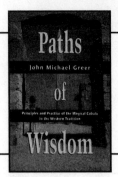

Unlock the hidden potentials of your self and the universe—of macrocosm and microcosm—with the key of the Cabala. *Paths of Wisdom* gives you complete instruction to perform Cabalistic magic. This general introduction to the magical Cabala in the Golden Dawn Tradition will be used by the complete beginner, as well as by the more experienced magician or Cabalist. But *Paths of Wisdom* also contains practical material on the advanced levels of Cabalistic work, based on a perspective inherent in most of the Golden Dawn-derived approaches to magic. Originating as a secret mystical school within Judaism, Cabala was transmitted to the great magicians of the Renaissance and became the engine behind the body of Western magical methods. From Cornelius Agrippa to the adepts of the Golden Dawn, the magicians of the West have used the Cabala as the foundation of their work. Central to this tradition is an understanding of magic that sees esoteric practice as a spiritual Path, and an approach to practical work stressing visualization and the use of symbolic correspondences. Through meditation, Pathworking, magical rituals, and mystical contemplation you'll incorporate the insight of the Cabala into your daily life.

1-56718-315-8, 416 pp., 6 x 9, illus.                    $20.00